Fran Rutt

CW00695115

SELF MANAGED LEARN
NEW EDUCATIONAL PARADIGM

Self Managed Learning and the New Educational Paradigm proposes revolutionary change to the educational system. The overwhelming research evidence is that the sum total of educational and training input accounts typically for only 10–20% of what makes a person an effective human being.

Balancing theory, evidence and practice, this ground-breaking book demonstrates that current structures in education are ill-equipped to support a learning-based approach. It establishes the case that learning, as a core human activity, is too important to be left to schools and other educational institutions. The book goes beyond just a critique of current practice in showing how a New Educational Paradigm can work. Self Managed Learning College (for 9–17 year olds) has no classrooms, no lessons, no imposed timetable and no imposed curriculum. This is a place where students can learn whatever they want, in any way they want and whenever they want. And it works – as evidenced by the lives of former students and from academic research. Dr Ian Cunningham, its founder, draws also on his extensive work in using Self Managed Learning in many of the world's largest organisations to show how this new paradigm can be put into practice.

The book blends the unequivocal research evidence that we need a New Educational Paradigm with a real live demonstration of what it could look like. It should be essential reading for anyone wanting to see how a new approach to education can be achieved.

Dr Ian Cunningham is a former Chief Executive of a business school and head of an international learning and development consultancy. He is the founder of Self Managed Learning College, Sussex, UK.

SELF MANAGED LEARNING AND THE NEW EDUCATIONAL PARADIGM

Ian Cunningham

Routledge
Taylor & Francis Group

LONDON AND NEW YORK

First published 2021
by Routledge
2 Park Square, Milton Park, Abingdon, Oxon OX14 4RN

and by Routledge
52 Vanderbilt Avenue, New York, NY 10017

Routledge is an imprint of the Taylor & Francis Group, an informa business

British Library Cataloguing in Publication Data
A catalogue record for this book is available from the British Library

Library of Congress Cataloging-in-Publication Data
Names: Cunningham, Ian, 1943- author.
Title: Self managed learning and the new educational paradigm / Ian
Cunningham.
Description: Abingdon, Oxon ; New York, NY : Routledge, 2021. | Includes
bibliographical references and index. Identifiers: LCCN 2020015124 (print) |
LCCN 2020015125 (ebook) | ISBN 9780367219659 (hardback) |
ISBN 9780367219666 (paperback) | ISBN 9780429269066 (ebook)
Subjects: LCSH: Self-culture. | Independent study. | Continuing education.
| Adult training. | Organizational learning.
Classification: LCC LC32 .C86 2021 (print) | LCC LC32 (ebook) | DDC
371.39/43–dc23
LC record available at https://lccn.loc.gov/2020015124
LC ebook record available at https://lccn.loc.gov/2020015125

ISBN: 978-0-367-21965-9 (hbk)
ISBN: 978-0-367-21966-6 (pbk)
ISBN: 978-0-429-26906-6 (ebk)

Typeset in Bembo
by Taylor & Francis Books

CONTENTS

ILLUSTRATIONS

Figures

Tables

ACKNOWLEDGEMENTS

In mentioning some people here, I am particularly keen to recognise and give thanks to those who have supported our work at Self Managed Learning College. Getting the College going and keeping it going has been a real collaborative effort and that needs recognising. I have learned a great deal from so many people that it's impossible for me to acknowledge all of them here. Much of what I have learned has come from other people's writings   some of that is reflected in the references in this book, and I hope that other authors who read this will recognise my debts to them.

Other learning and support has come from direct contact with people and I will mention some names here. I want to start with special thanks to Anne Gimson and Graham Dawes, who are long-standing friends, and in this context have been brilliant readers and commentators on this book. They have read it all and given me great feedback.

The people who I have worked with in Self Managed Learning College and our parent charity the Centre for Self Managed Learning have been important to me. The students I have learned from are too numerous to mention. As to the adults, current staff of the College includes David Lilly, Lars Schuy, Joe Allen, Jason Pegg, Julie Eren-Wilson, Charlie Dunkerton, Eleanor Mayne and Claire Parkman. They have been important in believing in this work and making it happen. They have developed work initiated by their predecessors in our College, including Gillian Trott, Alison McDonagh, Barbara Benson, Nicky Sankey, Jan Jemson, Paloma Hanlon, Bec Garland, Tanya Bartlett and Dan Benson. The latter people made certain that we progressed Self Managed Learning, even in difficult times.

The College is supported by dedicated trustees and governors, without whom we could not function. Specifically Sam Story, Liz Barlow, Ben Bennett, Vikki Mathews, Avis Carter, Moira Nangle, Emma Dean and Gavin Emsden have provided me with great support. A special mention is due to our president, Rose Luckin, for many valuable conversations about learning.

Outside our College and charity, I have had many stimulating dialogues with lots of people over the years. Yaacov Hecht deserves thanks for persuading me to work with the schools attached to the Institute for Democratic Education in Hadera, Israel, and allowing me to show, for the first time, that Self Managed Learning works in schools. Michael Fielding was similarly crucial in letting me set up Self Managed Learning programmes in English schools and for his enthusiastic energy in supporting these. Of the senior leaders in schools who have shown particular interest and help with developing Self Managed Learning have been Andrea Hazeldine and Gayle Adams. They took real risks to trust me and my colleagues to work in their schools, and for that I am extremely grateful.

Nationally there have been valuable allies from two specific organisations. Firstly, Peter Humphreys of the Centre for Personalised Education has led the fight for real change in education and his help with our College has been invaluable. Secondly, Danny Whitehouse and Sally Hall and their team at Phoenix Trust – and also through the Freedom to Learn network – are carrying forward what I am calling a New Educational Paradigm, and have been great allies of the College.

Two other national figures also deserve a thank you. Harry Gray and John Burgoyne are based in the Lancaster area and are pushing forward with ideas and activities. Harry is a long-standing friend and colleague from the early 1970s and has always offered a clear vision of what education should be like. John provided me with great help while I was doing my PhD at Lancaster University and has remained a friend since.

Internationally, Jerry Mintz has been an amazing stalwart figure who undoubtedly has more knowledge of radical educational activity than anyone on the planet. His organisation, the Alternative Education Resource Organization (AERO), is a crucial node in a global network. He has been personally supportive of me and my work in England from his office in New York.

Lastly, I need to thank my family. My son, David, and my daughter, Lucy, have taught me more about learning and education than they probably realise. Jane, my wife, has been with me all along with this current book and it could not have been done without her.

PREFACE

This book is about Self Managed Learning and its part in what I am labelling a New Educational Paradigm. In this preface I want to try to indicate my choice of particular concepts and ideas, and a language that goes with that. I hope that this will help the reader in recognising that there is a reason for my choice of language, even if the fuller rationale for these terms lies in the main body of the book.

Self Managed Learning

My late wife, Caroline, and I invented the term 'Self Managed Learning' in 1979 as we searched for an appropriate label for the approach to learning that we were developing. I use SML (Self Managed Learning) in capitals to distinguish the processes we developed from the use that has grown of 'self managed learning' as a generic label for a range of vaguely learner-centred approaches that are not specific about the kind of processes that will be described in this book. We were careful to pick the label and did extensive searches to see if anyone had used the term already and there were no published sources that had used Self Managed Learning by 1979.

New Educational Paradigm

A paradigm is a tricky concept in that many have used the term since Thomas Kuhn popularised its use in 1962.[1] His book was about scientific revolutions. The idea is that in 'normal science' there are agreed ways of working, an agreed language, agreed problems that researchers work on, how experiments should be conducted and what should be observed and measured and what predictions would be expected from theory. A scientific revolution would be when these taken-for-granted dimensions of scientific activity are challenged.

I have chosen to apply the concept of 'paradigm' to identify the key differences between research, enquiry and practice in the Schooling Paradigm from what I am calling a New Educational Paradigm. I could have suggested that paradoxically I am promoting an old paradigm in that schooling is a relatively recent invention and for at least 95% of human history there were no schools. Still today the remains of hunter-gatherer people do not have schools and learning is conducted in ways that go back for over 100,000 years. However, what I am calling the New Educational Paradigm is a response to the now manifest problems of the Schooling Paradigm, so it is perhaps an appropriate term.

Young people not children

I prefer to use the term 'young person' to that of 'child'. The taken-for-granted notion in our culture is that there is a very clear distinction between a child and an adult. It is very much the belief that you only become a real person at age 18 (in England). Up until this age you do not need to be treated as a real person but as some lesser being. You have fewer rights and you are compelled to be in education whether you like it or not. Over 18, people have choices and can be treated as autonomous beings; below 18, children are not seen as capable of autonomous decision making.

I have often run into problems by talking about the 9–17-year-olds who we work with in our College as 'young people'. Those in authority tend to think (and official documents can back this up) that a 'young person' means someone aged, say, 18–25. You only become a person at 18 in this view of the world. Of necessity in places in this book I will talk about children because I am citing authors who use this term. Or there are ways of talking that impel me to use child or children in a specific context.

Students not pupils

The young people in our College are students in that they study (whatever they like). For our young people the term 'pupil' belongs to school language and is anathema to them.

College not school

In England there is a rough definition of a school in law, which is used by the state to indicate that such an institution must be registered with the state and obey certain rules. There are no legal definitions of a college in England, so we use that term for our learning community. This was a choice of the students as they like to be seen as doing something normal, that is, going to college ('which is kind of like school' – to use our students' rationale). Peer group acceptance is crucial for young people and as most of their friends away from the College go to school, we are OK about using a more formal term than 'learning community'.

Learning community not formal organisation

There is a difference between a community and an organisation. At one level most people would recognise that their local community, for example, is not an organisation. It does not have a formal structure, rules and laws written down, an explicit hierarchy, agreed formal roles for people, and so on. Communities can be by location (streets etc.) or by particular interests or by family connections. In a pure form they do not have any of the arrangements deemed necessary for an organisation.

In our case we cannot claim that we are purely an informal community. We have, for instance, registered ourselves as a charity in order to provide a secure basis for our operations. Also, there are defined roles for adults working within the community. Some of these are laid down by the state, such as those for safeguarding, so we have policies to reflect the state's requirements. However, in day-to-day working we are closer to a live community. Everyone is on first name terms, there is no dress code for anyone in the community and everyone attends a daily community meeting which is relatively informal (there is a chair but the person in that role changes every day).

Ownership

School heads or principals often talk about 'my school', as though they own it (which is rarely true). The language also makes clear that learners are not part of what is owned. Teachers often say 'my class', and it distinguishes the person in power from those who they have power over. Our College is ours – it is never a 'my'. Similarly, students are in groups with one adult to support them. The group is for all in the group, so it is inappropriate for the adult to say 'my group'. In order to assist this process all groups choose a name for themselves which is agreed by all the students in the group. (Our groups are made of a maximum of six students and one adult. This format is explained later.) It can seem a trivial point, but if we are to be true to the idea of a learning community that is self-governing then adults must not claim ownership of any aspect of the community, and so imply a power difference that should not be there.

Conclusion

All of the above will be explored more fully in this book but it seemed important here to explain my use of language. Language is important – it is not a trivial issue, for instance, to call a young person a child. The word itself shows that schools are dealing with the difference between children and persons.

Note

1 Wikipedia has a good summary of the notion of paradigms and the work of Kuhn. For interested readers it also does a good job of exploring critiques of the concept as well as of other relevant concepts such as incommensurability. (Accessed on 20/8/19.)

Reference

Kuhn, T. S. (1996) *The Structure of Scientific Revolutions*, 3rd edition. Chicago: University of Chicago Press.

1

AN INTRODUCTION TO THE BASICS OF SELF MANAGED LEARNING

Introduction

The central subject of the book is young learners, and what and how they can best learn. Earlier books on Self Managed Learning have addressed the organisational world and the role of Self Managed Learning processes in companies and public sector organisations. (See, for example, Cunningham, 1999; Cunningham et al., 2000). This book is more about the application of Self Managed Learning to those who might normally be in school or college. The case of Self Managed Learning College is used in this book as an exemplar of what I am calling a 'New Educational Paradigm'. It is just one example of a growing international movement that is challenging the School Paradigm. In later chapters I will refer to some other examples of other kinds of learning-based approaches that are also examples of this growing trend.

At the start of the chapter I will discuss some relevant concepts that can feature in a New Educational Paradigm. I will follow this with some information about Self Managed Learning College that will provide a context for later chapters.

Some basic concepts

In discussions with philosophers of education it seems as though the most common notion of the role of education is to develop autonomous individuals who can live and work within their own societies. Hence ideas of autonomy also need to be considered and what that actually means in practice. At an educational conference some time ago, I was in a discussion group with a number of academic philosophers of education. When they talked about **autonomy**, I suggested that means and ends needed to be synchronised. How can individuals become autonomous in a process which doesn't allow them to be autonomous, namely the process of schooling?

I suggested that schooling needs to change if we are to be serious about developing autonomy. This was regarded as a laughable idea. Somehow the notion is that people become autonomous through a process which does not develop autonomy.

Linked to the idea of autonomy is the idea of **independence**. In discussions in schools there is often reference to the desirability of independent learning. The problem is that independence is separated from interdependence. In this book I will argue for a balance of **independent** and **interdependent learning**.

The issue of who has **power** and how it is used is an important factor when we think about learning. Typical dictionary definitions of education emphasise the notion of instruction, training and teaching. Implicit in this is the notion of an adult instructing a child. That might be a teacher or instructor or tutor, or it might be a parent or someone else in a position of authority. The overwhelming majority of writings about education discuss teaching and learning as though these are symmetrical processes. Somehow it is assumed that what is taught equals what is learned, even though all the evidence shows that this is a false assumption. This book is about learning rather than teaching, although of necessity I address the reasons why I have concerns about schooling and teaching.

The literature on the notion of power tends to suggest there are different modes that need to be analysed. For instance, 'position power' suggests that a person has power over others by virtue of their position. A headteacher or school principal would be a good example of the use of position power. Another kind of power is that of 'expert power'. Teachers claim expertise in a particular subject or subjects and that this gives them power over learners by virtue of that expertise.

Notions of **empowerment** cover two key aspects. The first is the idea of not taking power away from the individual but giving them the opportunity to exert their own personal power over their own situation. A second dimension is the idea of helping individuals who have been de-powered by virtue of aspects of the social situation they found themselves in.

In terms of what is called 'autonomous home education', empowerment is in the first domain: that is, that individuals in the family (typically the children) are not subjected to overbearing authoritarianism from adults (generally parents). The second idea of giving back power to young people comes more in the kinds of programmes that I have been involved in where often young people come out of school and need assistance to regain their own personal power over their learning.

In this context I am not talking about 'position power' or 'expert power', but about 'personal power'. A key notion is individuals having power over major issues in their lives, particularly here about choices of what to learn, where to learn it, when to learn it and, most importantly, why learn it. I appreciate that the term 'empowerment' has been sometimes used to justify taking power away from people and then giving a bit back. In school that might mean 'empowering' students to have a school council with representatives empowered to raise issues about the school, so long as it does not involve students having power over their own learning. This notion of empowerment is used to justify minor tidying up of school arrangements, but it does not genuinely empower students in the way that I mean it.

Alongside the idea of empowerment there are other concepts which are relevant. The idea of **freedom** for the individual is central to much of the literature on what is termed alternative education. For me freedom is conceptually close to autonomy and empowerment. Carl Rogers' book *Freedom to Learn* (1969) was an influential text and the Freedom to Learn Network in the UK is an important collaboration of educational organisations interested in freedom for young people in their learning. This network, I believe, constitutes an example of the New Educational Paradigm as it supports organisations and communities where the principles discussed in this book are manifest.

The International Democratic Education Conference (IDEC) is another significant body that draws together people under the umbrella of democratic education. The fact that there are literally hundreds of schools and learning communities committed to the notion of **democracy** is again part of this New Educational Paradigm. IDEC is an interesting non-organisation. At each conference there is a general meeting which agrees where the conference will be in two years' time. Whoever is organising a conference makes the local decisions on arrangements. There is a generally agreed understanding that the conferences will rotate around different continents but other than that there are no rules, there is no constitution and no central organising group.

Learning not school education

The title of this text indicates that it is about learning and not school education. This is quite deliberate, even though it may surprise some readers. After all most people in authority believe schooling is a good thing and there are organisations attempting to create compulsory education worldwide. The espoused basis for this is the idea that there is an entitlement to education for young people. So, I have to explain what I mean by a different approach. My fundamental stance is that humans are crucially learning creatures. Human babies are born with the least range of inbuilt abilities of any animal. Babies have to learn hugely in the first few years of their life and, even then, they are not able to survive on their own. Learning is central to being human and absolutely crucial for our survival. And the learning of a baby, whilst extensive and crucial, is not generally categorised as education.

Education, on the other hand, is currently seen largely as an institutional process where teachers teach in classrooms against a defined curriculum with a narrow range of assessments of performance as a central part of the activity. Education and schooling are seen as one. It is this problem that I am addressing here. I am aware that people may cite the saying 'I never let schooling interfere with my education' – the saying that has been ascribed to Mark Twain, though that is not certain – but even such a stance is in itself recognising that school and education generally go together as concepts.

Let me take a couple of dictionary definitions. The *Concise Oxford English Dictionary* defines 'educate' as 'give intellectual moral and social instruction to (a pupil, especially a child), especially as a formal and prolonged process'. 'Education' is defined as 'the act or process of educating or being educated; systematic instruction'. *The Chambers Dictionary* defines the verb 'to educate' to mean 'to bring up and instruct; to teach; to train'. 'Education' is defined as the 'bringing up or training e.g. of a child; instruction strengthening of the powers of body or mind; culture'. A New Educational Paradigm sets itself against this educational model.

I do accept that there are people who want to broaden the definition of education to include learning outside institutions. There are also examples of many parents home educating, where clearly such activity occurs outside an institution. However, the judgement of the efficacy of such activity tends to be against educational standards. This is not inevitable, of course, and it is possible to recognise that through home education children are learning a wide range of things that would fall outside what schools provide. However, it is really difficult to attach the word 'education' to what might be seen as day-to-day learning. We learn all the time and because it is such a ubiquitous process it tends to be missed as part of our normal living activity. At a trivial level I had to learn that the bus timetables had changed recently. This would not normally be seen as education, but it is important to know that we need to learn practical things that affect us in our daily lives. This is the implication of a New Educational Paradigm.

Another interesting example of learning not formal education came up when 13 of us who had had the greatest involvement in research and practice on learning in organisations in Britain came together to see if we could agree about learning. We drew up a Declaration on Learning which we all felt we could agree on, even though the 13 of us came from different backgrounds; for example, some were very much university-based researchers, and others worked in consultancy or in organisations. What linked us is that we had all written numerous books and papers and done significant research and practice over a considerable amount of time. At one meeting of the group we were discussing an aspect of the Declaration. One person suggested that as we were thinking about learning, then education and training should only be used as a last resort. We suddenly found that we could all agree to that statement. In organisations education and training activity tends to be very expensive and often ineffective because there is no attempt to measure what has come out of the education or training activity. The assumption that one size fits all and that everybody has the same learning need at the same time is completely erroneous.

I will take just one piece of evidence here, though more will follow. I have spent most of my working life supporting learning in organisations. (Only recently have I been involved in the learning of young people in what we call Self Managed Learning College.) In my organisational work I gathered together a team of experienced researchers to look at learning in organisations. We researched many thousands of managers and professional people across organisations around the world. We wanted to know what makes them effective at work. They all talk about things that they have learned but very little reference is made to education, training, colleges, universities, courses, and so on. Indeed, not just our research, but that conducted by a number of universities in the UK and in the USA has shown that the maximum contribution of education and training to the performance of a professional person is about 10–20% (see Burgoyne and Reynolds, 1997; Cunningham et al., 2004; Eraut, 1998; Eraut et al., 1998; McCall et al., 1988; Wenger, 1998). Most of the useful learning that we gain comes from what tends to be dismissed (by officialdom) as informal learning, such as that from peers, family, travel, reading, and so on. In our own research we have identified over 80 useful learning modes outside schooling. Some of these are summarised in Cunningham et al., 2004.

This evidence can come as a bit of a shock to people in the educational world. One reason for the shock is that by and large educational institutions do not follow up the people who have attended them to find out what impact that education has had on their lives. We started from the opposite end, which was to find out what made adults effective and particularly what learning had helped them to become effective.

In our research we questioned people about what particular processes had helped them to become effective. The most often mentioned word was 'experience'. When we pursued in greater depth, through extensive interviews, what people meant by 'experience' the answers were many and varied. Reference was made to having had challenging projects, having had a good boss to work with, travelling to other countries, getting help from a coach, and so on. There was no obvious pattern to these answers – people varied enormously in terms of those experiences that had helped them to learn to be effective.

This research has been in the world of work. When I have done sessions with adults outside the world of work asking them about their wider life, including family and community, the value of education and training drops to an even lower figure. For instance, parents often comment on all sorts of ways that they learn to be a parent. These include having role models, reading books, watching TV and films, talking to other parents, and so on. I ask these adults about their role in the wider life of the community, with friends or with sports teams. Then things get mentioned such as their own friendships that have helped them to understand how to get on well with other people or how they have learned to take up leadership roles through being mentored by somebody.

A late colleague of mine, David Gribble, asked audiences that he was presenting to to come up with one thing that they use on a daily basis that they learned after the age of 11 in education. People struggle to think of one thing. It is another example of this syndrome whereby the claim that education is preparation for life in our society becomes problematic.

There can, of course, be times when there are some common learning needs; but even then, there is generally not a common starting point. One client of mine was a well-known and very successful international investment banking company. Graduates who joined the organisation were given a test on their first day on both the company's policies and practices, but also the general financial rules within which the company had to operate. Most of the participants could answer very few of the questions. That was not the issue. The new entrants were then told that they had two weeks in which to go and find the answers to these questions and that they would be given the same test at the end of those two weeks. This time they would be expected to get 100%. The company found that not only did this save them a lot of wasted effort in running lectures and giving out boring reading matter, but also that the participants had to spend time learning about the business by going out and talking to people. It particularly highlighted the value of social learning and the ability to ask good questions. It is a mark of the success of the business that they had such sensible practices. And the focus was on learning not courses. Also, there was rigorous assessment of the learning – as opposed to the typical company induction course where individuals are taught a great deal but there is no assessment of learning. The lack of a relationship of teaching to learning will be a feature of aspects of this book.

A universal need is that of the driving test. In England anyone can take the test once they are an adult and they can find any mode that they wish to learn how to drive. The state is not interested in the learning mode used by the individual. The person could have spent 1000 hours on the road with a driving school or they could have had just a few hours driving around the block with their mother and father. The mode of learning is irrelevant. What is required by the state is, quite rightly, that the individual has to demonstrate on a real road in a real car that they can actually drive safely. Although passing a written test is also required, if the person cannot drive safely, as evidenced by performance on the road, then they do not get their licence. Outcome measures are important, but measures of input may be irrelevant.

I can remember, in particular, one conference on mentoring in the National Health Service that I was speaking at. I was observing doctors sitting in the back row reading the daily newspapers. They were attending the day conference in order to tick a box in their Continuing Professional Development scheme, but they clearly had no interest in learning anything from the day's events. Of course, they were not being assessed as to whether they had learned anything. This is one of the typical examples of the irrelevance of training. A slightly amusing, but also slightly worrying, fact is that I know people who have been caught speeding, done a speeding awareness course in order to avoid getting points on their licence, and then three years later have been caught speeding again and done another speeding awareness course. The notion that people can every three years get caught for speeding and do a speeding awareness course, from which some people may learn but others do not, seems to me somewhat unhelpful.

The case I want to make is that we should pay a lot more attention to learning – and how people learn and what they need to learn – but pay a lot less attention to education and training in formal institutions. Indeed, we have to wonder whether as a society we should be spending the billions of pounds that it costs to run educational institutions when they are clearly not at all cost-effective. Note that my stance is not that formal instruction is always wrong or irrelevant. I am back to our Declaration on Learning. If we cannot learn cheaply and effectively through other modes, then a course or some other formal arrangement may be needed. But most of the time it is not.

Also, I recognise that we sometimes have to play the game of 'getting trained' to satisfy bureaucratic rules. A recent example for me was attending a one-day course on acting as a 'Safeguarding Lead'. There are rules that are laid down in England that dictate that as, at the time, I acted as 'Safeguarding Lead' in our College (that is to say, I had an overview of arrangements to keep our students safe) I had to be trained. I learned nothing from the trainer running the course, though informal chats in the breaks with people from other charities were useful as we shared experiences. There was no assessment of whether I could actually do the job and the course made no material change in how I worked. I did it so that we can tick the box that says I have been trained. Whether I learned anything is of no relevance in the rules.

By this comment, note that I am in favour of appropriate assessment. We do want to know that people are effective in what they do. For example, having a driving test is hugely important.

Context

One of my interests has been about processes that have a general applicability. The approach that I have called Self Managed Learning has been used with most of the largest organisations in the world over the last 40 years. It's only since the year 2000 that we have used Self Managed Learning processes with young people. However, I will argue in the book that these learning processes have a longer provenance and I will draw evidence from learning approaches developed prior to the use of schooling. I will also mention the use of Self Managed Learning in a number of countries where I have assisted with its development for young people. These include Finland, Sweden, Canada, China, India, Taiwan, Puerto Rico, Israel and Spain.

In England we run both Self Managed Learning programmes in schools and operate Self Managed Learning College. Self Managed Learning College will be used as a specific case study within the book. Currently, the college has 39 students aged between 9 and 17 and is located on the English south coast in Sussex. By virtue of being located in England there will necessarily be some reference to particular educational structures in England such as the public examination system. However, my case is that, despite these particular technical aspects of its operation, the College does provide a genuine example of the principle of Self Managed Learning that is applicable elsewhere. Visitors to the College from a number of different countries have asserted this to be so. These countries include Australia, Korea, USA, Japan, Germany, Chile, Greece, Spain and Hungary.

New Educational Paradigm

The case made in this book is then that the structures and processes of Self Managed Learning (SML) have general applicability. An element of this is the notion that SML is part of this international movement that I am labelling a New Educational Paradigm. As is predicted by paradigm theory, the adherents to the current model are so used to working in their own ways that the growing research evidence is still not recognised.

It is likely that teachers will absorb the current dominant paradigm about the nature of education. For most teachers it will be taken as read that there are classrooms where children are taught as a group, there are time-limited lessons, there is a timetable for both students and teachers, there is a formality between the role of the teacher and the student, there is a fixed curriculum that the teachers will be working to, they will plan and deliver lessons, and decisions in the school will be made through the hierarchy. This is the dominant paradigm in education.

I am deliberately invoking the concept of a paradigm because it seems to me to be rather important. Paradigms are the 'taken for granted' aspects that operate within a particular sphere. The original use of the term came out of science and the work of Kuhn (1996). A classic paradigm in physics until the end of the 19th century was a Newtonian view of the world and universe. Early in the 20th century we had the work of Einstein and of the quantum theorists. This challenged the paradigm and gradually a new paradigm was accepted. As Kuhn points out, in a period of normal science there is a generally accepted way of doing science and a revolution in thinking may take a while to be accepted or catch on, and to be absorbed. When that new way of thinking is absorbed in general in the scientific community, it becomes a new paradigm.

As proponents of the paradigm approach would predict, it may take time for those used to the existing but flawed paradigm to recognise the relevance of both the research evidence and growing practice in a new way. During revolutions there is turbulence and disagreement as the majority hold sway through the existing published works.

In this sense the world of education is different from the world of science. Science is not democratic. Eventually new modes take hold because they explain better the facts. In the social context of education the facts that could disturb the status quo are more easily ignored, especially as the media and others, such as politicians, are likely to have benefited from the current system and also, having experienced it, find it difficult to accept evidence that contradicts their experience.

Despite the difficulties, what I am arguing for in this book is a new paradigm in the way we think about learning and about education. The taken-for-granted in the traditional paradigm that I have indicated above is that the teacher will have a generally agreed view about the nature of teaching, classrooms, school lessons, timetables, formality, and so on. This is a view that I do not accept – and it is not supported by evidence that will be presented in later chapters. In our College we do not have a fixed curriculum, we do not have teaching in classes, we do not have a timetable where people move around from lesson to lesson, we are informal and students use first names when talking with adults, we work as a community rather than making decisions through a hierarchy, and so on. It is a different paradigm and it is important that the existing paradigm in education is juxtaposed against that. Table 1.1 indicates some basic differences between the two paradigms.

Beliefs about what to do in working with young people will be located within either the traditional paradigm or the new paradigm I am proposing. We act out of

TABLE 1.1 Traditional schooling paradigm versus New Educational Paradigm

Traditional schooling paradigm	New Educational Paradigm
Learning is organised by institutions such as schools and colleges. This is the only proper learning.	Learning anywhere – and not necessarily in an organised setting.
Young people have to be controlled otherwise they won't learn – extrinsic motivation is required.	Young people naturally want to learn given the right support. Intrinsic motivation works.
Imposed content curriculum.	Free – no imposition.
Teacher in charge.	Learner in charge – works with adults as needed.
Imposed timetable – pupils must follow.	No imposed timetable – students learn as and when they choose.
Decisions made hierarchically.	Joint decision-making between adults and young people.
Teachers impose tests.	Students choose if they want to take tests.
Formal relationships between teachers and pupils.	Informal relationships – all on first name terms.
Steady progression of learning expected.	Learning goes at a pace that suits the learner.
Taking public exams expected.	Taking public exams if the student chooses.
Dress code or uniforms.	No dress code or uniforms.
Students required to be in fixed rooms. No access to toilets or refreshments without permission from staff.	Students free to access rooms, e.g. toilets, as needed. No permission needed.
Learning is preparation for life, so it stops at some point and people start living.	Learning occurs from birth to death – it never ceases while you are alive.
People who can memorise a lot of facts are better people than those who can't.	Everyone is important and can contribute in different ways to communities and organisations.
Homework is required.	Learning can occur anywhere and there is no compulsory homework.

NB Some ideas taken from R. Meighan (2005) *Comparing Learning Systems*. Nottingham: Educational Heretics Press.

our beliefs. Hence exploring these is crucial. However, alongside our beliefs are our values. This is what we care about. Again, in terms of traditional schooling, teachers will obviously say that they care about their pupils. This may come to mean that their role is to make certain their pupils learn subjects to take on with them into university or into the world around them, and that somehow that subject-based knowledge is what it means to be educated. There is an implicit assumption that this will then equip all pupils for a good, fulfilling and healthy life beyond school. In the new paradigm I will show that there are faulty beliefs and there are faulty values involved here.

Of course, I agree with teachers that we should care about young people, but once we tease apart this notion of caring, there is a different theory and practice involved here. In our College we would say that it is about working with the whole person, it is about helping people to learn to work in all sorts of ways and to develop a level of autonomy that provides them with choices in life. Within that whole person assumption is the fact that we value, alongside academic learning, the abilities to engage with other humans in a positive way. This is often called social and emotional learning but, though this label moves us beyond just valuing knowledge acquisition, it does not do justice to my sense of the new paradigm.

The distinction between **values** and **beliefs** is very important. I often see these two terms put together as though they are one topic. As I have mentioned above, teachers in traditional schools can say that they **value** their pupils – that is, they **care** about them. **Values** tell us what a person **cares** about. **Beliefs** are what we hold to be **true**. Teachers **believe** that teaching in a classroom to a defined curriculum is a valid basis for education. I don't. My **beliefs** are based on the evidence of the failure of the current Schooling Paradigm, and also come from the research evidence that supports a different model of learning.

Grayling (2003) suggests the following aspects of the 'Good Life'. These are his **beliefs** and they make sense to me. They are in outline as follows:

1   *Meaning* – most people welcome having meaningful work that is based on achieving their values and goals.
2   *Endeavour* – people like to make things happen – to achieve their goals, to see a job well-done. I once talked with a skilled craftsman about his work making chairs and how he always made the underside of the chair look good, even if most people never saw it. Pride in work is, in part, what it is about.
3   *Truth* – the good life includes living with intellectual honesty and respecting real evidence – hence my concern about evidence being ignored.
4   *Freedom* – we know that, generally, people like having autonomy and responsibility, and authoritarian control undermines this.
5   *Beauty* – aesthetics do impact on people. It is not just about a few paintings or sculptures in a reception area; it is about working in a pleasing environment. It can also be about access to nature and the enjoyment of it.
6   *Fulfilment* – this is about integrating the above factors in a coherent way and feeling fulfilled in career, family, and so on.

Shouldn't education address issues such as these?

Perhaps the well-known quote from a Holocaust survivor can give us a pithy sense of what worries me about education. It is identified as a letter to teachers:

> I am a survivor of a concentration camp. My eyes saw what no person should witness: gas chambers built by learned engineers. Children poisoned by educated physicians. Infants killed by trained nurses. Women and babies shot by high school and college graduates.

So, I am suspicious of education.

My request is this: Help your children become human. Your efforts must never produce learned monsters, skilled psychopaths or educated Eichmanns. Reading, writing, and arithmetic are important only if they serve to make our children more human.[1]

It would be good if the purveyors of the traditional schooling paradigm responded to this request.

Conclusion

This introductory chapter has outlined some key concepts for what I have labelled as the New Educational Paradigm. I have indicated some major differences between the two competing paradigms in education. Later chapters will flesh out these basics, starting with the next chapter, which introduces Self Managed Learning College as an example of the New Educational Paradigm.

Note

1   The quote is cited by Haim Ginott (2003).

References

Burgoyne, J. and Reynolds, M., eds. (1997) *Management Learning*. London: Sage.

The Chambers Dictionary (2014) London: Chambers.

Concise Oxford English Dictionary (2008) Oxford: University Press.

Cunningham, I. (1999) *The Wisdom of Strategic Learning*, 2nd edition. Aldershot, Hants.: Gower.

Cunningham, I., Bennett, B. and Dawes, G. (2000) *Self Managed Learning in Action*. Aldershot, Hants.: Gower.

Cunningham, I., Dawes, G. and Bennett, B. (2004) *Handbook of Work Based Learning*. Aldershot, Hants.: Gower.

Eraut, M. (1998) Learning in the workplace. *Training Officer*, 34(6), 172–174.

Eraut, M., Alderton, J., Cole, G. and Senker, P. (1998) Development of knowledge and skills in employment, Research Report No. 5. Brighton: University of Sussex Institute of Education.

Ginott, H. (2003) *Between Parent and Child*. New York: Three Rivers Press.

Grayling, A. C. (2003) *What is Good?* London: Weidenfeld and Nicolson.

Kuhn, T. (1996) *The Structure of Scientific Revolutions*, 3rd edition. Chicago: University Press.

McCall, M. W., Lombardo, M. M. and Morrison, A. M. (1988) *The Lessons of Experience*. Lexington: Lexington Books.

Meighan, R. (2005) *Comparing Learning Systems*. Nottingham: Educational Heretics Press.

Rogers, C. (1969) *Freedom to Learn*. Columbus, Ohio: Charles E. Merrill.

Wenger, E. (1998) *Communities of Practice*. Cambridge: University Press.

2

AN INTRODUCTION TO SELF MANAGED LEARNING COLLEGE

I will now introduce the workings of the College, through a route where there was an important interchange with the adherents of the current schooling paradigm, namely Government inspectors. This, hopefully, shows some ways to address the Schooling Paradigm. I then explain the main aspects of the College as an introduction to later chapters.

An unusual morning at College

On October 20, 2016 I was sitting working through my emails at Self Managed Learning College. I heard banging on the door that led into the building. I went down and on the doorstep were two people who said they were from the Office for Standards in Education (Ofsted). The man, who was clearly the more senior inspector, said to me, 'We understand that you are running an illegal school and we are here to close you down.' This came as a bit of a shock, but I let the man and woman in and asked them to stay by the door, while I checked their credentials. Ofsted is the Government's inspection arm; I knew that the Government was keen on a purge of what they called illegal schools and they had created a team within Ofsted to take action on this.

Once I had checked their credentials with their office, which took a little time and therefore gave me a bit of a chance to think as to what to do, I let them in and let them carry out their inspection, since they had a legal right of entry. Initially, we sat at the table in the corridor, where I had been working, and I was asked about what we were doing. I explained that whilst we call ourselves Self Managed Learning College we were, in our view, not a school. There is a legal definition of a school, but not of a college, so that is why we picked that name. We did not have an imposed curriculum, we did not have an imposed timetable, and we did not have any classrooms. We had at that time 18 students aged between 9 and 17 on the roll and we were renting a floor within the Brighton Youth Centre to run the College. Our students attended in the mornings between 9am and 1pm and learned whatever they wanted to learn. Generally, students did choose to take some subjects in the General Certificate of Secondary Education (GCSE) but, although schools usually put their pupils in for these exams at around age 16, our students could choose not only which subjects they took (if any) but also when.

I explained that we spent the first week with students finding out about them and what they were interested in and their thoughts about the future. They then wrote what we call a learning agreement at the end of the week, which they shared with their learning group. The group consisted of six students and one of our team, who we call a learning group adviser. The other adults in the College were what I would term 'learning assistants', although at that time we tended to use the term 'tutor' because parents understood that better. I explained that we had three students with us who had been sent either by schools or by the local council and the other students came as a result of parents' initiative, either because of dissatisfaction with school or because they favoured the Self Managed Learning approach that we use.

The lead inspector then said that he wanted to talk to the students, which he did. The inspectors went around the different rooms that we used and interviewed individual students as they went. In the room where we had our computers and resources, the lead inspector sat down by someone who was on the computer and asked him what he was doing. The student explained that they were working on creating a computer game and showed him some of the graphics that they had created. At the back of the room Jimmy was sitting strumming on a guitar, so the inspector asked him about what he was doing. The latter explained that he had been learning music, even though he had not done anything musical before he came to the College. He also talked about the maths and English and other things that he was studying. The inspectors split up and continued to go around, and I followed round the lead inspector. They saw people doing artwork and working in the music room, writing stories, sitting in groups talking – a whole range of activities were going on. The general atmosphere was calm and relaxed.

After the lead inspector had been round most students, he ended up with Terry, who was doing some maths. The inspector asked him about what he was doing, and Terry explained that he was now in year 11 – the year that 15/16-year-olds occupied in a school. However, he mentioned that he had taken three GCSEs the year before and he was taking three more this year. He had gained A grades in his GCSEs, but he felt slightly annoyed about that because he had to go and sit them at a private college, since our College is not an exam centre (and he wanted A* grades). He had felt a bit daunted by the place and he felt that had affected his performance. However, he was confident of better results in the GCSEs he was going to take in the summer of 2017. When the inspector asked about career options, he said he wanted ideally to do computer science at MIT in the USA. I interjected that Terry had opined that no British university was adequate for what he wanted, and therefore that was why he was planning to go to MIT.

After this last conversation the lead inspector stopped his quizzing of our students and said to me that, although I had said there was no imposed curriculum, his view was that we had a broader curriculum than any school, given the wide variety of things that our students study. He and the other inspector then asked to go off to a room to discuss their visit. I showed them into the quiet room at the back of the College. They spent ten minutes in discussion before they came out and said that, clearly, we were not running a school and they would report back accordingly.

They indicated that their report would go to the Department for Education, and this must have taken place because, in December 2016, we received a letter from the Department for Education saying that we were clearly not a school, and that this was accepted by them. So, it is almost that we became the first recognised non-school in the country, which delighted us. However, the initial experience of their showing up unannounced was not very pleasant.

It may be worth adding here that we have conducted programmes for school students in five other local authorities, including in the neighbouring council (East Sussex County Council), where we have been inspected and approved by the Council as an external provider.

Students' views

If the inspectors had quizzed students in more depth, they might have found even more evidence of how students really learned in the College. In later chapters, such as Chapter 8, there is evidence from a range of external research studies. However, I will provide here an extract from a report done for us by an independent researcher, Luke Freedman (Freedman, 2019), as a precursor to introducing aspects of how the College works. These case histories came from in-depth interviews with past students and are direct quotes from his report. They give accounts of experiences in the College and the implications for life after the College:

Kate's Story
SML College was Kate's first experience of an organised educational setting. Before joining she had followed an 'unschooling' approach to life and learning; being supported by her parents to access interesting and stimulating experiences and follow her passions whatever they were. At around age eight she decided she wanted to learn to read, which she did rapidly, and around age nine she began playing music. Until age eleven when she joined the College, pursuing these activities, along with socialising with other home-schooled children, occupied the majority of her time.

Her decision to join the College was driven by a desire to access new opportunities, engage in more formal academic learning, and be a part of a structured learning community. Although she didn't imagine she would find the rules or structure of mainstream school problematic, the idea of being in classes with people who did not want to be there, were not interested in learning, and might not appreciate her passion for learning put her off. SMLC '... *seemed the perfect compromise between school and full home education.*'

Arriving at the College, Kate found exactly what she was looking for; new opportunities to learn and do things she had been previously unaware of, adult tutors who were caring, passionate and knowledgeable, space and time to pursue her interests and studies with support available when it was needed. Although she had not been aware of it, Kate had been self-managing all her life and found it easy to adjust and make the most of the freedom and opportunities on offer.

'*I was absolutely like ... Just ecstatic like at how many things I could learn and how many things they would help me with ...*' [sic]

Unequivocal in her appreciation of Self Managed Learning, her reflections on the group processes at the College are more nuanced. On one hand, she appreciated the importance of learning groups, especially for students new to self-managing, and having a say in the way the College was run was empowering. On the other, she questioned the value of learning groups, at least for herself, and on some occasions she found the democratic resolution of inter-personal issues harsh. Ultimately however, she credits her experience of group processes at the college with the development of important personal characteristics.

'*It gave me the confidence to kind of stand up and potentially argue or reject someone else's opinion, if I thought that it was wrong or if I thought that it was unfair in some way and it gave me that confidence to do that and also to feel like I could do that to adults as well. Even if I felt like they might patronise me or if I felt like they knew more than me or that I was probably wrong. It was like ... it ... it definitely gave me that ability, which obviously is massively important, and I think for me, it was probably more important than the actual Self Managed Learning.*'

Driven by a desire to further her passions, Kate left the college after 3 years to pursue a course in horse care and the beginnings of a career in music. Later, after completing GCSEs independently, she joined a prestigious local 6th form to study English Language and Literature alongside her ongoing music studies at a conservatoire in London. Torn between continuing formal education in English or Music, she chose music.

Now twenty-two she is currently on course to complete a BA in music. Although she occasionally finds their passion for drinking alienating, preferring reading and creative pursuits as a means of relaxation, she has good friends and an active social life in Leeds. Deeply committed to music, she is crystal clear about her life's direction and unperturbed by the knowledge that pursuing her passions may not bring about huge material rewards. Kate has grown into many things; musician, reader, singer, dancer, thinker, caring moral human, and much more besides. Connecting all aspects of her life and character is a unifying thread; a deep and profound love of learning.

'*It's just like learning is the reason I'm alive really, like, I mean, the thing that keeps me going, regardless of anything, is always that feeling of just like how much there is to learn and that I can never stop learning, and in a way, I definitely felt that at the College because I was exposed to so many different areas and so many different subjects whether they were academic or creative or even just areas that were just personal, that personal development, like, I think that idea that you never stop growing and you've never learned everything and that if your purpose in life is kind of just to constantly get better and constantly learn more, then that can never be exhausted and I definitely, definitely got that at the College.'*

Johnny's Story

'In primary school, I used to bully. And I do believe it's because I wasn't getting what I needed from the institution to begin with. Like you know, I had learning needs that weren't being fulfilled, therefore it was frustrating constantly being in lessons. It frustrated me continuously. And then also there was lack of empathy to try and get help which led me to be worse than I really would have been, if it would have been in a pleasant environment. I don't really believe most children, primary school students, really, with OK upbringings, you know, really have it in them just to be absolute assholes just for the sake of it, there has to be something else, I don't really agree with the kids will be kids mindset.'

After leaving the primary school described in this quote, Johnny went on to a Steiner school. He disliked this experience as much as if not more than his primary school, resenting the compulsion to engage in activities he found no joy or purpose in, such as expressive dance. In social terms, while the teacher-student relationships were improved, he found the student-student relationships poor. The combination of these factors caused him to dread attending school and regularly feign illness to avoid it, and his poor attendance eventually resulted in him being expelled.

Initially attracted to the humane atmosphere of SML College, he hadn't really considered their pedagogy before he began. Happily, although he had never previously experienced anything resembling a self managed approach to learning, he found it incredibly easy to adjust, describing the process as taking just a few days. It seemed as if self-managing came naturally to him, and now that his studies were no longer compulsory his relationship to them rapidly began to change.

'I started to enjoy them a lot more. I started to pick up more stuff as well. I started learning the piano. I was just enjoying learning more. I started enjoying English which is something I really really hated but I ended up enjoying it because they let us write about we wanted as long as we fulfilled the criteria of what we needed to do.'

He also adjusted easily to the social environment which was refreshing in comparison with past schools.

'It was a little bit unusual because it wasn't what I was used to. Everyone was very loving and kind and empathetic. So it was quite unusual to be treated with humane respect. A kind of mature level of respect and kindness throughout the whole community … It's quite a natural thing to become accustomed to.'

Johnny had always had an interest in playing the piano but had never had the confidence to try. At the College, the combination of his growing self-assurance, and the availability of a tutor he trusted enabled him to finally take a step which proved to be pivotal. He was soon practising at every available opportunity and decided to pursue further education in music. With the help of the College, he identified a suitable course in music production and prepared an application which was accepted. He flourished on his music production course, finding himself to be much more self-motivated than the majority of his peers.

'I feel like that was a big thing I had from an early age because of SMLC. I knew that if I want to get anywhere doing what I want to do I actually have to put the effort in and do stuff on my own. Be proactive. And I feel like at college that really helped me, because in the music industry and most industries if people don't see you actively working towards something, they are not going to let you in on whatever they're doing or help you get to that place either. I felt like because I was always proactive, and I was always trying to do something, and I was always doing the thing that I want to do, I was given a lot of opportunities that other people weren't.'

Now aged 19, Johnny has just completed his music production course and is working as a live sound and lighting engineer at a variety of venues around Brighton. Doing a job he 'absolutely loves', pursuing his passion for music, enjoying a rich and active social life, and two years into a joyful romantic relationship, to say Johnny is happy with his life would be an understatement. He directly credits all of these things, as well as his confidence, strong moral compass, empathic caring attitude to people and the world, and his sense of personal responsibility, to the experiences he had during his two years at SML College.

'I believe I was only able to get to where I am now because of SMLC. SMLC has helped me develop into a person I feel happy to be. Without that guidance I believe I would be an unhappy and less emotionally mature person with little to no skills.'

Mike's Story

Mike never struggled to find purpose in the activities and lessons he was obliged to do during his time in mainstream education. However, he found the social and physical environment – big schools, big classes – intimidating, and decided to move into home education for a more intimate and personal approach to learning. For four years, home education worked well for him, but aged fourteen his family did not feel able to provide the support necessary to study for GSCE's and together they decided to look for other options.

Mike was attracted to the combination of freedom, flexibility and support, and the small size that SML College offered. Although he had been out of formal education for some time, his home-schooling had been organised and directed by his parents and tutors. The concept and practice of self-managing was entirely new to him.

'I definitely did struggle to manage my own learning … managing my timetable … making sure that I actually did the work or stuck to my timetable. There was so much freedom at SMLC as I'm sure you're aware of … yeah … and … trying to commit

yourself to your studies while there is also sort of the social element; it was tricky. It was very difficult as a teenager to do that yourself. Of course at school you'd be disciplined if you're talking in class whereas at SMLC instead of doing what's on your timetable you had the flexibility to do something else, without punishment. So. I guess that was quite tricky.'

At the same time, he reports appreciating the flexibility to study whatever he wanted whether or not it was academic, receiving support without judgment to pursue his interests, and being able to use online resources to study at his own pace. He also valued the social dynamic of the College, the way tutors related to students, and the capacity to have a say in the way the College was organised.

'You definitely had a voice at SMLC. I don't know if it's still the case now. But back then every morning we have a meeting, actually it was twice a day, at the beginning of the morning, at the end of the morning we'd have a meeting. We could express how we feel about things and any issues that we had. So I think that was definitely a bonus. You weren't … It wasn't the typical teacher-student relationship where the teacher tells you what to do. The teachers were listening to your opinions. They gave honest advice. They treated you perhaps in a more mature way than would be at a conventional school.'

As he came closer to his GSCEs, which he considered important at the time, Mike was able to motivate himself to commit to his exam preparation. He achieved good passes in Business, French, English Language and Maths, and along with the personal statement the college helped him to write, these grades got him into the college he wanted to attend. However, a combination of factors including lack of support and the intimidating scale meant he did not get on with 6th form and dropped out after 3 months.

After leaving, Mike joined an apprenticeship in digital marketing. The combination of real-world activity, small group size, being paid, and having the good fortune to be placed in a company which like SML College valued his voice, meant that this programme worked incredibly well for him and he flourished. Since finishing his apprenticeship he has continued to progress in the digital marketing industry and is now the head of SEO for a marketing agency, an impressive feat for a 21-year-old.

'I tell you what I love it. And again you're probably going to think oh stop comparing yourself to your peers. But when I look at myself in comparison to some of my peers who are just coming out of university. So many graduates are looking for apprenticeships. It's crazy. It's almost like those three years, or even college five years that they've spent doing that just to be in the same position that I was back then … Definitely I don't know. I don't know what the word is. I don't know whether pride is the right word.'

Looking forward, Mike hopes to further his career, pursue his passion for travel, learn more, and eventually start his own business, reasonable aspirations for someone in his position. Reflecting on his time at SML College he considers its greatest benefits to be developing social skills and learning the importance of motivating yourself:

'... although I found it a struggle at first the lack of structure and lack of being told what to do. In reality that's something I was going to face at some point in my life anyway so ... I think ... I guess SMLC did help me in that, and help me to realise that I am the master of my destiny or whatever and that only I can choose where I go.'

The next story is one that relates to when we had the programme in my house. For four years I had 12 students and two staff occupying all the ground floor of the house. We also built a music and art room in the garden. I had already built an office in the garden (which students called 'the shed'). After four years we moved into the Brighton Youth Centre so that we could expand as we had a long waiting list for places.

David's Story

The bullying began in David's first year of secondary school. Unfortunately, despite drawing the school's attention to the abuse he was suffering – first verbal and then physical – he received no meaningful support. Over the course of several years, the bullying not only persisted, but worsened, and as it did so David's anxiety and depression increased as well. Just before he left mainstream education, David was being physically assaulted regularly. Never knowing when the next attack would come, he existed in a state of constant fear. He avoided eye contact with other students, ate his lunch in the toilet – the only place he felt safe – and often considered self-harm and suicide. Clearly, attendance at school was incompatible with even the most basic level of wellbeing.

After six months at home, David's family began to look for educational environments that might be able to meet his needs. Away from school, his depression had improved somewhat, but his anxiety was still extremely debilitating. SML College seemed a good fit for his educational needs, but at that point, just leaving the house was a real achievement.

'The thing that I liked about it when I did start going was just how gradual and how comforting the environment was. I would walk past the window and cover my face so I didn't have to see or look at any of the other students and I would go straight to his shed and he would do like 1–1 sessions with me. He would do Maths and stuff and ... I mean it was quite difficult even though obviously it's ... looking back it doesn't seem that much but it was a big step ... and then ... it was very gradual so ... but it was progression so we would ... I would progress over time ... and then I would be exposed to the other students and then I would actually be able to go into the house and do some stuff there and like talk to other people ... cause I basically had a phobia of people my age and the way they slowly introduced me and understood ... like Ian really understood what I needed at that time and that's what I think was the best part about being there.' [sic]

At SML College David found a place where he felt accepted for who he was. The attentive attitude of tutors led to David being formally diagnosed with autism, missed by his previous schools, which helped him to better understand himself. Although he did take part in formal study at the college, including gaining a good English GSCE, in his view the most important thing he achieved at the college was a transformative positive shift in his psychological wellbeing, a shift he understands as being enabled by the combinations of flexibility and structure, and freedom and support, which characterised his experience of SML College.

After SML College he went on to a mainstream 6th form and then University where he earned a 2–2 honours degree in Psychology. While it was initially a struggle returning to larger and more formal learning environments, which reminded him of his traumatic experiences in school, the personal development he achieved at SML College enabled him to make a success of both the academic and social aspects of 6th form and university.

Now aged 24, David enjoys a stable long term romantic relationship and participates in a variety of hobbies including learning how to code and playing the piano. He is currently working in two part-time jobs at a pharmacy and as a tutor. While he is not yet fully satisfied with his work life, he is proactive about improving it and optimistic for the future:

'It's just like minimum wage stuff but it's better than nothing and it's a lot better than what my parents and what a lot of people thought that I would be doing 8 or so years ago. They thought I would never leave the house or I'd never really be able to function ... like I could barely function as an individual person let alone manage to get or maintain some kind of income. I think it is a big improvement. Obviously I'm very ... I'm really wanting to work more and find a more stable income so I have been looking at lots of different options.
I might even go back to college. I've been thinking of doing an electrical engineering ... like that type of [vocational] degree.' [sic]

David only spent two years at SML College. However, he clearly understands his time there as a pivotal period of his life. Without it, he imagines he would have been less comfortable and confident in himself, less socially skilled and active, unable to function in paid employment and for all these reasons a less happy, less psychologically well, and less successful person.

Aspects of how the College works

These case studies indicate the differing experiences of just a few of our ex-students. I will now explain a little about how the College works so that the lived experiences of ex-students might be better understood and analysed.

My role in all this is technically as Chair of Governors of the College, though I also led the creation of the College 18 years earlier, and that creation was as a result of a long history of developing Self Managed Learning for our work in organisations. Hence, I will also need to say something about how that whole process occurred. In this section I will introduce some key aspects of how we work, and then other examples will be provided as we go along.

The College is located in the south of England so comments about the context of our work will recognise this. However, I have worked around the world

developing the approach in various educational contexts. So, although some specifics about the English education scene will necessarily come into my discussion,
the Self Managed Learning approach has proved widely applicable across cultures.

An example of the English context in the above is the reference to the use of
GCSEs. The acronym stands for the General Certificate of Secondary Education
and is the standard public examination for 16-year-olds. Also, I have referred to the
grading in GCSEs, which went from A★ to A to B, and so on. At the time of
writing the Department for Education in England has started to change this to a
numerical scale 9 (at the top) to 1 (at the bottom).

In the section above I mentioned that the College was at that time located in
Brighton Youth Centre. Since then we have moved to our own premises and have
expanded from 18 students to 39. It is not our intention to grow much larger and
possibly we will limit our size to 48 students aged 9 to 17.

Structure not control

In a typical school the main structural arrangement is the classroom. This is also a
location for providing control over learners. My contention is that structures are
important so we should try to create forms of them which not only reduce control
but actually facilitate the capability for each person to self manage.

There is much confusion about the difference between structure and control. In
some earlier work in the 1970s a group of us created the School for Independent
Study within a higher educational institution. What we found was that students
asked for more structure. Each person was pursuing their own individual learning
and what students wanted was more support for them to achieve their own ends.
Unfortunately, the faculty interpreted this as meaning more control and so pro-
ceeded to be more instructional in the way they operated.

My argument is then that we need to have structures because life in general is
structured. People have structures to their daily life. For instance, getting up in the
morning, having breakfast, having a wash, getting dressed – all of these processes
generally occur within a structure. Most people do not necessarily think of it as a
structure, but I would want to use the word structure in this wider context.

The most common analogy I have used is that of a glass. A glass has a rigid
structure which allows you to put something in it. This could be milk, beer, wine,
water – whatever you choose. If the glass was made of, say, cotton wool, then it
would not be much use. Any liquid put into it would readily escape. So, there is a
value in having a rigid structure in this particular case. However, the next most
important feature of the glass is that it is empty. There is a space in which you can
put liquid. Empty spaces are crucial. It is not the person who invented the wheel
who is important – it was the person who invented the hole. A wheel without a
hole is largely useless. Once you put a hole in it you can create an axle and then
you can produce vehicles that can move. So, you could say that usefulness comes
from nothingness – a Taoist concept. In writing this I'm sitting in my office and it
is useful because it is a rigid structure with walls and a roof, but it allows me to sit

in my chair at the computer. If the room was full to the ceiling of tables and chairs, then it would not be much use. Usefulness comes from the bounded free space.

A further feature of the glass is that it is transparent. This is really useful because you can see what is in the glass. So, there is value in rigid transparent structures which provide space. The final feature of a glass is that it needs to be robust. Its value comes from being able, for instance, to withstand temperature change. If you put a glass that lacks this robustness into a dishwasher or into hot water, it will crack. So robust, rigid, empty structures that are transparent are crucial.

This analogy applies to learning. We need rigid, transparent, robust, empty structures. Such structures assist the person to be autonomous. They have the freedom to put into the space what they need. Unlike a classroom, which is filled with what the teacher wants to fill it with, we use approaches that provide a structure which allows the young person to say what they want and to learn whatever they want. Our aim therefore is to minimise controls, and certainly to provide the kind of freedom missing in most schools.

A learning community

If you came to the College in the morning you would find that at 9 o'clock we have a community meeting. We also have such a meeting at the end of the morning. The meeting is chaired in rotation. It could be an adult who is chairing the meeting, or it could be a nine-year -old. A community meeting creates its own rules, so that there is a boundary and a structure to the meeting. For instance, we agree that one person speaks at a time so that everybody can be heard, if they want to be. Therefore, a person wanting to speak needs to put their hand up so that the chair can recognise them and pass them a beanbag. The person holding the bean-bag is therefore entitled to speak and say whatever they want, provided they stick to the rules. The major rule that the community agreed is for respect: respect yourself, respect others, respect the building, respect the environment, and so on. Hence, for instance, abusive language isn't allowed.

The freedom of each person to be able to speak uninterrupted does, of course, limit the freedom of others who want to interrupt. This could be categorised as giving the freedom to do things, but also the freedom not to be oppressed by others. This is recognised in society where a person is not free to rob another person because in doing that the other person's freedom is restricted. If you rob someone of an item, then they're not free to use that item anymore.

In our context it is important that people recognise, within the community, the need to be able to be yourself and part of that is the freedom from fear or ridicule – or any other aspect that may limit the individual's freedom.

In the community meeting there are rules about how the meeting should operate but they are very minimal. A lot of the time it is actually common sense and does not need to be articulated. However, for new people coming into the community, it can seem a strange place, and they need help to recognise that it is a place where people can raise anything in the meeting: they can ask for help; they can make suggestions about things that need to be done within the College, and so on. They also need to understand that freedom cannot be disrupted by interrupting an individual when they are talking.

Learning groups

Another important structure we have is that of the learning group. Learning groups are typically made up of five or six students and one adult in the role of learning group adviser. The idea of the learning group is that each person can plan their own learning with support from others. Those 'others' will be fellow students as well as adults who are within the community to support learners. In the first week of the year there are three objectives that have to be achieved in that week. First of all, we need to make the community work effectively and that means discussing rules and agreeing how we can operate. Secondly, each individual needs, by the end of the week, to have worked out some plans about what they want to do whilst being members of the community, and beyond. Thirdly, we need to make certain that learning groups are created such that there is a bond between group members and that they are able to provide support for each other in their learning. The learning group is not a team or seminar or a tutorial or any of the normal structures that you might find within a school. The group is a place where each person has time to talk about whatever they need to talk about and get help on a whole range of things that they may want to raise.

Learning agreement

We have a very clear structure for how students are helped to plan. During the first week we go through a series of questions that students need to answer. Note that each person is able to answer those questions in any way they want and the questions themselves are like the glass in being a robust, transparent, empty structure. The five questions that we ask students to address during the first week are taken in order. These questions are as follows:

1   **Where have I been?** What has been my experience of learning so far in my life? What other things have happened to me in my life that make me who I am now?
2   **Where am I now?** What kind of person am I? What are things that I like or don't like? What do I enjoy? And also, what do I find unpleasant? What skills, abilities and knowledge do I have that are important to me? What do I value – what do I care about? What do I believe in?
3   **Where do I want to get to?** Who do I want to be in the future? What kind of life do I want to lead? What kind of work would I like to do? What things do I need to learn and develop now to help me in life and work?
4   **How will I get there?** What precisely do I need to learn and how will I learn? What processes will I use to learn things I want to learn? What help might I need? What other resources might I need?

5   **How will I know if I've arrived?** How will I assess my development? How will I know if I've learned to the level that I need? How will I recognise that I have gained the capabilities and knowledge I need?

In Chapter 8 I will go into more detail about the research evidence about how the particular structures and processes work. I will say here a little bit more about the five questions that we use so that the rationale for using this approach is a bit more apparent. In later chapters I will indicate more about the way we actually do it in practice.

The reason for asking the first question about a person's past is that anyone today is 100% as a result of the past. Crudely, we can say that we have experienced three things in the past that make us as we are today. Firstly, there is our genetic makeup, which clearly indicates many features of the person in the present. Secondly, there are things that the person has learned from birth (or maybe before birth) through to the present day. Thirdly, there are physical changes each person goes through, for instance, gaining height, gaining strength, increasing manual dexterity, and so on. Hence if we are to understand the person in the present, it can be really valuable to get an understanding of their past.

In terms of the learning dimension, there are a number of contexts the person will have experienced. Initially, the family plays a major role. Or, if they are not in a family, appropriate caregivers will be influential. It is likely that over time there will be then increasing influence from the environment around the family including media, relatives, other adults, and so on. If an individual goes to school, then that becomes another influence alongside the others. What we are interested in teasing out is some idea of the implications of all those influences. We are not trying to do an extensive rigorous survey of the person's past history but rather to identify perhaps key moments or key influences.

A good example is where individuals might have been told things within the school context. For instance, we have students who come to us having been told they are no good at music, no good at art or no good in another area of their learning. Recently, I was talking to a new 10-year-old student who said that he was not good at English. When I questioned him he talked about what he was reading and, clearly, he read well (for example, he had read all the Harry Potter books when he was younger). He had written various things and his writing was clear, and his grammar and spelling were quite good. So, I said to him that it seemed like he could read and write, so what was this about not being good at English. Then he indicated that this had come from his previous school and was to do with the extent to which he conformed to the teacher's requirements in English. He was, for instance, not a fan of tests and found the emphasis on knowing grammatical rules pointless.

Another example was a student who had tried to learn the cello and been told that he was not musical. Our music tutor found out that he was interested in music and so suggested that he might like to just have a go with a guitar and learn some chords. He was keen to do this and gradually learned to play the guitar and four other instruments over the next year. Eventually he went on to university and gained a degree in music. Hence finding out about a person's past is important. Often, it is to disabuse them of negative opinions that they have absorbed. They can then make a fresh start in the College.

Sometimes students want to talk about issues within their family – for instance, the separation of their parents and what impact that had on their learning. Others comment on the implications of travelling around with their parents and therefore moving school a great deal. There are others who have not been to school and are more likely to comment on their home education.

It is our contention that we cannot possibly engage in the process of helping the person to learn unless we know the point at which they are starting from. The second question about where the person is now leads logically from the first question. What is disappointing, and indeed frightening, is that young people coming to us from school tend to have more negative assumptions about themselves, and their abilities, than positive ones.

I remember one new girl saying that she was not good at anything and she meant it. She had had a bad experience in school, and she had been labelled as someone with learning difficulties. Certainly, her English was patchy, and she could not do maths at all. However, we found that she was a dancer, and had been entering dance competitions. She was also someone who contributed greatly to the community because she was always someone who, as I would put it, would 'tell it like it is'. She was a kind of moral compass within the community – for instance, she wasn't afraid to speak out about important issues. It was essential for us to help her to start to value herself and to understand that she could learn, but it would need to fit in with the way in which she did learn.

The point about valuing all students equally is important. Schools tend to value those who are good at 'doing schooling'. This would include those who are good at tests, though sometimes it might be sporting or musical ability, for example. Young people know who is valued and who isn't in the school system, and this impacts hugely on how their identity develops. We are clear that we value all students equally. We don't force students to take tests, for instance, and certainly not ones where they inevitably compare themselves with others. It is crucial that we establish at the start our stance. As students share the answers to these five questions in their learning group, they develop a recognition of this.

The third question we ask is about thoughts they have for the future. We appreciate that some students may have given very little thought towards what they might do in the future, especially those in the younger age range. However, we find that asking people about the kind of life they might like to leave when they become adults does get a lot of responses. For instance, people will talk about wanting to travel, or not, and wanting a family life, or not, to earn money, or not. These judgements of course come out of past experience and their exposure to media and other influences, and they may not be helpful notions.

Certainly, we have had some students who started out by saying they wanted to have jobs that earned them a lot of money and then gradually they moved towards jobs that would give them the satisfaction they wanted in life, with the hope that they would earn enough to lead the life they wanted to lead. One boy's parents had divorced some years ago, and he had only really met his father in the circumstances where the father's wealth was rather apparent. He had been brought up by his mother, who was not wealthy. His initial ideas were around taking on the same kind of career as his father because he had a notion of that being a more glamorous and more satisfying life. He is someone who changed his mind through the course of attending the College, and not because we pushed him. We gave him the space to think things through for himself.

The important point is that we challenge people to think about the future because there will be some future for them. It is not about whether they get it right or not, but more that they start to think about the way that they think about things. Often young people have an implicit idea of some kind of glowing future, which they don't articulate. Once they have articulated it, they may start to see flaws in it, and they may start to think more widely about what they might do.

In all our work with young people exploring these questions our objective is to get them to explore for themselves – to really learn how to learn. Learning to learn is not about learning, for instance, study skills techniques for passing exams. It's about young people developing the confidence that they will be able to learn what they need to learn as they go through life, given the changing nature of the world. We are not necessarily suggesting that they plan for a particular kind of job, although some may want to. Given that the world of work is changing rapidly, rigid assumptions about future work opportunities may not be helpful. Later I will return to this and explore the issue of the changing nature of the work environment.

The fourth question asks students to think about how they going to move from where they are (question 2) to where they might like to be (question 3). In a school context this might be labelled a syllabus or a curriculum. Even if the goal that a person might think is appropriate is one that could be challenged, it can be very important to look at the gap between where the person is, and where they would like to be. An example was working in a school with a group of seven-year-olds. One boy said he wanted to be an astronaut. It's quite possible that this might not be his career choice in future. However, what it gave us was an opportunity to then question him about what he would need to learn to be able to do that. Then we could get into a productive dialogue about learning and about how that boy could use the school context to learn things that he wanted to do. Such a discussion raised questions such as: Would an astronaut need good English? Would they need to be physically fit? Would they need to know science, for example, to understand how rockets work? What about astronomy? This led on then to considering what he now might start to learn that might lead to that career, or to something else.

Another example was in a school where we were working with 11/12-year-olds. One boy said he would like to be a film director. It's one of the things that appealed to him. Since we were making a film about our programme in the school, we suggested he might like to attach himself to the film crew to see first-hand what a film director did. He thought this was a great idea and the film crew agreed to it. Largely, he was fetching and carrying things for them and observing their work. We had given him the task of learning from that situation and to be able to report back on this to his group.

When he came back to the group, we quizzed him on what he had learned. Then I asked him to identify on a flipchart the particular abilities and skills that he saw the director exhibiting. One of these was being organised, so then I asked him to rate his own ability in terms of being organised on a scale of 1 to 10. He rated himself 3 out of 10. His colleagues in the group agreed with him. Incidentally, this is a good example of why groups are so important because peers can engage productively in this kind of discussion.

He recognised through his peers and his own self-evaluation that he was someone who was quite disorganised and, for instance, often did not do his homework and was generally seen as a somewhat messy student. We could then say, 'Well if you want to be a film director, how are you going to learn to be more organised?' This could get him either to loop back to his original choice and say perhaps that he didn't want to be a film director, or to challenge him about what kind of learning he might really need to engage in.

Hopefully this little incident shows the links across the questions we ask. The information from question 2 (where he was then) showed a lack of organisation. The options in question 3 (where he wanted to be) showed the challenge of the gap and that led to question 4 (how he would bridge the gap). Generally, students are able to make good progress on the first three questions, given help from the group. Young people can come up with goals for learning that can make sense. Where they often need more help from us (learning advisers) is in the 'how'. They may have very limited ideas how to learn what they need as they may well have been exposed to a limited range of options, for example, a classroom or reading. We have found from our research at least 57 learning modes available to young people.

The fifth question we ask is about assessment and how students can judge if they have achieved what they wanted to achieve. In schooling much of the assessment is based on tests and examinations. It's rare that our students think of these as important measures. However, where people feel the need to take GCSEs because they lead onto the particular career, like being a scientist or a doctor, then clearly exam results come into this. However, what we hope is that students will understand that there is a wider picture here. In a recent conversation with an ex-student now age 17 the difference between GCSE results and career needs became very apparent. He said that he rather regretted devoting so much time to getting good results in his GCSE subjects. He is someone who actually did well in his exams and got very good grades. He wants to go into working in computing and originally had set his goal of going to university to do computer science. This changed through time as he started to do projects and create a portfolio. He gained a presence for himself on the internet by the age of 16. This meant that he was asked to work with a company engaged in blockchain development based in the USA. He started doing this and working out of his home in Brighton.

He is very clear that his GCSE results are an irrelevance in terms of his current work. He gained a reputation through doing projects with us that then went out into the wider world and he now feels that it would have been better him to spend more time on that activity, rather than slogging away to get good GCSE results – especially as for most students these days it has become a rather stressful and unpleasant experience. In judging his achievement of his goals he is now quite clear that going to do a degree, in the way that he had thought of, is not relevant and that in answering now this question 5 it is obvious that he is getting paid to do work that he enjoys and is doing rather well at it – and that this is a good assessment of his development and what he achieved.

Conclusion

In this chapter I wanted to indicate some aspects of the different ways in which I and my colleagues think about learning and about education. My contention is that learning is crucial within our society, both collectively and for individuals. In the next chapter I will say more about that. I'm clear, however, both from our research, and that of credible researchers who I have come across, that the current educational model has very little to offer. It's not that it has nothing to offer. But we as adults can do a lot better.

In advising my son and my daughter through school I suggested that they needed to use the school, and not be used by it. I made it clear that I would stand by them when they decided not to do what the school wanted and I would support them. They both had challenges, especially at university, to their ways of wanting to undertake their learning. In the end both were successful at university (as judged by the system – e.g. with first-class degrees – and by themselves) and both are now enjoying life in widely different careers.

I specially wanted to establish here the importance of having good structures and processes – particularly ones that reduce control from adults and in essence are liberatory and more conducive to the freedom of the learner. In arguing for Self Managed Learning I also want to say that in reality young people do manage their own learning anyway when they are in school. For instance, students make choices about what they want to learn and what they don't want to learn. They may spend their time in classrooms daydreaming or fooling around. These are choices individuals make and, in general, are choices that, from the individual's point of view, seem to be the most desirable at the time. They may not, of course, be sensible in the long term as school pupils generally get little help in thinking through how they approach learning. When we go into schools and introduce the Five Questions approach and the use of learning groups it is a revelation to both young people and their teachers.

Finally, I want to offer Self Managed Learning as an example of what a New Educational Paradigm looks like. It is only one example amongst hundreds of programmes and projects around the world that emphasise freedom and rights for young people.

Reference

Freedman, L. (2019) The Self Managed Learning College Study, Phase One Report. Brighton: Centre for Self Managed Learning.

3

THE CENTRALITY OF LEARNING

Introduction

This chapter is not meant to provide a complete encyclopaedic exploration of learning. That belongs elsewhere. Rather, what I need to do is to identify some issues around learning, such that later chapters can be based on an understanding of key facets of learning that will impact on what is to be explored later.

I used to think that it was fairly obvious that people learned all the time and that, for instance, anyone who has watched a baby grow up can see the extent to which the baby learns hugely in the first few years of its life. What is interesting about that learning is the role of adults. A child will only learn to talk if it has been exposed to language. It's clear that during those first five years of life the child can only be helped if the parents and other adult carers are prepared to learn about the baby, before the baby can learn from them. Babies make noises, attempt to do things like walking, and adults need to observe and respond appropriately by learning about this other human being. Unfortunately, this whole process gets turned around from about the age of four or five in the UK when play and natural learning is overtaken by the role of the formal education system.

I have to admit that it's very difficult for me to take seriously some of the statements that I will mention here. Firstly, *The Guardian* newspaper has had as a headline in its education section 'How early should learning begin'.[1] I thought that *The Guardian* was a reasonably well-written and thoughtful newspaper, but that just showed how, in their education section, it's been taken over by an educational establishment that has the notion that learning and education are somehow joined. The idea that formal education should be the start of learning is bizarre.

The Chartered Institute of Personnel and Development (CIPD) claims a key role in the matter of learning and development at work. In August 2018 it had a survey on its website which had the following question, 'Do You Participate in

Formal Learning Programmes to Boost Your Career?' Three possible answers were given:

1   *Yes*
2   *No, but I would like to*
3   *No, I can't find the time.*

That's it. Just three options and no space for comments.

The notion that so-called informal learning has value is not accounted for. I will show that actually it's the informal learning that matters.

In an article in the CIPD magazine the author (Kirton, 2018) cites the Department for Education as saying that '19% of adults are currently engaged in some form of learning'. So, 81% of the adult population are assumed not to be learning. Anything at all! And this is the Department for Education. This government department clearly buys into the educational model that if you are not on a course you can't be learning anything.

Please note that here the educational view is that it's not just that the other learning is irrelevant. It is that it isn't actually learning. Otherwise we would not have a government department saying that only 19% of the adult population is learning. A key focus of this chapter is about showing that the educational establishment, including the Department for Education and daily newspapers, are completely and utterly wrong. It is why this book is about learning rather than school-oriented education, since we can see what the educational model does in terms of underestimating the daily learning that goes on for adults who are not in a coma. We know that learning even goes on while you sleep (Walker, 2018). And such learning is actually rather important. As Walker shows, NREM sleep is the reflective dimension in sleep where raw data and skills can be stored; REM sleep is involved in integrating this material and enabling innovation and problem solving to occur.

In a visit to a school for extremely disabled children, I was able to see the amazing work of those adults helping the children to learn. What was odd was that there was an expectation that the children there would follow a modified version of the National Curriculum. The principal of the school explained that they were supposed to, for instance, test the children on knowledge such as what was the difference between a triangle and a rectangle. These could be children who were unfortunately destined for a short life and for whom the most important thing was helping them to be happy and fulfilled in the time that they were alive and in the school.

One assumption in the past was that if the child was completely paralysed and unable to speak or use their hands, they couldn't write and therefore couldn't think. With the use of computers to help children use eyeblink to write stories, they found that such children learn very well and that they were able to write using the eyeblink mode on their computers. It didn't actually involve pen to paper or fingers to keyboard (Bryan, 2018). People who have a notion of learning to write as something that is done as a psychomotor task are misguided. Due to a serious bicycle accident that for some time put my left arm out of use, I learned to do voice to text writing and this is how this book is being produced. There was a wonderful TV programme entitled *The Singing Detective* that featured a private detective who had a disability which caused him to be in hospital. As he was lying seemingly motionless in bed, the nurse asked him what he was doing and he said that he was writing. And so he was. Writing goes on in your head, not on a piece of paper and in this day and age having to handwrite examinations, which is imposed on children, is unacceptable.

Returning to the special school with highly disabled children, I provided a small help to the principal in making a case, to use the educational jargon, 'to disapply the National Curriculum'. It seemed to me strange that he had to do this, given the enormous difficulties for the adults supporting these children. It's another example of the imposition of an educational model that seems to disregard the needs of particular individuals.

Learning is not all one process

It is reported that Bishop William Temple said that education has been about learning 'to think together and feel separately' whereas what we need is people to learn 'to feel together and think separately'.

The educational model has been one where the requirement is to learn knowledge and skills and to exclude wider issues of learning. The thinking together dimension of education is linked to classrooms and examinations, all of which require testing of standardised knowledge and skills which are imposed on the collective of young people. Schools in England certainly see 'feeling stuff' as belonging to pastoral care and if somebody has a problem with feelings they are sent to a counsellor if they're lucky, or if it's really bad (for example, mental health issues), sent to a psychiatrist or psychotherapist.

The emphasis on learning within a restricted domain means that education cannot fulfil the needs of young people. The increase in suicides amongst young people is indicative of this problem.[2] Children are not born suicidal. They learn things which may force the unfortunate few to develop feelings that their life is not worthwhile, and they can kill themselves. What we do know is that for young people, especially in their teens, the biggest influence on them is their peer group.[3] What is necessary for them is to fit in, to be accepted by their peers and to get on with them. When an individual is picked on through overt bullying in school or via social media such that they believe that they do not fit in or are not accepted by their peers, then at the very least it causes mental health problems and at the very worst it causes suicide.

We know that schools complain about this problem and see it as interfering in the education of children. However, in reality, for children in distress, the learning that is most important for them is around how they deal with that distress; how they can have a meaningful and fulfilled life.

For the rest of this chapter I will elaborate on just a few specific aspects of learning. I will focus on those areas which seem to me to be troublesome and problematic, especially for the education establishment. Hopefully, they help indicate the stance I take on learning and therefore how Self Managed Learning has evolved.

Defining learning

Some clues as to how I might define learning may be evident from the discussion above. However, perhaps a starting point to this section would be useful to show an equation that I put up when making presentations.

$$U = f(G,L,P) + X$$

You (U) are a function of the interaction of G (genes), L (learning) and P (physical factors). The X stand for a potential unknown or an aspect that could be disputed. An example of this would be the notion of the soul or spirit, which those who have a spiritual or religious orientation will regard as a factor in who we are and how we behave.

I appreciate that this is a slightly phony equation, but it can be useful to focus people's minds on what I think are the key factors that we need to address. Clearly, there's always been a debate about the balance between what is in our genes and what has been learned. As far as I'm concerned, I'm not interested in an argument about the relative proportions of these two factors. There is no doubt that our genes have a huge impact on who we are. However, we also need to be aware of the growing evidence from epigenetics which indicates that genes can be switched on or off (Carey, 2012). The metaphor of switching is not particularly valid as the process is a chemical one of methylation. However, what is undeniable is that a narrow and old-fashioned view of genes is no longer credible.

The physical dimension is often forgotten. We age. As a result of that we change purely by virtue of the processes of ageing. I'm aware that at my current age of 76, I'm not able to do the things that I could do at the age of 26, like playing sport. I might like to fool myself that I can do things I could do then, but I am fooling myself. Also, if someone has had an accident where they lose legs or arms, this impacts on who they are and what they can do. Therefore, we can't ignore the physical domain and, with current interests in areas such as the impact of obesity on children and the role of diet, it would be foolish to put this dimension into the margins.

One way of progressing is to say that if we consider what's in the genes, what has occurred physically for a person and any other unknown factors, then what is left in explaining who a person is and what they do comes from learning. Due to the fact that learning occurs all the time every day in all sorts of contexts it is easily forgotten as a process, as I showed above. Also, it is easier for an education establishment to say that education and learning are one thing and that, if pushed, say that any other learning outside the classroom does not really count. My stance is the opposite and research shows that indeed, as mentioned in the introduction, the majority of useful learning that people undertake has nothing to do with education, training, courses, classrooms and lessons.

In our Declaration on Learning – produced by 13 of us involved in organisational learning (see Chapter 1) – we said that, 'The ability to learn about learning and to harness the learning process is the key to our ability to survive in a complex and unpredictable world.' We absolutely meant this. Given that we can't do anything about our genes and our physical ageing processes, then the only way we can deal with changes in the world and to make appropriate changes is through learning. There is no other process available to us as humans. If we are to make better decisions about dealing with social and global problems that we face, then we have to learn better. This is a factor for individuals and society at large. We just have to get a whole lot better at individual and collective learning.

Here is just a small example of the link between individual learning responses and social problems. In an early Self Managed Learning programme we had one participant from the British Civil Service who was being fast tracked to a senior position. As is often the custom in the Civil Service he was asked to do an initial draft on a matter of policy that would go up the chain and end up with the Minister. His manager asked him to draft something on what at the time was called vagrancy, which now would be more associated with homelessness, begging and other issues affecting our inner cities. He said to his manager that he probably ought to go out onto the streets and learn about vagrancy practically from the people experiencing it. His manager expressly forbade him to do this. He said that his role was a policy one, and that therefore he had to work on policy and that such practical activity was forbidden. Being a conscientious and new person in the Civil Service, he decided to disobey his manager, and to go on the streets at weekends and meet with people who at the time were labelled as vagrants. He learned a great deal talking with individuals. I doubt, though, that whatever policies he drafted based on that had much influence by the time it got up to the level of the Minister. It is indicative of how individual learning needs to feed into collective learning and I will say more about this later on.

Education, work and learning

It was common in my school, and I believe it still is, for teachers to chide pupils who were not working. Working meant working at a prescribed task from the teacher. Also, in modern parlance, there is reference to having pupils 'on task'. If you are not working at a prescribed problem or task, then it is assumed that you are not learning.

Recently, a parent asked me what we would do if a student was not working. I indicated that we may do nothing, since it's not apparent that it's a problem. Often when I was criticised in school for not working, I would be thinking about something not to do with what the teacher was prescribing – but it was productive thinking as far as I was concerned. The notion that work and learning go together is strange to me. For instance, I worked on a production line once. After the first day I wasn't learning anything. In school, I might be given ten maths questions to answer. But if I had understood what the learning point was, and had answered the first couple of questions correctly, I could not see the point in another eight that may be increasing in complexity, but did not enhance my learning. 'Working' in school is not necessarily equal to learning and on the other side learning does not necessarily equal working.

Our approach allows us to escape from the irrelevance of prescribed tasks. I remember taking a couple of students to a hack event that gave them the opportunity to work on the programming of simple devices such as Arduinos. They were given a booklet with ten tasks of increasing complexity. One of the students just went to the tenth task and did it; he knew then that he hadn't needed to do the preceding nine.

I repeat that there are lots of times I've worked at things and have not been learning and lots of times when I've been learning but not working at things. Many writers have indicated the importance of play in learning. Gray (2013) provides a comprehensive analysis of the importance of play, especially for children, but also for adults. Many educationalists head to Finland to find out about the education system because it is seen as successful. One thing they seem to miss is that children in Finland do not go to school until they are seven. The importance of the kindergarten experience and play seems to get missed because people go with blinkers.[4]

Another use of the notion of work is in the imposition of homework on young people. Note that it is not about home learning. The assumption is that person will work on school-directed tasks while they are away from the school. What we do know is that young people learn a huge amount within the home and from people they interact with outside school. One example from our research on both young people and adults is the value of travel. Unfortunately, schools in England fine parents who take children out of school to travel in term time. The Government has demanded that headteachers of schools take a draconian attitude towards this and fine parents. At present, the norm is for parents to be fined £60 for a day out of school for a child who is taken out without permission. This rises to £120 if it is not paid within 21 days and after 28 days parents can be prosecuted. In England overall in 2017/18, there were 260,877 penalty notices issued for unauthorised absences from school. There were 19,580 prosecutions for non-payment of fines. This has gone up from the previous year of 13,324. There have also been ten parents (usually mothers) sent to prison for lack of attendance from their children. The idea that a child will be helped by their mother being sent to prison seems completely bizarre to me.

In our College we encourage parents to travel, if they can afford it, because we see the value in it. A good example was a 14-year-old student whose parents were working for a few months in India. She was able to go with them and carry on with her learning. A lot of the learning was, of course, about being in India and learning about the culture, language and norms of another society. For the two months she was away she remained in contact with her learning group via a weekly Skype session. Her group was able to engage for most of the morning with her while she was sitting on a beach in India with her laptop.

This negative attitude towards travel seems to be linked to the whole notion that young people should be working – either working in school or working at home on prescribed school tasks. The idea that there could be important learning taking place by being in another culture seems to have escaped authorities. We do know, of course, that many parents want to take their children on holiday out of term time because of the increased prices of holidays during term time. The assumption is that there can't be useful learning on holiday. This notion that you don't learn anything on a holiday is directly contradicted by our research on young people. There are the experiences of different food, a different language, a different culture, and so on, which are all valuable learning experiences. Our research with senior leaders in organisations has indicated that they have gained a great deal from travelling, not just abroad but also within the UK. Hence, we encourage parents to utilise the opportunities to travel with their children and for students when they come back from travelling to reflect on what they have gained from any new experiences.

What has been interesting is how ex-students refer to what they learned at the College. Many talk about gaining social skills, although we don't teach social skills. We create a learning community where students learn to interact freely with others. Some of the learning comes from structured experiences, such as the fact that each and every student gets the chance to chair our morning community meeting. However, much of this learning is from the seemingly non-working side of the College, that is to say, learning through engaging with others and learning what works and what doesn't. The weekly learning group also provides a space for each student to reflect on their experiences during the previous week and to consider what next to do.

Here are some direct quotes from ex-students from independent research conducted during 2018–9.[5]

'I feel as if the SMLC developed my social skills greatly – perhaps due to the mixed age groups and alternative nature of the people who attended. I didn't do too much academic study, but I don't think I suffered in the long-term from that at all.'

'Friendships, social skills, the importance of motivating yourself.'

'Although I don't think I got a lot out of SMLC academically, I think it really helped me to increase my confidence and connect back into society after having been very isolated. I think socializing was the biggest and most positive thing I got out of my experience.'

The research also showed how much ex-students valued having a real level of freedom and what they gained from that:

'Allowed me to make decisions about what was best for me and I don't regret a single thing.'

'By allowing & thriving for independence. If I had not attended SMLC, if I had not been given the opportunity to try and test new things, especially the invaluable work experience, I would be very, very lost.'

'Easing my way into education and social environments has helped me learn and change on my own terms, and be myself more comfortably. Being an accepted part of a community, whilst being strange and ever changing, helped me grow immensely.'

'It allowed me to focus on what I wanted to do with my life and provided support for that.'

'I think it gave me some time as a teenager to figure out what it is that I actually enjoy doing, I may have forgotten that for a while but have gotten back to it of late. I don't know I'd be as sure of what it is I want without having attended. Not to mention I'm still close with one or two people from there.'

'I made new friends; I got to learn what I want to learn.'

Self-confidence was mentioned often as an outcome of the way the community works:

'Build my confidence by being respectful, no shouting or any fear-based learning. Before SMLC I was sick to my stomach, sick at school, always sad and in the toilet. After leaving SMLC I was full of confidence and caught up with all the school work that I had missed which was about a year out of school. I had the confidence to go to any school and not let authoritarian teachers get me down as much as they used to.'

'It helped me to be confident in being myself and knowing that I was free to be interested in and love whatever I want. I would say it helped me a little in managing my own learning and reaching my goals but I also know that those things are quite natural for me as I've always had a really clear idea of where I wanted to be and what I wanted to be doing. SMLC definitely did a lot for my confidence.'

This latter quote in its mention of learning to manage one's own learning – and life – is supported by other comments:

'I have made many different friends during my time at SMLC. I have also learnt how to better use my time and organise myself. This has come in very useful when trying to juggle college, work and social life.'

'It definitely helped me with art. I think it also made me more independent.'

The last area I want to mention here is on the emotional learning that goes on, that is, students feeling valued and supported, and developing emotional maturity with that:

'It made me feel like an actual individual rather than just another name on a sheet, I have so many good memories from SMLC.'

'Well I probably would have killed myself [without SMLC], I wasn't enjoying being home-schooled, I had no friends, it also helped me achieve the necessary qualifications to move on to college which I also didn't really like.'

'I find myself to be much more emotionally mature than my peers. I know myself – who I am, what I need, what I want – much better than anyone else I know. I know, appreciate and respect the value of education because it has not been forced upon me in a careless and rigid way. I have experienced freedom in my life and my education, which I don't think many people do or at least feel they do and this has reinforced my belief that "doing life" in your own way and outside of the norm, in a way that benefits and suits you, isn't naive or stupid. I can say that everything I've done has been my own choice. And knowing that I have this freedom continues to inform my decisions and thus makes me very happy. I can't blame anyone else for these choices and I can't be "sour" because things haven't worked out for me. Further, in terms of higher education – having studied for my GCSEs more or less of my accord and in my own way, I found the work at College to be relatively easy in terms of reading etc and especially in terms of University – I have the motivation to read etc and then apply and evaluate that.'

'I made four good friends, two of which I am still very close with now. The staff were very supportive but not pushy. I felt comfortable and secure there. I felt valued and important. I was able to get GCSEs to progress to college (which I thought I wanted at the time).'

The learning and development that ex-students cite has not come from 'working' in the way that many parents and teachers would demand. The learning looks almost accidental and yet it is the core of what is important. Young people are developing their identity in this period of their lives and they are learning to develop what has become labelled 'emotional intelligence'. This emotional maturity has been shown to be more important than IQ or academic qualifications in adults' satisfaction with life and success in their careers (see, for example, Clark et al., 2018).

Motivation to learn

The idea of the motivation of young people to learn is an important one. However, we have to distinguish between extrinsic and intrinsic motivation. Too often, the notion of motivation comes from a physical metaphor – that it's about pushing the person in a specified direction. The analogy would be if you kick a ball, it is likely to move in a predictable direction based on the principles of physics. If you kick a person, that's not necessarily true. People are not like balls or any other physical object. We get parents often talking about the need to push their child to do various things. Of course, sometimes that can work as a short-term response to, for instance, the need to pass an exam. However, the long-term implications may be that the person becomes too used to having to respond to external pressure to do things and is unable, in the extreme case, to make their own choices about how to live their own lives (see, for example, Mathewson, 2019).

One theoretical framework for this is the notion of locus of control. A shorthand way of indicating the basis of this theory is that if you have an internal locus of control you are more likely to see the choices that you create coming from you, i.e. they are internal. An external locus of control would be the assumption that what is happening to you is a result of things external to you. A typical result from research comparing students with internal and external loci of control is summarised as follows:

> At the end of the research it is concluded that learning performances of the students with internal locus of control are high, and they are more proactive and effective during the learning process. On the other hand, the ones with external locus of control are more passive and reactive during this period (Kutanis et al. 2011).

Hence encouraging young people to develop an internal locus of control is extremely valuable. The problem often for young people coming out of school is that they have been encouraged to develop the notions of external motivation and an external locus of control. Part of the unrecognised impact of schooling is that it can persuade young people that they should expect direction from adults: that a clear direction as to what to do with their lives is necessary and that the adults have the role to create this for them (Jackson, 1968). Initially, students coming to us with this external focus, where they look for direction from others, especially adults, will struggle to self manage their learning in a more effective way. Note that I'm saying self manage their learning in a more effective way. They will have been managing their learning, often ineffectively, in school. They may sometimes rebel against this external direction, but this will be based on having something to rebel against. It's like the teenage boy saying, 'I'm not influenced by my father. I just do the opposite of what he says.' The reality is that this rebellion is against something specific rather than a personally chosen course of action.

It can often look to both the young person and to their parents during the phase of de-schooling that they're not doing any proper useful learning during this phase, but that is wrong. The young person's exploration can lead them to come out the other end with a clear sense about how they do manage their own learning and a clearer sense of what is important to them in life – what is important therefore for them to be learning. This, then, leads to much more internally focused motivation. The motivation is coming from inside the person going out into the world utilising all the resources of their environment to support them, as opposed to an external model that encourages them to look to the world around them to tell them what to do.

Occasionally we have had students see us adults in the teaching role, and therefore believe that we should tell them what to do. They demand instruction from us. Having explored with an individual that they really mean this, I might say, 'Okay, I'm going to give you an instruction which is to learn what you think is important for you. That's an instruction and you must make your own choices and I am instructing you to do that.' Of course, I do it in a somewhat jokey way to try to indicate that they really do need to work at things themselves.

The other thing to bear in mind is that the peer group is enormously important in this process, not only within the wider College community, but also in their own learning group. The value of the learning group is that these are people of a similar age and therefore they are having often similar struggles with what to learn and how to lead a good life. It is not that peers tell individuals what to do in a broader sense, but rather that by being in a group and hearing of other people's thoughts and ways of addressing a problem, individuals can start to think for themselves in a deeper way about what they need to do.

Whilst mentioning the value of the peer group, it's important not to deny that we as adults have a role. A good example about motivation with one student might give some clues here. Rory was aged 14 and his mum had commented that Rory was a really nice boy, but he didn't seem to have any focus and that he struggled at school. In talking with him it was clear that he didn't find academic learning particularly congenial. However, one of the things that he had been enjoying was creating a computer game. I asked him to show it to me and to explain what he was doing. It struck me that this was something quite interesting, even though I am no expert on computer games. The aesthetics of it seemed to me to be quite creative, irrespective of the game itself.

I asked him if he was interested in taking his game-making ability forward and he said yes. So, we did a number of things. First of all, I took him to sit with me at a computer and we went on the local further education college website to look at what they did in the game-making and design area. The college did a diploma course for 16 to 18-year olds and they had a really nice video of the activity of their students doing computer-game making. Rory suddenly became very excited by looking at this. He became aware that this wasn't a strange thing that he was engaged in. One could get a qualification in this. He had never thought this was possible, and his school had not explored this with him.

The second phase was to start looking practically at what was involved in game-making. Through our contacts we got somebody who runs a game-making company locally to come in and see what Rory had been doing. He was quite impressed, and he gave Rory some ideas about the things he could do and other software he could use. Rory was then also able to work with our computer expert on the staff. This gave him some more ideas about a direction to go in.

We had a collaboration at the time with a local university and their Masters degree students had to do a project out in the real world related to their learning. This was a Masters degree in Informatics, and I arranged for a project group to come and visit Rory and see what he was doing and what they could offer by way of support to him. Within the project team there were people who were experienced IT practitioners in their 30s who were working in a local financial institution and were doing a Masters degree as a part-time study. They then agreed that they would be a project team to support Rory and come regularly to work with him. They also used this project as part of their Masters degree, so it was of mutual benefit.

As a result of suddenly being energised with possibilities, we then checked with the college what they required for entry to a computer design diploma, which seemed like a good starting point for him when he was 16. They said that they required four passes at GCSE level. We knew that colleges often set entry requirements that are not necessarily rigidly held to, so we worked with Rory so that he took maths and English GCSEs. He also did what is called an Arts Award, which is a GCSE equivalent, and he created a portfolio of work. He was able to make a case to the college to admit him to the course on the basis that this was equivalent to four GCSEs. He successfully completed his diploma course and I got a card from him saying that he was starting at a university with a degree in this field. His mother was clear that none of this would have been possible if he had stayed at school and also that this motivation to learn in this area really made a difference to him personally in terms of improvements in confidence and self-esteem.

This example could be repeated many, many times from our experience with young people. It's helping them to develop that internal motivation where they can have a passion for something that is meaningful to them. Then they can motor with it. Often what they are being taught in school, which is encouraging the more external focus, isn't actually providing a motivational environment at all.

Another way into this idea is to think about the concept of an amateur. The origin of the term 'amateur' is from the French 'one who loves'. The word is to do with the fact that people take on things to do simply because of the love of it, rather than from the point of view of being paid (the professional focus). It is clearly linked to this notion of internal not external motivation. The amateur is somebody who so loves doing something that they may have to accommodate personal cost in order to do what they love.

Learning levels

It's clear that there are different levels of learning. For instance, learning that the bus timetable has changed and what the new arrangements are is quite different from learning to be self-confident. Learning a new bus timetable is a simple, practical issue. However, knowing that bus timetables can change and that therefore you have to keep an eye on them is slightly different. So, we can see that there are different levels of learning.

The most useful author in laying down a theoretical case with this is Gregory Bateson (Bateson, 1972). His writings are not a model of clarity and ease. For my purposes here, I want to take quite a simple route through his theory. His approach indicates that learning within a context is Learning 1 and learning that takes you across contexts is Learning 2. Back to the example of self-confidence, we can say this is Learning 2. It's a generalised quality for a person that will take them across different contexts. A person who is more self-confident may be open to new learning more readily than someone less confident. They may be able to evaluate and take sensible risks more appropriately than someone who is not so confident. Just gaining lots of Level 1 learning may not make you more confident. The Level 2 learning necessary to be more self-confident is of a different kind.

Learning 1 can often be purely additive. The focus may be on adding new knowledge or skills to the individual. It is the general model of schooling. There is a debate about the balance between knowledge and skill learning, but in a way it's probably an irrelevant argument, as both are Learning 1. Adding new knowledge or adding a new skill to a person is still within an additive mode and does not necessarily address Learning 2, such as self-confidence. One way of thinking about becoming more confident or having greater self-esteem is that it's more of habit change and about creating a new quality.

There are the habits that we find that we perhaps want to change, and which are quite different from adding in new knowledge and skills. An example with young people, and indeed adults, is to stop procrastinating. To work in a different way requires a change of habit. It's not about adding new knowledge and skills, but rather a person not only realising that they need to change, but also addressing more widely the issue of procrastination. Sometimes that procrastination is context dependent, such as people procrastinating about their homework. However, it's often more generally an issue that an individual can easily identify. In adults it may be putting off a difficult phone conversation or not dealing with work problems.

In arguing for the importance of Learning 2 and habit change, this is not to say we neglect Learning 1. Developing new knowledge and skills can be important. However, it can often be seen that it is easier to learn new knowledge and skills if you feel more confident to do that. For instance, the notion of lifelong learning is best conceptualised as an approach to life where a person is prepared to learn new things as they go through life as opposed to a Learning 1 approach, which implies learning new skills like study skills. This can be an error that schools make in trying to teach children specific skills of learning, but not addressing the wider issue of the person's lack of confidence in their ability to continue to learn throughout their whole life.

The notion of metacognition can come within the Learning 2 framework. Part of this second-order (Learning 2) domain is about thinking about the way we think. This may mean reframing a way of doing things. The use of the learning agreement is an example of encouraging real metacognition. The student has to examine why they want to learn what they say they want to learn. They may be challenged in their learning group to re-examine long-held assumptions about the world and their place in it.

One aspect of Learning 2 is that it underpins taking a more strategic approach to learning. I have made a broader case for a strategic approach to learning elsewhere (Cunningham, 1999). Suffice it to say here that it is to do with taking a broader and longer-term perspective on learning. It's also about being able to choose what learning to undertake and what not. A strategic approach to learning would include the idea that we learn about what we need to learn and can therefore have a secure basis for learning rather than just responding to, for instance, imposition from school or from the marketing ploys of the world around us.

An example of the latter would be the fact that I have a smartphone which is some years old and I keep being pestered to update it as there have been three new versions of this smartphone since I bought it. I am resisting these marketing pressures as it would require me to learn how to use a new piece of technology and I don't see the value in that. It's also like my choice when changing my car. I recently changed my old car to a newer one, but I have the same make and model as it means there is less I have to learn in the new vehicle. Most of the controls are pretty much as they were in the older version. Of course, someone who is very into cars would take an opposite view to mine and might enjoy learning how to drive a totally new model of car. Similarly, those who are interested in having the latest version of a smartphone no doubt enjoy the new learning that is required. It's all a matter of choice in the context of a strategic stance to learning.

The couple of examples I've mentioned are small fry compared with some of the big decisions that people have to take, especially in the context of work. Working as I have done for nearly half a century with senior leaders in organisations, I have seen that they have to be careful about their choices of what to learn and what not to learn. For instance, learning about new technology that is coming into their field or learning about new markets are big issues. For leaders, one of the issues is whether they need to learn things or whether somebody else will do it and that they will work with that person. When I was a chief executive, I was reliant on my personal assistant to learn any new technology that came along that we had to deal with and then she could teach it to me once she had mastered it. Alternatively, in some cases she could learn something, and I would just rely on her to have that skill that I could call upon. Elsewhere, I make the case for the importance of team working and one of the most fundamental points of team working is how to share knowledge and skills, but individuals need the recognition that not everybody can learn everything that is relevant to their role in a modern organisation. This requires a strategic approach to learning. Leaders of teams have to step back and consider who in the team may need to learn what.

An interesting example of team learning occurred when I was working with a group of senior technical people within a large international high-tech company. A new methodology had appeared which they all needed to know about. As is often the case in this field, training companies with the expertise were charging high prices to run one-week programmes to train people in this new methodology. I had been working with the team on a Self Managed Learning programme where they were looking at what they needed to learn. They realised that they needed to find a solution to the problem that the company could not possibly spare their time, and that of many of their colleagues, or the cost for everybody to attend this training course being run by external consultancies. The group solved the problem by agreeing that one person would attend the training course and get the material and take copious notes. After the course, they would return and hold a half-day coaching session with the team on the new methodology, since, as is often the case, you don't really need all the material that's been provided during a one-week open course.

The most important strategic learning that they gained from this experience was that they could use this approach for other learning that they needed to undertake. For instance, the group agreed that they needed to know more about the financial arrangements within the business and especially future financial plans. They delegated one of their number to go and spend some time with the finance people and with the strategy side of the business so that then the person could pull together what was relevant for the team and again conduct a short coaching session with the team on what it was that they really needed to know.

Note that by taking a more strategic approach it's possible to save time and money, and this does not just apply to business. I save time and money by changing phones and cars as little as possible.

A major problem with the notion of a more strategic, habit-changing model is that it can be difficult for people in education to accept that this is actually legitimate learning. I ran a Self Managed Learning programme for heads of schools. It had been set up by my colleague Michael Fielding and the Institute of Education in London. The six participants in the group came from schools that were attempting to be more innovative and to resist the kind of pressures coming from the British government for a more rigid approach to learning. They were experienced heads, but recognised the need for a development process that would give them the chance to think through what they needed to learn to improve their schools, and also get the support of five other heads for this. For a day every five weeks over about a nine-month period we met, and the process was as I have described in Chapter 2.

As part of the evaluation of the programme, Michael Fielding interviewed the participants part way through and wrote up an interim report. He then repeated the process at the end (Fielding, 2010).

Here is a quote from Michael's interim report on the programme from one head:

> The process has been very valuable, but at the same time difficult as there have been a lot more questions than answers which has been a challenge to my analytical side. The fact that my goals have had to be articulated, revisited, refined and challenged by such experienced colleagues has meant that they have evolved in a completely different way to that which I originally envisaged. My original focus on student voice has become much broader in scope and I think has moved much closer to the transfer of some of the significant power within school to the children. More children are involved in the process, including the less articulate and the non-conforming – this has come directly from my discussions within the group.
>
> The impact in my own school has been huge, in that as I've clarified my own goals and directions with the group, this has somehow been

communicated to the rest of my staff and has resulted in significantly changed leadership behaviour. Two of my senior teachers have independently taken on some of the structures and systems I've been wrestling with within the group and made them their own in their improvement foci in school. Most significant is that I'm increasingly not needed!

This has probably been one of the most 'impactful' experiences of my teaching career so far which sounds incredibly gushing but isn't meant to be. The process of multiple sessions with 'action time' and 'reflection time' in between has provided a sustainable pace to the process and also an accountability to the group which I really could not have predicted at the start. My goals are now much more aspirational and more openly targeted towards democratic classrooms and authentic choice for children.

Here is a comment from the final report from another participant:

Participation in the Self Managed Learning group of fellow headteachers during 2008–9 provided me with one of the most rewarding professional development opportunities of my career to date.

I have reflected deeply about the process and structure of our encounters. I consider myself to be someone who is passionate about the purposes and principles of education. I am often called upon to provide support and guidance to others and to respond to requests for information, to offer visits to my school, to give lectures or to write reflectively on my practice. In order to continue to 'give' meaningfully school leaders also need to be nourished and (sustained). This group of colleagues enabled me to believe in myself during times of doubt and to maintain the courage that is needed to swim against the tide of central government policy implementation which at times challenges my values and beliefs.

Membership of the group meant that I was at times reassured and yet challenged, supported and yet pushed beyond my comfort zone, encouraged and yet held to account. Leadership and facilitation of the group by Ian Cunningham reminded us of our shared purposes and values. His presence, and the inspirational support of Michael Fielding, enabled us to experience a collective sense of self-worth and purpose beyond our own individual stories. We approached meetings in the belief that our shared reflections were of importance. At no stage did the process feel self-indulgent or lacking in direction. We are all busy people with many competing demands on our time, but the work of this group enabled an intense opportunity for reflection and enlightenment.

We desperately need colleagues who have the courage to offer a principled approach to education that focuses on the importance of human values. Colleagues with the courage and conviction to stand up for what they believe in need spaces in time to re-energise and sharpen their resolve, hold their nerve and continue with renewed purpose and energy. Membership of the Self

Managed Learning group provided me with this opportunity, and I shall always be grateful. In the future I hope that I shall hold their voices in my head when faced with adversity.

Note that in the quotes above there are various references to learning that can be categorised as Learning 2. For instance, developing courage, being re-energised and clarifying goals were developed through fundamental change that re-shaped their mode of working.

It was then felt that, because there were national interests in improving innovation in schools, there should be a meeting in the University with professors of education from other institutions and also other people who might have a voice on such matters.

At the meeting, the heads still talked enthusiastically about changes in what they had achieved. It was very much in the Learning 2 mode. They all talked about having to step back and think through the moral purpose for the institution and also the way in which they needed to reshape their behaviour. None of this learning was about additive approach – we didn't run any teaching events as part of the programme. The individuals all saw that what they needed was, given their experience, to utilise that experience in a fuller way and to be able to develop the confidence and courage to tackle much-needed changes.

In response to comments of the heads, one of the visiting education professors launched into an attack on the programme, saying it was merely therapy and therefore what was the value of it. It was a bit of a shock but, on reflection, I shouldn't have been shocked given the educational model is largely an additive model. The assumption is of empty buckets that need to be filled, but the problem is that there are leaky buckets and therefore they need regular top-up activity. This is perhaps what this professor and others present were used to doing. They would deliver lectures and pontificate on what heads should or shouldn't do. The notion that this programme was therapy was quite an insult to the six heads present. None were ill and in need of therapy. The problem lay in the educational model of an additive approach, which was seen by some to be the only valid one, and the reshaping and realigning and reframing of skills and knowledge couldn't possibly be of value. It was another lesson for me in underestimating the rigidity of the education establishment.

Conclusion

In this chapter I have established that Self Managed Learning is based on a view of learning that leaves behind the narrow approach of education as articulated by authorities such as the UK Government. In SML we approach learning as a fundamental human activity, and I have argued for its particular role. I have defined learning in a broad way and indicated how we need to look at learning as not all one process. There are levels of learning and the more important Learning 2 is a sine qua non for real personal development that carries a person through life.

I have made the case for dismissing an approach to learning that requires 'work' – typically prescribed in educational establishments by teachers and others in authority. In SML we recognise that natural informal learning is the mainstay of our development as human beings and we promote processes and structures based on that stance. In SML we help learners to develop an intrinsic motivational pattern and to develop on the basis of an internal locus of control. This means that we reject the notion of smooth linear progression in learning and support learners to grow at their own pace and in keeping with their needs.

All the comments above are features of what I have called a New Educational Paradigm. It requires a drastic reappraisal of current educational practice and a completely different approach to how we help young people to learn. As is common in paradigm shifts, this is not about tidying up or improving current practice. Current practice is not fit for purpose and only a new way of thinking will suffice.

Notes

1 This appeared on June 1, 1999 as a headline in *G2, The Guardian* newspaper supplement. This kind of statement has been commonplace in all newspapers and Government announcements. The Chartered Institute of Personnel and Development is the official body for the HR world in the UK and it continues to misrepresent the nature of learning.
2 There is a vast literature now on suicides among young people. For instance, the Office of National Statistics is tasked with looking at well-being among young people and the worrying statistics about obesity are now well known. However, other factors are less well known. One example is that in 2012 suicide overtook traffic accidents as the major cause of death in 16–24-year-olds in England and Wales. The Office of National Statistics comments that 'Suicide rates can be used as an indicator of acute mental health problems'. Acute (and also less acute) mental health problems have clearly increased among children. This is not to say that schools necessarily cause suicides. There are many social factors involved. However, in terms of the claim of education to prepare young people for their place in the world, not paying sufficient attention to mental health in schools means that those who kill themselves are clearly not prepared for living in the world.
3 The influence of peers on learning for young people has a well-developed research base. The most recent and wide-ranging research is from Blakemore (2018).
4 Jordan Baker (2019) cites a Finnish parent saying that in Finland play time is a time for learning whereas in Australia play time is wasted time. Another take on the non-working dimension is daydreaming. A good summary of the value of daydreaming is K. Schwartz (2014).
5 The evaluation research on past students is being carried out by Luke Freedman, an independent researcher. The interim report from the first stage of the research is available from Self Managed Learning College at www.smlcollege.org.uk.

References

Baker, J. (2019) From play to pressure: A Finnish perspective on Australian schools. *Sydney Herald*, March 17.

Bateson, G. (1972) *Steps to an Ecology of Mind*. Chicago: University Press.

Blakemore, S.-J. (2018) *Inventing Ourselves: The Secret Life of the Teenage Brain*. London: Doubleday.

Bryan, J. (2018) *Eye Can Write*. London: Blink Publishing.

Carey, N. (2012) *The Epigenetics Revolution: How Modern Biology is Rewriting Our Understanding of Genetics, Disease and Inheritance*. London: Icon Books.

CIPD Newsletter (2018), August.

Clark, A. E., Flèche, S., Layard, R., Powdthavee, N. and Ward, G. (2018) *The Origins of Happiness*. Princeton: University Press.

Cunningham, I. (1999) *The Wisdom of Strategic Learning*, 2nd edition. Aldershot, Hants.: Gower.

Fielding, M. (2010) Supporting people in working in ground-breaking ways. Report to the Esmee Fairbairn Foundation. London: Institute of Education.

Freedman, L. (2019) The Self Managed Learning College Study, Interim Report 1. Sussex: Self Managed Learning College.

Gray, P. (2013) *Free to Learn*. New York: Basic Books.

Jackson, P. W. (1968) *Life in Classrooms*. New York: Holt, Reinhart & Winston.

Kirton, H. (2018) Are your staff too skilled for their jobs? *People Management*, Nov, 36–37.

Kutanis, R. O., Mesci, M. and Ovdur, Z. (2011) The effects of locus of control on learning performance: A case of an academic organization. *Journal of Economic and Social Studies*, 1(2), 113–137.

Mathewson, T. G. (2019) Intrinsic motivation is key to student achievement – but schools can crush it. https://www.kqed.org/mindshift/53337/intrinsic-motivation-is-key-to-student-achievement-but-schools-can-crush-it.

Schwartz, K. (2014) Why daydreaming is critical to effective learning. https://www.kqed.org/mindshift/37711/why-daydreaming-is-critical-to-effective-learning.

Walker, M. (2018) *Why We Sleep*. London: Penguin.

4

HISTORY AND BACKGROUND

Introduction

In this chapter I want to give some background information about how we have developed the Self Managed Learning approach specifically for young people. There is also some discussion of the setting up of SML College so that later material can make more sense.

One reason for giving some background is that it is interestingly a frequent question from people who come to open days to the College. They ask about how it is that I came to set up the College and what the basis for using Self Managed Learning with young people is. So that will be my starting point for this chapter.

Why we started SML College

I have a number of versions of the story of how we came to start up a college for young people at the start of this century. In a way each individual story provides a valid reason for doing something, but when you put them together it becomes clear that it seemed to me to be impossible to not take action. However, for most of my adult life I have not wanted to have anything to do with the educational world because it seemed impossible to change and improve what was happening with young people. For over 30 years I worked almost solely with adults and mainly within the context of large organisations, as well as often with senior leaders in such organisations. My own research had been focused on adults, starting with the time I went into a business school and then later doing doctoral research on management learning.

The change in the direction of my work was a surprise to many of my friends. We had established a thriving business working with major organisations around the world. We had demonstrated the value of Self Managed

Learning in a number of contexts. I was earning good money doing this work, enjoying it and also seeing the fruits of that in improvements in the way organisations worked.[1] The notion that I would do something with young people, which would actually cost me money, seemed strange to many of the people I was working with.

Reasons to get involved in education

The following are the reasons that I tend to give for getting involved with education and why I was prepared to make the shift from organisational work to working with young people.

First reason: organisations and the world of work

A lot of my work in organisations was around organisation development in a broader sense, rather than purely the learning of individuals. Self Managed Learning contributed to organisation development by bringing together people from different parts of the business to learn together. Such social learning went beyond individual learning and contributed to making the organisation more successful and being a better place in which to work.

There were clearly other methodologies that were available to help to improve organisations. One of these was helping teams to work more effectively and I was often asked to do team development for top management teams, such as boards of directors of companies and public bodies. Much of this work was about helping people to learn to get on with each other and to have better insights into how and why people behaved the way that they did. It seemed to me that it would have been a good idea if senior people had learned this when they were younger. Most often the major reasons that boards were having trouble was to do with personal relationships within the board. Indeed, when I interviewed board members as individuals about what was stopping the organisation in fulfilling its mission, the most commonly answered term was 'people'.

One motive, then, for getting involved in the educational world was to say that we needed to help people to learn better to not just work independently but interdependently, and in a later chapter I focus more on those issues because they are crucial to making organisations work. Suffice it to say here that we had always had great feedback from SML programmes in companies about how the programme had created better relationships in the organisation and how people had developed improved ways of working with colleagues in departments other than their own. Also, I had developed an approach to team development that emphasised that people needed to develop **teamworking skills** rather than just fixing a problem of team **building**. Indeed, I had written about how team building was too limited as an approach as people needed to be able to work in any team especially as over a typical career people very rarely stayed in one team.[2]

Second reason: social class and difference

I had come from a working-class area in the south of Manchester into a grammar school and then the university system. What I resented was to see how the class system worked to keep out people from what are seen as top jobs.

During the late 1950s I was a member of a gang. It didn't seem to me to be anything unusual because that's just what you did if you lived in an area like mine. In the gang were people with equal ability to me, but somehow did not escape the council estate and its constrictions. I remember a boy, Mike, who died at the age of 17 in a motorbike accident and the person who was closest to him said he pretty much killed himself through his recklessness. What was interesting was that he was very skilled at making bombs. I should say that he never used such bombs against people but did make use of the destructiveness of bombs for vandalism purposes. These were the days when there was no internet and no computers. And yet somehow not only had he found out how to make simple pipe bombs, but he had also made nitro-glycerine. I have no idea how he learned that because it's complicated stuff. I could not think that there were books to access and certainly there were no other sources that I knew of that would explain how to do this. However, somehow, he had learned this. I thought what a waste it was that someone with ability had had a difficult family situation and never been helped to get out of his own situation. I am not here praising bomb making per se. It was obvious that he had real ability and that he could have gone on to have a glittering career if he had only been born in another context.

My own experience in attending a very selective boys' grammar school from 1954 was that it was a real cultural shock. I never felt that I fitted in, and some of the teachers made it clear to me that they didn't welcome my presence in the school. I almost had to learn a new language and way of communicating. I felt that I lived in two worlds: the gang outside school and my artificial life in school.

Since that time I have learned much more about the impact of the class system and how even to this day there has been no real improvement in supporting working-class people through the education system. Schools are designed as middle-class institutions and if you don't fit in then you have a problem. Mike was better than me at chemistry (clearly), yet I managed to get onto a chemistry degree and he didn't have a chance.[3]

Another example of class issues is the way that the school curriculum is created. I wrote the following letter to the editor of the *Observer* newspaper as a result of a misleading article:

> The headline 'Why Lancashire backed the Confederacy' (4th June 2011) was staggering in its inaccuracy. The truth was more complex. If anything, it should have read: 'Why Lancashire opposed the Confederacy'. Your headline represents one of the many distortions in the way history is presented. It foregrounds the behaviour of the rich and powerful over the working class.

The real facts are as follows. The blockade of the Confederacy in the US Civil War meant that cotton could not get to the mills in Lancashire. Naturally the mill owners were not happy – and many did indeed back the Confederacy. However, the real sufferers were the mill workers and their families who experienced extreme poverty. There were many deaths in the families as they had no income due to the closure of the mills.

The mill workers called a meeting at Manchester's Free Trade Hall on December 31st, 1862 and agreed to side with the Union against the Confederacy. They wrote to Abraham Lincoln in support of the abolition of slavery. The following is an extract from their letter:

'the vast progress which you have made in the short space of twenty months fills us with hope that every stain on your freedom will shortly be removed, and that the erasure of that foul blot on civilisation and Christianity – chattel slavery – during your presidency, will cause the name of Abraham Lincoln to be honoured and revered in posterity.'

On January 19th, 1863 Lincoln responded. His letter contained the following words:

'I know and deeply deplore the sufferings which the working people of Manchester and in all Europe are called to endure in this crisis [...]. I cannot but regard your decisive utterances on the question as an instance of sublime Christian heroism which has not been surpassed in any age or in any country.'

Your headline therefore represents a view of Lancashire that only features the views of the rich and powerful. Ordinary people were prepared to sacrifice their own families to support the abolition of slavery. The rich and powerful wanted to see it survive. Your headline is typical of how history is taught in schools. I went to school in Manchester until I was 18 and I was regarded as pretty good at history. However, I only recently learned the facts about the role of ordinary working Lancashire people in the struggle against slavery. I was well schooled and ill-educated. I had walked past the statue of Lincoln in central Manchester many times and never stopped to read of the reason for its existence in that square.

One reason then for creating SML College has been to try to develop a fairer mode of learning that honours difference, not just about class but about all the differences that the educational system uses to separate young people and give some an easy passage into adulthood and some a rough ride. We know that there are whole groups of people who are discriminated against through the way in which school operates. These include summer born children, who are likely to drop at least one grade in public examinations; autistic children; children in care; and minority groups.

Part of the idea of setting up Self Managed Learning College included the notion that we start where the person is when they arrive. Instead of assuming that the person will fit in with a middle-class educational culture, we start with what the person brings. We ask them about their experiences in life so that we know the person and we know where we're starting from. The fact that everyone's different means you have to respect that, and it was clearly a fundamental reason for us to do what seemed risky, namely setting up this new venture with young people.

Third reason: later experiences in education

My own experience in school had been one that I found difficult. I agreed with the Oscar Wilde quote that 'I love to learn; I just can't bear to be taught'. I learned a great deal about things that interested me but much of the school curriculum made little sense to me. University was an even greater disappointment in terms of the narrowness of the teaching and of the legitimacy of what you could actually talk about and learn about.

Here is one example, from a lecture from our professor of physical chemistry (I was doing a chemistry degree). I asked, 'What exactly is an electron?' We had been taught a great deal of complex maths about the sub-atomic world but none of this explained what an electron is. I was told pretty much to shut up because such a question was philosophy. The idea that we had to stick to a narrow focus in our learning was something that I resented. I had been the first person in our neighbourhood to go to university and I had swallowed my school's glowing picture of a broadened education at university. I discovered the opposite.

Later when I was doing a Masters degree in an occupational psychology department, a professor cited some research around people's attitudes. I offered an alternative interpretation of this research evidence and the professor also more or less told me to be quiet because my proffered explanation was sociological (and therefore not acceptable in a psychology programme). Again, that seemed to me to be an unhelpful, narrowing and anti-intellectual stance.

My growing concern about the educational world was that it wasn't doing what it claimed to do. I rather sympathised with a friend's definition of a university: that it was a bunch of departments loosely connected by a central heating system. The silo mentality of universities infects the organisational world where departments don't work well together due to people's experience in school and university.

Caplan (2018) does a wonderful demolition of university teaching, drawing on a modified version of the old Soviet aphorism from organisations, 'We pretend to work, and they pretend to pay us,' which is, 'University professors pretend to teach, and students pretend to learn.' He shows how the university world has traded on its ability to provide qualifications as a meal ticket for individuals but that there may be little of value in the education provided. As an economics professor, he suggests that only a tiny part of the university economics curriculum is of any use in students' careers (unless they become economics professors). He argues that most of what is taught in such a degree is based on what the faculty want to teach as opposed to what would be useful for students to learn.[4]

Another aspect of the academic and educational world that I have found a problem is its focus on detached abstract academic learning. Matthew Crawford (2009) does a brilliant job in undermining the detached uninvolved academic curriculum.

After his doctorate, he had a career in the world of policy and wrote elegant papers on major policy issues. He started to realise that this detached, ephemeral world disconnected people from doing practical stuff with their hands. He moved to running a motorbike repair shop. But this was not a retreat into working with your hands and then not thinking. His argument, quite rightly, is that when you're repairing motorbikes or doing other craft activity it requires a great deal of thinking. It requires good knowledge of what you are doing and highly developed skills which you have to think about using.

His development into running a motorbike workshop reminded me of Pirsig's *Zen and the Art of Motorcycle Maintenance* (1974). One of the fascinating points within that book is the notion of 'stuckness'. He elaborates on the fact that something might go wrong in a motorbike and it might be inside the casing. If you then try and open it, and the nut shears off, you may be stuck because you can't get inside to solve the problem. He shows that this requires another level of thinking because the mechanical thinking that you might have used in the past doesn't apply when you're stuck. You may have opened many casings and done repairs but this time you can't run the same routine.

This is an example of what I've argued as Level 2 learning in Chapter 3. This situation makes you move out of the existing context and have to rethink, reapply, and maybe reframe your knowledge and skills in a new way to be able to solve a real problem. This is both real intellectual activity as well as working with your hands.

An example of my frustration with this was in a chemistry degree where practical work was oriented towards research and not practical application in the day-to-day world. One example was that I learned about the chemistry of oxyacetylene welding but we, of course, never did any. It was only at the age of 67 when I went to do a qualification in welding that I learned practically what it meant to use oxygen and acetylene to be able to weld metal. I also used this qualification to be able to make metal sculpture. Such creative activity requires the ability to think and to use your skills in a particular way. It is not merely working with your hands to create a chunk of metal.

Currently, we are seeing in England the decimation of arts and applied areas in schools and particularly secondary schools because of the emphasis on academic learning and the valuing only of detached academic subjects. Teachers of art, design, dance and music are being dispensed with as part of a narrowing of the curriculum.

As I will show in Chapter 6 the major growth area of employment in the UK and of economic activity in general is in the creative and digital sectors and not in those set as subjects that are being taught in school. However, there is, of course, a broader reason for what can be seen as applied areas because it's part of being human. You can't go into the caves in France and Spain and see paintings and drawings from 30 to 40,000 years ago without realising that art is central to our humanity – not some dispensable add-on.

Dance is common to cultures across the globe. Again, it isn't some charming but useless frippery. My academic grammar school didn't do any of this stuff and it was only at the age of 68 when I took up performing contemporary dance that I was able to start to learn and develop ways of using my body in a creative way. To reiterate Crawford's point, this is not merely a physical activity. You have to think about what you're doing; you have to think about theories of dance and understand the conceptual framework within which contemporary dance operates. And you are learning through all sorts of different routes about how to be better at dancing.

In summary, my experience of the educational world prompted my thinking about creating a new kind of facility for young people that honours all human learning and does not make crass distinctions between 'proper' academic learning and learning that is creative and expressive. In the educational press there are derogatory remarks about 'Mickey Mouse' degrees – which seems to cover any kind of applied or active learning. We stand counter to that kind of criticism.

Fourth reason: students

I had been involved with the National Union of Students of England, Wales and Northern Ireland during the 1960s. I was on the executive for two years from 1966 to 1968 and then I was full-time National Secretary from 1968 to 1970. The President's role in the union is political and outward facing, whereas the National Secretary's role is to do with education and welfare issues and the running of the commercial enterprises that we had at the time. The reason I wanted to have the National Secretary role was to make an impact on educational issues, not just in universities and colleges, but more widely. At the time there was a great ferment about young people's roles and this had had major international political implications with what was happening in the USA in opposition to the Vietnam war, and also in Paris, where it almost seemed as though the student action would bring down the whole Government.

The first sit-in in the UK was in 1968 and I was necessarily involved with student action at the time. I was disappointed with the focus on such things as getting students onto the senates of universities or on to major committees. This seemed to me to be trivial compared with addressing the major issues in education. I was involved in producing reports and campaigns focusing on educational issues such as on the iniquity of the examination system. It was only really in the art colleges that students took militant action against more authoritarian educational models. When I left in 1970, I went into a training post because I wanted to take the focus away from just working with young people. That period of the 1960s and into the 1970s was a period of much radical thought and I was, along with many others, influenced by that thinking about how current educational models were not fit for purpose.

The outcome from my dissatisfaction with education led to my joining a polytechnic. My choice of North East London Polytechnic (NELP) was because there seemed to be a chance to make radical changes in higher education. The separation from the university world helped that, along with the Director of NELP being someone who was prepared to stick his neck out to support radical change. Having originally joined the business school part of the Polytechnic I quickly transferred to a new unit that was creating the School for Independent Study. This unit became a separate School and launched independent study programmes for undergraduates. Initially we had a Diploma of Higher Education as a two-year stand-alone programme and then we added a one-year degree programme on top of that.

The development of this work, and the link to setting up Self Managed Learning, is elaborated in Cunningham, 1999. Suffice it to say here that having seen how Self Managed Learning could work with undergraduates, I had the confidence to have a go at something for young people.

Fifth reason: self managing and play

Peter Gray's book on Self Directed Education (2013) makes a great case for learning through play and that was certainly part of my experience as a young person. In our neighbourhood we young people organised ourselves. We played kids' games and also sports games. We used to play football (soccer) for hours on the local playing field and it was all self organised. There was no adult in charge and no referee. We had coats for goal posts, and we worked out two teams – they might be for five or six aside. We learned skills playing football by doing it. We had no coaches. We created our own version of rules, if we needed, and we had a lot of fun in learning.

In the process we got to know each other well; we knew how to play with each other. However, we'd never played as an 11 in a team. One of our group knew a boy in the local league champions and he challenged them to a match. Being a group of poor kids, we had no proper kit and no shirts. The other team turned up for the match with nice clean kit and matching shirts. They had a manager, and a man with a bucket and sponge who came on to treat injuries. We had no captain or manager organising us. We just had to work out for ourselves how we were going to play and, as is common in these circumstances, the weakest outfield player was made to go in goal. We played a full match against this team and beat them 9–2. This was pretty annoying for their manager and his team given that they had been top of the league in the last few seasons.[5]

Our attitude towards games also applied in other areas like organising trips to go out into the countryside where we just agreed on a consensus basis what we were going to do and who was going. People had the choice of opting in or opting out of any activity. We also used to meet on a bomb site which had been a church. We were horrified to find that something was happening in this place that we felt was our own. The old graves were being dug up and there were clearly plans for the site. What apparently was happening was that they had decided to build two police houses on this site. We were particularly unhappy about seeing our site taken away from us, especially as it was for the police.

As far as local people were concerned, we engaged in what they would label as mindless vandalism. The press would certainly call it that these days. It wasn't from our point of view mindless, because we wanted to stop them building these houses on our patch. So, we would overnight as much as possible undo the work that had been carried out during the day, such that they had to hire permanent security people.

This is a good example where the authorities did not want to find out why we were doing what we were doing just to try and stop the building. Nobody had bothered to talk to us or even try to find a way to, for instance, meet our particular needs. It was just assumed that kids didn't matter and therefore we were not to be treated seriously.

So, my attitude to authority was obviously formed a lot by some of those experiences both positive, in the sense of being self organised, and negative in terms of the way that adults treated us. And it is still going on today. When young people do things that don't look sensible to adults it's because it seems the best option for them at the time. If you're in a gang, you go with the collective decisions of the gang because your identity is mixed up with being in that group of other young people.

In thinking therefore about setting up a new venture I was particularly keen that we would work with young people around what they wanted to do and to treat them seriously. We would also need to draw on experience of the fact that young people can self manage and that we as adults should find ways of working with them, not against them.

Sixth reason: school

Whilst I had resisted the idea of working in the educational world, I had always taken an interest in education. This was, though, very much as a spectator. I had read a lot of 1960s and 1970s radical ideas which emanated from school systems. The work of Carl Rogers (1969)[6] particularly influenced me and many of my colleagues, but there was a whole range of writers who came out of that era. I had followed the development of Summerhill School in England which, through the work of A. S. Neill, had developed an international reputation for a more democratic approach to education, with decisions being made jointly between students and staff. When Summerhill School was threatened with closure by the Labour government at the time, I thought this was potentially an appalling act that needed to be stopped. The government inspectors had made a critical report about the school and especially condemned the supposed idleness of the students and the fact that classes were optional. I attended an international conference at Summerhill in 1999 and kept track of what was happening.

Following the deaths of A. S. Neill and his wife, his daughter Zoe Redhead had taken over the running of the school. I contacted her about the school's campaign to stop it being closed or fundamentally changed. I suggested that governments were used to dealing with traditional campaigns (petitions and marches etc) and what it needed, perhaps, was, to use an American expression, to throw a curve ball. I suggested that I could set up an alternative inspection with better qualified people than the Ofsted inspectors and that we could write an alternative report that could go to the tribunal which was going to hear the case against Summerhill.

I gathered together an interesting collection of people, some of whom were very respectable academics, two of whom were heads of other boarding schools and others were respected figures in their own fields. This included an ex deputy school head who had been involved in over 80 inspections as part of Ofsted's work. We carried out an alternative inspection and reported to Ofsted and the school in 2000.[7] The school won its case in the tribunal and has remained open ever since. It has continued to work on the basis of the principles laid down by A. S. Neill.

Coming out of the conference in 1999, I had met Yaakov Hecht from the Institute for Democratic Education in Israel. He suggested that the Self Managed Learning approach would have something to offer for the growing number of democratic schools in Israel. He invited me to Israel, and I spent two weeks both going to schools and also running a workshop at the Institute so that people in schools could learn about the Self Managed Learning approach. I also did a university lecture and in general tried to spread the word that this approach might well have something to offer for young people.

The impact of the work I did there was extraordinarily fruitful and Self Managed Learning didn't only spread among schools, but also in other activities such as the Israeli Government's youth leadership programme. There is a mention of this contribution in Hecht's (2010) book.

When I came back from Israel it did seem strange to offer the benefits of our developments for another country and not to have done something in my own city of Brighton. This is when things started to happen locally.

South Downs Learning Centre

On my return from Israel I started to have meetings in Brighton with parents and other people who I knew might be interested in something different from the existing schools. Some teachers came to meetings as well as one school head and some people from the local council. We organised seminars, which included an event with Yaakov Hecht from Israel when he was over in the UK.

What became apparent was the need to respond to desperate parents. Some were home educating, but as their children grew older, they felt the need for an organised social setting that was not like a school. Others had children in school who are being bullied or who were just making no progress (including school refusers). So, we started running some groups in local community centres. We ran groups on a Monday morning where we did what we would normally do with adults, namely students wrote learning agreements and negotiated these within the group. We had some coverage in the local paper and one school on the edge of Brighton contacted us about taking on a 14-year-old boy, Jason, who was a selective mute. That meant he hadn't spoken for four years in his secondary school. He had not made eye contact with anybody. Nor had he done any schoolwork.

We met with his mother at her house and discovered more about his background. His mother explained that her son Jason had been told by a teacher in his primary school in his last year there that he was 'stupid'. 'Stupid' was the exact word that the teacher had used. Jason quite sensibly decided that there wasn't much point in talking to adults if they were going to behave like this and therefore throughout secondary education he had stopped talking in school. He talked outside the school and he was happy to talk with us.

Jason joined the group with a boy who'd been withdrawn from school, and others who had been home educated. We worked with Jason to explore both his unfortunate experiences in education along with possibilities for the future. Since he wanted to work after he left school, he realised the need to improve his skills, especially his English. I remember working with him at a computer one time and he was writing something which included a reference to the afternoon, except that he spelled afternoon 'arternoon'. He spoke in the local working-class dialect and that was a phonetic translation of how he would speak. If he talked about going out in the afternoon, he would say 'arternoon'.

I assume that in school this would be an example of him being seen as stupid. For me it was an example of where he was starting from. English is not a phonetic language and certainly standard English does not correlate with spoken working-class English. In helping him to understand what will be seen as the proper spelling we went back to his aim to gain employment when he left school. It was fairly easy to talk to him about the need an employer might have if he was writing a CV for himself in order to get a job. He fully understood the need to learn to be seen as doing the proper spelling, because he'd explored the kind of lifestyle he wanted to have in the future and he could see now that it would be a good idea to learn what seemed proper spelling.

It's interesting that in a presentation about our work some years later in one school, some teachers said, 'You need to have short-term targets for the less able.' My response was the opposite; you have to help students to commit to longer-term goals. This is especially important with those who are deemed this 'less able' because they haven't worked out for themselves a future within which school learning might be useful.

The upshot of Jason's changes was that we were able to go to school for a meeting that was required about his progress. The school was shocked to hear him speak and to talk sensibly about what he was looking for and what he needed to learn. These kinds of experiences gave us heart in recognising that we could offer something to schools, even if they are traditionally organised.

Another example in the same group as Jason was Tom. Tom had just opted out of school at age 14 as he could not read or write. He could just about write his name, but that was very much the limit. When talking with him about his past, he was able to tell us of some really interesting achievements. For a start he had been making a bit of money by making bicycles for his friends in the locality. He would find out what they wanted and then he would buy the parts and make the bike. When I explained that this was a real ability, he was a bit surprised. He didn't think of himself as having anything of worth and the notion that he had abilities which were beyond possibly 99% of young people of his age was a new realisation for him. In general, he had an extraordinary ability with machinery. As part of his growing confidence he and a friend found an old, rusting truck on a farm and completely renovated it, made it go and drove it around the farm. When we went on trips, such as to the Imperial War Museum, he was forever fascinated by machines and was able to work out how they functioned. He would excitedly clamber round tanks to understand how the tank operated and was able to talk to me about what the mechanics of the tank were.

With his growing confidence he worked in a local fairground helping to both install the fairground machinery and take it apart at the end, for which he was paid quite well. He even had the confidence to run a hoopla stall in the fair. This really surprised his parents since they had seen him as rather withdrawn and not able to do anything very much. Another way he earned some money was working in the pits in the banger car racing.

Alongside supporting him with his new ventures one of our team worked intensively with him on his English reading and writing, and also helped his parents with what they could do at home to support his learning. He left our programme after two years at the age of 16. Some years later I got an email from his father saying that Tom had managed to get through a basic course in the further education college and was now going on to a more advanced course. As he said in his email, if we'd have told him that his son was capable of going to college and achieving anything, he would have laughed in our faces.

The two examples were part of a group that only ran on a Monday since we didn't have any permanent premises. Although the community centre we worked in had some storage for materials, we couldn't leave things out as other users followed us. We just had to turn up on a Monday with any resources that we were using and then store them away for next time. Even with this limited facility we achieved a great deal with the students, and we had a lot of delighted parents.

During this time, we made a link with the University of Sussex and their Centre for Educational Innovation. Michael Fielding, who was running that, was sympathetic to the need for new ways of running schools. He tended to use the term 'personalised education' as his brand, but he recognised that Self Managed Learning in a sense was part of that personalised approach that he was promoting. The upshot of this was that we ended up being able to collaborate with the University running programmes in two local schools.

In one school they had identified a group of their 11/12-year-olds as 'gifted and talented' and had promised parents to run a special programme for them. However, this hadn't really worked out so well. Given that they had an orientation to improving independent learning, we were able to sell the notion of using a Self Managed Learning programme for this group. In another school we worked with slightly older students, but who again had been labelled 'gifted and talented'. Ideally, we wouldn't have liked to be working in a school with students with a particular label, especially one that separated them from other students. However, we decided that strategically this was of value since it would give us some leverage with the system in showing what we could achieve.

Both these programmes ran very successfully and had brilliant feedback from both the schools. A film was made about this by the University of Sussex and at the time of writing was still available on YouTube.[8]

One thing that comes out in the film is the fact that we managed to persuade one of the schools to have different kinds of groups in addition to the gifted and talented. Some groups included students who were seen as less active or involved, and the film shows one of these working with one of my colleagues. Another group was one for boys who were consistently in trouble in the school and who had experienced (or were currently experiencing) periods of exclusion.

As a result of the success of these programmes we went on to work in other schools with students ranging from 7 to 16 years old. Alongside the school programmes we continued to run groups in community centres around the city. In 2006 my wife died, and my daughter was away at university. I had a house to myself, so we started to run a Monday to Friday programme there every morning from 9am to 1pm.

This ran for four years in my house before we moved to rent facilities at Brighton Youth Centre, where we had one floor of the building every morning. We were also able to access other facilities within the building, such as the gym. In the afternoon, apart from the one room which was our office and learning resource area, the rest of the building reverted to the youth club. The advantage of working there was access to those facilities, but the disadvantage was that we couldn't leave stuff out in rooms which would then become part of the Youth Centre. The other advantage was that we could expand from the 12 students we had in my house since my house could not cope with anymore, so that at its largest we had up to 18 students in the centre. A downside of the Youth Centre was the level of vandalism in the building, which meant that it was becoming less usable, and also we were keen to have our own premises. So, although we had quite a good financial deal with the Centre, we moved out to the adjoining area of Fishersgate, where, at the time of writing, we are located.

Self Managed Learning College

Another change occurred when we moved out of my house, which was a change of name. Until that time we had the name South Downs Learning Centre. I like the concept of a learning centre and it certainly helped us to be distinguished from being a school. The downside was that the word 'centre' was associated in students' minds with a rather negative connotation. The Council's Pupil Referral Unit (meaning for those children who were permanently excluded from school and generally therefore had major behavioural problems) was called the Alternative Centre for Education. The students felt that whilst we had the complete range of young people, we should not be identified with a narrow band of young people in the Pupil Referral Unit, especially as they obviously had a negative label.

The term 'school' has a legal definition in England, and it is a criminal offence to run a school which is not registered with the authorities. The name 'college' is not one that has a legal attachment, and anyone could call what they do a college, so that's what we decided upon. We also decided that we would move from a title which mentioned location, namely the South Downs (which is an area of southern England), to saying it is Self Managed Learning College. We were also recognising that we were doing programmes in other parts of the country and that it was useful to have the generic term Self Managed Learning College rather than an association with a location.

Part of our strategy was to evolve slowly and carefully. Later I will comment on the need to maintain sustainability but suffice it to say here that we knew that the majority of alternative education institutions that had been set up in the last 50 years in the UK had closed fairly quickly. We are in this for the long haul and therefore wanted to make certain that we are financially stable and in every other way a sustainable operation.

When we were renting facilities in use in community centres this was very cheap. Moving into my house meant there were no costs of renting a place but obviously we were limited space-wise. The Youth Centre meant that we had to pay rent, but this did cover cleaning, heating and lighting, etc and meant that therefore we didn't have a large financial commitment. But we did have to make certain we earned the money to pay the rent. In moving SML College to Fishersgate we had to be sure that we could pay for a lease which was also more expensive, but considerably cheaper than if we had remained within the city limits of Brighton and Hove. Our potential next move is into our own facilities, which of course will be more expensive because we may need to buy a place.

Our status

I now need to elaborate on our status within the system as developing this has been a really important part of our history and of the development of the College.

In the 1944 Education Act it was established that every child must be in education. The actual choice for any parent was between 'school or otherwise'. Parents had, and still have, the legal responsibility for making certain that their child has a suitable education. In subsequent Acts of Parliament, it has been established that 'suitable' means 'suitable in terms of the age, aptitude, ability and any special needs' of the child. In the 1944 Act, and subsequent Acts up to the present day, there is little clarity about the interpretation of 'suitable' education. However, in all Acts of Parliament since 1944 the requirement for 'school or otherwise' has been maintained. Until the 1960s there was a presumption that school was really the only option. Then a parent who was home educating was challenged by their local authority in the courts as to why their child was not in school. The parent won the case on the basis that home educating was education and therefore was covered by the Act in terms of this 'otherwise' concept.

Since the 1960s it has generally been assumed that if a child is not in school it could be home educated. Both the Government and local authorities have tended to interpret the 'otherwise' notion as meaning home education. However, in law there is no mention of home education. There hasn't been since the 1944 Act or in any subsequent Acts of Parliament. The Government sends round guidance on home education to local authorities and local authorities themselves write their own guidance notes, which tend to assume that being 'otherwise' means being home educated. Of course, home education isn't necessarily at home. What it really means is that parents are taking charge of the education of their child, but that learning could be occurring in all sorts of contexts and generally is. One of the features of home education is that there have been groupings around the country, and these have often run, for instance, drop in groups where children might go together swimming or on trips.

In this scenario then the fact that we have been running a college that students attend from 9am to 1pm on five days a week is a bit of an anomaly. We have always argued that we come under the 'otherwise' category within the Acts and that therefore our work is legitimate. Parents who send their children to us are, as far as we're concerned, fulfilling their legal obligation to make certain their child has a suitable education. Indeed, I would argue that as most of the children who come to us have experienced being in school, parents have deemed school as not providing a suitable education. Therefore, it could be argued, though it hasn't been tested in the courts, that the parent is doing the right thing by making this choice, and that they would be contravening the law by keeping their child in a place where the education was not suitable in terms of 'the age, aptitude, ability and any special needs' of the child.

Given the extent of, for instance, bullying in all the schools in our area, especially those covering the post 11 age group, I would argue that school education is unsuitable for those children who are bullied. Indeed 'bullying' is probably too weak a word to use for the fact that in our local schools there are children every day being beaten up merely because they are different; for example, mixed race students get bullied as do those who are suspected of being gay. Bullied children are only one example of the fact that large local state schools are unsuitable for a wider range of children.

Our aim has been to provide a suitable education for young people in our area. For a while this was well recognised and supported by our local authority in the city of Brighton and Hove. Indeed, in a strategy plan produced by the Council a few years ago the work of the College was singled out as an example of a model which could show the future of what schooling could be like. It was the only organisation that was picked out within the strategy document for this kind of comment. At that time we worked with senior officials and politicians and had their support for what we were doing.

Even before we opened SML College the Director of Education for the Council had asked me to work with him and school heads/principals in exploring the use of Self Managed Learning across all local schools. This ended up with me doing a workshop in a school with teachers from a number of schools to show how the approach could be used. In the 20 years since then we have had schools and the local Council paying for students to come to us as they have recognised that school has not provided a suitable education for those individuals. We have worked, for instance, closely with the part of the local Council that works with children in care. This means either that the child is in a children's home or in foster care. Our record of success with young people in this situation was well recognised within that part of the Council, especially as it is well known that children in care tend to do very badly within the schooling system in general.

In some cases we worked with local schools not just to take on individual students, but also to do work within the school, showing how the Self Managed Learning approach could be used in the school context.

All of this is quite positive. However, political change in our local Council did change the situation. At the time there was a Conservative-run council. They supported us in tentatively putting in a bid to the Government to run what have been called 'free schools'. These schools were established to operate outside the local authority system and the Government argued that they could be set up by, for instance, parents or local community groups and they could meet needs that perhaps the local authority-run schools were not meeting.

There's a lot more that could be said about such free schools, especially as they have not been at all free, but that is outside the scope of this text. In this context when the Government made the announcement, we thought it would be interesting to test the water by suggesting a Self Managed Learning school that would be publicly funded under the free school arrangements. This was supported by the local Council, who could see the value in us taking up this offer from the Government. This is especially so in the context of support from the local Council for the notion that our approach was a model for how schooling could develop. We therefore put in a proposal under the Government's rubric, which at that time was a fairly open template that we had to complete.

We argued for the approach that we work with. We were able to say that we have been running these programmes both inside schools and for young people out of school in a successful way and have been supported by our local Council. Our radical approach, which said there will be no imposed curriculum or classrooms, or imposed lessons or imposed teaching, did not find favour with the officials at the Department for Education, so we had to withdraw our application.

Conclusion

I have outlined in this part of the book important developments in our history. Given our unique position within England and to some extent internationally, I know that many people have been intrigued as to how we have managed to become successful and to maintain our principles in only providing Self Managed Learning programmes for young people. Other organisations will have their own histories, and much can be learned from all of these.

In our case, our strategy of careful evolution is one we believe that could help other people wanting to set up similar kinds of organisations. Certainly, the poor survival rates of alternatives both in the UK and internationally do point to the need for careful development. My own way of thinking about strategy for sustainability is to consider the longest time horizon on which a student could stay with us. If we take someone at 9 and they leave at 17, then we need to promise eight years' existence at the very least for that child. I know that schools and other organisations that have closed down can argue that they have at least during their short history been really helpful to young people who otherwise would have not received that help. However, I don't only see it as an obligation to parents and children to be there. We also need to show that those of us operating outside the educational system can actually manage and operate educational provision that is effective and stable.

Notes

1   Some of the evaluations of SML programmes can be read in I. Cunningham et al. (2000) *Self Managed Learning in Action*. These include evaluations from AXA, Arun District Council, Barclays Bank, Cable and Wireless, Ericsson, Finland Post, Ladbroke Group, Norwich Union Insurance, Reigate and Banstead District Council, S Group (Finland), Shell and J Sainsbury.
2   'Team skills' not 'team building' is a direct challenge to the 'building' metaphor, which assumes that a team is a fixed thing to be built. My interest is in responding to the fluidity of how organisational life actually plays out. Teams in work are not the same as sports teams and attempts to replicate the sports model are unhealthy. Also, my case is that people need to learn to work in any team within which they are located – it's a learning process not a process of fixing a team and then everything is fine. Also, the narrow team orientation focuses too much on the bonding of individuals and not enough on the skills of bridging across teams. The former process can ossify silo working, which is damaging to organisational performance. SML has helped bridging processes by using heterogenous learning groups based around people from different parts of the organisation so participants learn to enhance bridging processes.
3   Friedman and Laurison (2019) in *The Class Ceiling* do a brilliant job in exposing the myths of a classless society through their research. For instance, they show that privileged graduates from elite universities with a 2.2 degree (often these days in England seen as a virtual fail) are more likely to get into top jobs than working-class graduates with a 1st.
    Evans (2006) provides a social anthropological analysis of the discrimination against working-class school pupils. She shows how middle-class children have a home environment that mirrors school culture, which makes the transition to school easier. Working-class children don't have this start in life so entering school requires them first to learn about this new form of learning called education. She cites specific evidence of the lack of impact of schooling on achievement. For instance, the child's overall developmental score at 22 months plus its socio-economic classification accurately predicts educational qualifications by age 26. As she comments, this means that education has had no impact on the person's position in society.
4   Caplan (2018) claims that the only marketable skills that the better economics students gain are elementary statistics and the ability to calculate a present discounted value. He argues that professors fill the rest of the time in a four-year degree with topics that interest the faculty but may have no career value (unless the student wants to be an economics professor). Note that Caplan is an experienced economics professor in a genuine university.

5 I'm not saying that you could always achieve this or that this is the way you could play professionally. However, I have worked with professional teams with their young players. Part of what I and my colleagues have been trying to do is improve the quality of football in this country by taking a different stance to the development of young players (up to the age of 16). Through work with the coaches at professional clubs, the orientation has been to liberate young players from excessive controlled coaching and instead to encourage increased self managed learning. It has also meant honouring seemingly unstructured play and fewer imposed drills and exercises.

6 My work as having responsibility for educational matters at the National Union of Students for England, Wales and Northern Ireland (1968–1970) had meant that I was in touch with radical ideas about education and had campaigned for reform of colleges and universities. The work of a range of radical writers in the UK and the USA had been important in exposing the errors of the education system.

7 'The Independent Inquiry into Summerhill School' (2000) is obtainable from the Centre for Self Managed Learning. There is an online version at www.evaluating-education.org. uk/archive/resources/ESRCArchiveDemo_203.pdf

8 If you want to know more and hear from the people involved, please watch the film: https://www.youtube.com/watch?v=TBybHthhwXE

References

Caplan, B. (2018) *The Case Against Education*. Princeton: Princeton University Press.

Crawford, M. B. (2009) *Shop Class as Soulcraft*. New York: Penguin.

Cunningham, I. (1999) *The Wisdom of Strategic Learning*, 2nd edition. Aldershot, Hants.: Gower.

Cunningham, I., Bennett, B. and Dawes, G. (2000) *Self Managed Learning in Action*. Aldershot, Hants.: Gower.

Evans, G. (2006) *Education Failure and Working Class White Children in Britain*. Basingstoke, Hants.: Palgrave Macmillan.

Friedman, S. and Laurison, D. (2019). *The Class Ceiling*. Bristol: Bristol University Press.

Gray, P. (2013) *Free to Learn*. New York: Basic Books.

Hecht, Y. (2010) *Democratic Education*. New York: AERO.

Pirsig, R. M. (1974) *Zen and the Art of Motorcycle Maintenance*. New York: William Morrow.

Rogers, C. R. (1969) *Freedom to Learn*. Columbus, Ohio: Charles E. Merrill Publishing Company.

5

AN EVIDENCE BASIS FOR ACTION

Introduction

I want to discuss here our approach to an evidence-based, research-based way of carrying out our work. I am critical of how much educational research seems to be involved with trying to prop up the existing system without making a fundamental examination of it. Also, I'm concerned about how unsubstantiated opinions seem to dominate a great deal of the discourse about education.

My starting point will then be about the problems of opinions dictating action and how subjective decisions such as those around the curriculum are not driven by real evidence. I need to say something also about the nature of evidence and about my view about taking a more scientific approach to educational decisions. This will necessitate also looking at epistemological problems and I want to indicate a particular epistemological model so that there is a basis for taking forward action based on real evidence. A concern is about the intensions of governments and others, which look fine on the surface, but in reality, are non-actionable. In discussing the nature of science, I will use the notion of the need for 'skin in the game' and I will explain how I use that idea.

I want to make the case that science in practice is about prediction and about using the best available evidence to make predictions in which to test the evidence. It is also a necessity for science and technology to integrate, though in general social sciences are poor at this and it seems especially to affect education. There is also the problem that political decisions tend not to be based on good science, especially again in the area of education, but there are many examples elsewhere of social policy emerging more from political expediency.

I am also concerned about the need for a more systemic and grounded theory that provides a basis for development rather than narrow piecemeal research. I am particularly unhappy that the paradigm for education in itself acts as a barrier to a more scientific and research-based approach. Finally, I will raise the question of how to operate professionally in assisting others to learn.

Opinions dictate action

A good example of the dominance of opinion is the opposition to involving young people in their own learning and the citing of William Golding's *Lord of the Flies* (1954) as supposed evidence that children left to their devices will descend into savagery. Golding's work of fiction was a response to an earlier fictional piece by R. M. Ballantyne about a group of boys being shipwrecked and doing well in coping together. The first thing to mention is that none of the educational processes that I am talking about involve leaving children so totally alone. In our College typically we would have 4 adults present for 40 young people. The argument that what we do will result in the 'Lord of the Flies' syndrome has no validity.

The other rebuttal of Golding's fiction is evidence from Agnelli, 1986, cited also by Ward, 1988. Here is solid evidence of a group of six boys from the Pacific island of Tonga who were shipwrecked on an uninhabited tropical island due to a storm. They worked well together, got on well and 15 months later they were all rescued. In other words, the evidence is that even left alone young boys can actually work together and will not descend into savagery. Golding's views have no merit other than as a work of fiction. There is no factual evidence whatsoever that I know of that shows that young boys would behave in the way that Golding's fiction describes.

I have mentioned in Chapter 4 about my own childhood in a working-class area of South Manchester, where we were left to roam on our own and we did get on pretty well together. But again, I would reiterate that in our College and in all other supposed alternative educational institutions, there is always adult presence and a very serious involvement of adults in supporting the learning of young people.

The refusal to consider evidence and instead base decisions on invalid opinions or historical ideas is not new. In a letter to Kepler, Galileo bemoaned the fact that the principal professor of philosophy was asked repeatedly to look through his 'glass' (telescope) at the moon and planets. The man pointedly refused. He argued that he based his ideas on Aristotle and did not need to get any further evidence than Aristotle's views. Such stances undermined scientific progress for many years and there are still those who want to avoid looking at the evidence about learning.

Kahneman (2011) points out that the most reliable way to make people believe in falsehoods is frequent repetition. The evidence of other researchers such as Cialdini (2009) also comes to a similar conclusion. Cialdini's extensive research on modes of influencing shows also that reference to authority is another way to get people to believe something. Golding was awarded the Nobel Prize for Literature, so he must be right, is the assumption. This evidence along with the continual repeating of the myth of the Lord of the Flies convinces people of its truth, even though there is absolutely no evidence to support the fiction.

If we take, in comparison, a more practical example of the influence of opinion, then the use of school uniforms is such an example. The Educational Endowment

Foundation does many thorough analyses of evidence and its conclusion is that there is no evidence that the wearing of school uniform on its own has a positive impact on 'academic performance, behaviour or attendance'.[1] Despite this many teachers and educational administrators support the imposition of uniforms in school on the basis of the opinion that it has a positive impact on the school. But it's just an opinion and there is really no basis for continuing with this practice.

Therefore, although in this part of this book I will be making a strong case for a properly research-based scientific and evidentially based approach to education, I unfortunately don't have a lot of confidence that in the short term it will make any difference whatsoever to educational decision-making. However, I'm not going to let my pessimism get in the way of attempting to make a good case for the evidence that is cited in the next part of this book.

The curriculum

Any choice of what is to go into a curriculum in school is a subjective choice. There is no objective basis to such choice, and this is evidenced by the continual changes in the English National Curriculum without proper evidence of the reasons for this other than political judgements. The current political choice is to have an academic basis to the curriculum for 11 to 16-year-olds. This has attracted a great deal of criticism, especially from people in the arts, quite rightly so since the choices are based on erroneous assumptions such as the faulty analysis of the needs of the economy.

There is ample evidence of the implications of subjective curriculum choices. I will just take one example from the English primary curriculum here: by the end of Year 5, namely for 10-year-olds, students are required to know about relative clauses and modal verbs, and by the end of Year 6, the 11-year-old students are supposed to know about ellipsis and independent clauses. Kahneman (2011) points out that the average four-year-old can speak grammatically without any knowledge whatsoever of these grammatical forms. There is no evidence that knowing these structures will actually make someone more able to write effectively in English. Indeed, a number of well-known writers have made this criticism of the curriculum. I write quite a lot and I take grammar seriously, I hope. I had no idea what these terms meant until I saw them in the primary curriculum. Seriously. No idea whatsoever – and I'm certainly not alone. It's quite clear that the majority of the population have no idea about this either.

The proponents of a knowledge-based curriculum, such as Christodoulou (2014), actually seem to have little knowledge of how the real world works. The idea that you have to know something before you can do anything is bizarre. A good example is riding a bicycle. There is a formula about how you ride a bicycle and it is an inverse square law, namely the relationship between the radius of the wind of the bicycle and the inverse square of the velocity of the bicycle. It is genuinely useless to know this since when you want to learn to ride a bicycle you get on it and you have a go at it, with assistance quite probably, and eventually you learn to keep upright. Nobody that I know who rides a bicycle has any idea of the scientific basis for riding a bicycle.

I once imagined a school having a bicycle riding curriculum. Students would be taught these physical principles and also the chemistry of the bicycle frames and tyres, quite probably the history of bicycle riding, and so on. Students wouldn't, of course, ever ride a bicycle. For these teachers, knowledge is more important than skills. Now the reality is that often knowledge and skills go together and it's futile to argue the precedence of one over the other. Unfortunately, there are plenty of teachers who buy into the arguments of Christodoulou and others. Their case for fact-based learning as the required dominant mode in schools will be looked at further later.

Even more bizarre than this fact-orientation is the whole issue of the testing of the curriculum. Assuming that even if the curriculum is somewhat subjective, that the testing ought to be quite objective is a basic assumption in education. Sara Holbrook (2017), a poet, commented that she found out that she couldn't answer questions posed about two of her own poems on the Texas State assessment tests. Young people were asked to forget the joy of language and the fun of discovering poetry and instead to do what she described as line by line dissection and analysis. The test questions as she indicates were incomprehensible to her and presumably to many of the children who had to answer them.

The evaluations of teachers would have to be based on guesses as to what the correct answers might be, yet Holbrook was clear that the 'correct answers' that the teachers had given did not relate to what she meant by the poems. She points out that teachers generally get away with this nonsense because they mostly test the work of dead people who can't protest. As she says, she's not dead and nobody bothered to ask her about her motivation for writing the poems or what they actually meant to her. Such testing is highly subjective and indeed currently as I write there is a lot of concern about public exams into areas like sociology and English and the subjective views of markers. Ofqual (the Government's exams regulator) has accepted that in such essay-based subjects, markers only agree on the grades a student receives 52% to 58% of the time (Duffy, 2019).

Sometimes bizarre answers were actually required in what might seem more objective areas which are not subject to the subjectivity of the marker. A Japanese colleague explained to me that when he was at school, he had to write April as the answer to the question as to when the cherry trees blossom. However, in the north of Japan blossom is not out until May, in the south it will be out in February. If anyone in the north wrote May or in the south February, it would be marked wrong. They had to put April, even though for large parts of the country this was clearly nonsense. Everyone could see when cherry blossom is out.

What knowledge – epistemology

We all have an epistemology – that is a theory about the nature of knowledge; what we know and what we don't know. I have a simple descriptive model which

I hope will be helpful here. I think about it in terms of personal pronouns, namely first, second and third person. First person knowledge is what 'I/we' know or believe we know. Second person knowledge is the result of a dialogue between 'I' and 'you'. Third person knowledge is that which is about 'they, them and it'. It's the abstracted knowledge about the world and is often recognised as academic or text-book knowledge.

I can exemplify how this works with a reference to a leadership course that I ran for a Masters degree in the USA. From a first-person perspective each person has their own views about leadership. People are in leadership roles and they believe that they know things about what it is to lead. Of course, these may be beliefs that don't stand up to test, but it is the beliefs that people hold, due to some evidence, that guide action. People in leadership roles are daily at work undertaking leadership activity from within their own sense of what makes a leader. In the programme that I ran I used my Self Managed Learning model, so each individual not only identified their own beliefs and epistemology regarding leadership, but they also dialogued with five other people in the group.

Other people have their ideas about leadership and their experiences from which they draw so the interactions between the person and others were a key part of the dialogue within the learning group. This is the domain of 'I to you'; the interaction between first and second person knowing. However, they also needed to explore third person knowledge – that is, that there is a huge and growing literature on leadership, and it was important that people drew on that literature in order to then juxtapose the three dimensions. They had to then look at leadership theory against their own experience and against the dialogic learning that they undertook as part of the discussions with the group, where each person would be sharing aspects of their own leadership style and their views about what makes a leader effective.

The bringing together of these three domains is crucial in making progress in an area like leadership. Just to work on the basis of one of these alone would be dangerous. Clearly, most of us would accept that working just on your own personal view without testing that with others can be an egocentric activity that has low value, but just engaging in dialogue with others may result in an individual making changes purely based on the evidence of other people. Those other people could be misguided. Testing those ideas against theories and models and the research literature is important. However, just accepting a leadership role based solely on the theory from the textbooks or the research may also be misguided. Leadership involves personality and the abstract generalisations of much of the research, if implemented purely on their own without any recourse to testing with others and testing with your own world, can lead to mechanistic, but ultimately flawed, learning.

To bring this now into the world of school teaching we can utilise these three domains. The first person learning for the trainee teacher may well come from their own experience in school, from their parents or from the media. They will take this first-person knowledge into a training course to become a teacher. During that course, they will engage in dialogue with colleagues on the course as well as during teaching practice discussions with teachers who are already qualified. This will then develop their view of teaching in all probability. Alongside the practical experience in school, the trainee teacher will probably attend lectures and have a taught course in a university around education and the role of teaching. They will be exposed to theory and have to pass examinations. Ultimately, they will enter school with some kind of integration between these three domains.

Values and beliefs

In terms of the notion of science as about prediction we would be predicting that none of our students at Self Managed Learning College should end up in prison, engage in antisocial behaviour of any kind and, on the contrary, we would expect students to move from our community into wider communities where they will play a positive role not just because of what they know. Independent research[2] so far shows that our predictions are valid.

I am suggesting that the combination of values and beliefs is a basis for action in an educational or learning context. One of the problems is that espoused values, for instance from the Government, end up with non-actionable advice and exhortation. There are many examples one could draw on of this problem. Just to take an example from the Integrated Communities Strategy Green Paper 2018, under the heading of what the Government is going to do, the first sentence is, 'All young people – whatever their background – should have the opportunity to go as far in life as their talents and hard work will take them.' There is no reference in this document anywhere to the problems of implementing this. First of all, there is the issue of the class system; secondly, of disability; thirdly, the fact that summer born children will do worse in exams; or fourthly, that children in care, autistic children and whole lot of other groups do worse in education. No matter what their talents and hard work bring, it will not bring them the same level of success as those from privileged backgrounds.

To this value based exhortation (which is clearly meaningless) if we dig into practical aspects, then the reference to schools' contribution to integration says that schools should 'promote fundamental British values of democracy, the rule of law, individual liberty, and mutual respect and tolerance of those with different faiths and beliefs'. The experience I've had, and many others, shows that schools as currently conceived are incapable of achieving this. First of all, schools do not seem to value democracy since children don't have much of a say about what goes on, they are forced to go to classes and to go through a particular curriculum. Secondly, individual liberty is definitely constrained in this context. Some people have made the criticism that schools are like prison, but others would say that they are even worse because at least in prison you can choose whether you go to lessons or not.

Mutual respect is clearly missing in terms of the relationship between teaching staff in many schools and those who have different beliefs. When I was at school my beliefs were about the need for me to have the liberty to learn what I wanted to learn and not to be constrained by the curriculum or by teachers. That belief was certainly not respected and is not respected in the average school. We have espoused values from Government that clearly are not being actioned and are merely interesting exhortations that have no real merit in the real world.

Skin in the game

I rather like the use of the notion of 'skin in the game' as used by Taleb (2018). He suggests that 'how much you truly believe in something can be manifested only through what you're willing to risk for it' (p. 219). Further, he quotes Sextus Empiricus, who said, 'those who talk should do and only those that do should talk' (p. 29). His criticism of what I'm labelling as the third person world on its own is captured in Taleb's statement that academia has the 'tendency when (unchecked from lack of skin in the game) to evolve into a ritualistic self-referential publishing game' (p. 146). Crucially, what underpins having 'skin in the game' involves the integration of the first-, second- and third-person knowledge. We have to test the generalities by investing in making things happen and then testing whether they are really valid. One way of viewing what we've done with creating Self Managed Learning College is to say that we believe in the research and scientific basis. We believe in it so much that we are prepared to risk doing it and if we are wrong, we will fail.

Science

This isn't the place to do a full exploration of the nature of science. What I want to do is more to focus on what I mean by being scientific in this particular context. The first feature of the application of science is the notion that it's about prediction. As a chemist I could predict that if we put salt in water it would dissolve, and that would happen anywhere in the world provided there were the basic conditions of the same temperature, atmospheric pressure, and so on. If at any time I tried to dissolve salt in water and it didn't dissolve, we would then have to revise our theory.

This is close to what the followers of Karl Popper[3] say with the notion of falsification. You can have a theoretical generalisation that all swans are white, but if you come across black swans you have to modify that theoretical generalisation. You have falsified your initial generalisation and must change it. Note here that I am not wanting to debate the full Popperian methodology or his notion of falsification. I want only to suggest that in this particular context I am at one with the Popperians.

I will show with the next part of this book the evidence and research that we have drawn up. I hope that by first indicating the status of that evidence in this chapter it will be clearer as to the basis on which we have used the evidence. I have done what Taleb suggests as 'skin in the game' by actually putting my 'money where my mouth is'.

I want here to exemplify Taleb's stance by first taking what might seem an extreme example from scientific research in the field of medicine. In 1982 Barry Marshall and another scientist, Robin Warren, published a paper showing that the causative factor for ulcers was *Helicobacter pylori*. The two authors showed, from research, that most gastric ulcers and gastritis were caused by the colonisation with this bacterium, not by stress or spicy food as had been assumed. Their research was initially poorly received so in an act of putting 'skin in the game' Barry Marshall drank a petri dish containing a culture of organisms extracted from a person with an ulcer and five days later he developed gastritis. (He did take the antibiotics to kill the bacteria.) His experiment was published in 1985 in the *Medical Journal of Australia* and is amongst the most cited articles from the journal (Marshall et al., 1985).

In 2005 he and his partner, Robin Warren, were awarded the Nobel Prize in Physiology or Medicine for the discovery of the bacterium *Helicobacter pylori* and its role in gastritis and peptic ulcer disease. This is a good example of 'skin in the game' and of the important role of experiment in science. Most experiments, of course, are not as dramatic as this one, but the point I want to make is as a former research chemist. If you are predicting something could happen because of a particular theory, then you may need to try it out and not pontificate without the evidence.

In my doctoral research I studied the role of someone like myself in assisting the learning of others. This was in the context of management development. I did first-, second- and third-person research. I had already had a lot of experience of working on the way described in this book. I reflected on my work a great deal before starting on the PhD. During the PhD research I engaged with others who were experts in the field by both interviewing them and carrying out group dialogic sessions. I utilised academic research in bringing together the first-, second- and third-person knowledge to come out with models and predictions. In order to demonstrate that I was actually carrying out that prediction I filmed myself working with a group with an annotated document attached to it to indicate what I was thinking of at different points in the film so that anyone watching the film could then understand what was going on. Most of what was going on was in my head as I was pondering what to do at particular times, as well as the actual things that I did visibly. The university had a bit of a problem dealing with a video tape. I was very keen to put the film with the thesis because I needed to show I had 'skin in the game'.

An early experiment to test my growing view about education was when I was a young chemist. I went to work in a further education college in 1967, supposedly to teach chemistry for the English Advance Level certification, largely for the 16 to 18-year-old age group. I felt that lecturing and standing at a board was not the way to go. I copied out notes for the topics in the syllabus and distributed them to the students. I discussed the notes with them. To me it made more sense to do it that way than lecturing. I hoped that they would increase their understanding through this approach. I predicted that this approach was likely to be more enjoyable and would be approved by the majority of students. I also predicted that it would not lower the exam results.

At the end of the year I distributed an anonymous questionnaire to all of them to ask them how they felt about the difference between the two approaches (lecture versus discussion). The majority were more favourably disposed to the discussion approach. Also, I checked the exam results and the results for the students were slightly better than normal (that is, in previous years). Given the small numbers it couldn't be seen as statistically valid, but certainly they had not gone down. I wanted to put 'skin in the game' by actually showing that there is another way to do things than standing at a board and writing.

Another example later on was when we set up the School for Independent Study at North East London Polytechnic because, again, we made predictions about the work. We said, for instance, that we would take anybody without any qualifications whatsoever and then after three years we would get them to a degree level with about the same dropout rate as the rest of the Polytechnic. We employed a researcher to study both how it would go, and also to make certain we had all the data. Interestingly, the dropout rate was about the same as the rest of the Polytechnic, even though we were taking people with no qualifications whatsoever. In a few cases, they had just come out of prison or a mental hospital. In other cases, they were unable to read and write very well. But not only was the dropout rate about the same as the average for the institution, we had a higher proportion with first-class honours degrees at the end of the programme than the rest of the Polytechnic, even though we had a much more stringent examination board because of the unusual nature of the programme. Our skin was in the game. If we had failed, it would have potentially been disastrous for our careers as we were very visible because of the radical nature of a degree with no syllabus and no entry requirements. Other studies have discussed this work, for example, Robbins (1988).

Linking science to technology

As a chemist I was well aware of the importance of the linkage of science and technology. As an example, we were able to develop sophisticated analytical techniques due to new spectrographic tools. These tools were an important technology. But that technology could only be created because it used scientific evidence about the nature of materials and so on. The scientific developments supported new technology and the new technology supported new scientific developments. Science has progressed through the development of technology as technology progressed through the development of science.

This seems to be lacking in areas such as education, where there is scientific research and evidence but applications of it seem sparse. If there were more applications, then there would be more testing and the science could improve. What we try to do with Self Managed Learning College is to say that this is a piece of social technology. If you like, we are applying scientific evidence and putting it all together to produce an applied demonstration of the implementation of that. What would be good would be if the research we are doing evaluating our work then could feed back into further research that could take us forward. The difficulty is that in school there seems to be little or no connection between the broader research world and the practice of education.

If we turn to current educational research, it's largely about how to improve classrooms and how to improve teaching and what to put in the curriculum, all of which use the existing structures and the existing technology. However, the world has moved on. Unlike school. As some people have suggested, the only major change from the Victorian times in school has been from black to white – that is, from blackboards to whiteboards. The social organisation is largely the same as you would see in a Victorian school: classrooms, desks and the teacher at the front. Attempting to improve classrooms is the equivalent of improving typewriters when word processing has been invented. Or improving the stagecoach when buses and trains have been invented. There is no need to continue with the old social tech-nology. But because fundamental research seems to be ignored in the educational world, then of course the social technology continues.

Please note that by using the concept of 'social technology' I do not mean what is pejoratively called 'social engineering'. I am not proposing the application of science, such that we try to mould the population in a particular kind of way, as is alleged with social engineering. My use of the term technology is from the scien-tific and technological world and relates to the notion of technology as the appli-cation of science.

Note also that this interplay of science and technology is based on the idea that science is about using the best available evidence at any one time. We can talk about the search for truth, but that's just too abstract. Bateson (1972) cuts through the deductive and inductive arguments about science by saying it's basically a pincer movement between theory and the evidence. If the two go together, then you have confidence about using the theory. But if they don't, then you have to do something. As he points out, it may be that you were observing the stars in some way and imagine that you've got some data which challenges existing theory. It may well be that you have done a poor observa-tion and that therefore you have to check it. You can't just rely on that one piece of evidence. Maybe you have made a breakthrough in science. Maybe you just got it wrong. On the other hand, if the new observation, as with the black swan example, indicates a need to change the theory then it's important to do it.

Counting and what counts

I hope I've done enough here to indicate a view of scientific working without going into a complete thesis on the nature of science. All I wanted to do is to justify a particular way of thinking and working with sufficient evidence. I am not saying that we always have to use scientific evidence. As Einstein has been quoted,

'Not everything that can be counted, counts. And not everything that counts can be counted.' Love can't be counted but it surely counts in relationships.

In terms of looking at what is counted and what counts it's clear that the dominant counting currently practised in England is of test and examination results. Schools are judged and judge themselves on getting passes in public examinations and appropriate tests. But how many schools do research on, for instance, seeing whether their ex pupils have a good life 5, 10 or 20 years later and that that good life has been positively influenced by the school? Isn't that future life something that really counts? It may not be judged in number terms but if schooling claims that it contributes to a good life, it should be the basis of the evaluation of schools.

A neat example of this counting problem is given by Colin Powell (1995) in his autobiography. He served as an officer in the Vietnam war. All the figures they were sending back to Washington, such as body counts, said that they were winning the war. However, people on the ground, who had 'skin in the game', knew that they were losing. If the objective was to win the war, clearly it didn't work out. The same problem bedevils education where the evaluation is of an intermediary point, namely exam passes when the person is in school. My case is that it is after school that we should be looking at and seeing to what extent school has had a positive influence.

When I'm challenged on why we don't enforce the teaching of English on students I mention the evidence that around half of the occupants of Her Majesty's prisons are judged to be functionally illiterate.[4] Presumably, most of them went to school. To what extent do schools therefore look at themselves to think about what they have failed to achieve if somebody is illiterate and also ends up in prison, in part because of illiteracy? It's a serious social issue. We know that imprisonment can be as a result of other factors, but if half the inhabitants of the prisons are functionally illiterate, that does tell us something really important.

Professionalism

My simple model of what it is to be professional requires at the minimum both an ethical basis and the application of the best evidence in practice. Both are needed – it's a sine qua non. When I first worked in local government, back in 1970, I asked a senior civil engineer as to what made his role professional. His reply was that if his employer asked him to build something that he knew would be unsafe he would refuse to do it. His professionally based theory and evidence would tell him what was safe, and his ethical position would be to refuse to ignore the evidence. Being professional requires both – and this takes us back to the quote from the concentration camp survivor. It also links to the best of the medical professional; the Hippocratic Oath and scientific knowledge have to go together. One without the other is dangerous (and I accept that medics are not always prudent on such matters).

The question to consider as we go into the next chapter regarding evidence is – is the current mode of teaching at all professional?

Conclusion

In this chapter I wanted to make a case for the need for good evidence of the right kind and also to indicate how this might come about. My overall concern about the current situation in education is that the basis of much of the practical activity is either from opinions or from narrowly based research attempting to improve existing practices, rather than looking at research which undermines the use of those practices. In the next chapter I will cover a range of research areas, which seem to me to undermine much of the taken for granted practice in schools, universities and colleges. The situation is serious and hence my plea for a new paradigm which encompasses approaches that are based on what we know about learning and about young people.

Notes

1 https://educationendowmentfoundation.org.uk/pdf/generate/?u=https://educationendowm entfoundation.org.uk/pdf/toolkit/?id=145&t=Teaching%20and%20Learning%20Toolkit& e=145&s= Accessed August 15, 2019.
2 Independent research on SML for young people has been carried out through a number of studies from the University of Brighton. The most extensive was conducted by Nicola Sankey in 2008 and was incorporated into a report by her and Graham Dawes (2008). A recent study on past students has been conducted by Luke Freedman (2019). A specific study on self-motivation of ex-students was conducted by Chelsea Mathews (2016).
3 See J. Swann (2012) for an interesting exposition of the use of Popper's ideas in education.
4 There are debates about the exact figures for illiteracy in prisons. A good summary of the issue and one that also shows how using peer-to-peer learning is having a positive impact is in Moss (2017). It is another example of skin in the game as it features real prisoners and real work with them to address the problem. A more standard piece of academic research is in Creese (2016).

References

Agnelli, S. (1986) *Street Children*. London: Weidenfeld and Nicolson.
Bateson, G. (1972) *Steps to an Ecology of Mind: Collected Essays in Anthropology, Psychiatry, Evolution, and Epistemology*. Chicago: University of Chicago Press.
Christodoulou, D. (2014) *Seven Myths about Education*. London: Routledge.
Cialdini, R. (2009) *Influence: Science and Practice*. Boston, MA: Pearson Education.
Creese, B. (2016) An assessment of the English and maths skills levels of prisoners in England. *London Review of Education*, 14(3).
Dawes, G. and Sankey, N. (2008) The Student Experience of Self Managed Learning: Evidence from Research. Brighton: Centre for Self Managed Learning.
Duffy, N. (2019) Half of A-Level students could be getting 'wrong' grades. *i newspaper*, August 11. https://inews.co.uk/news/education/half-of-a-level-students-could-be-getting-wrong-grades-analysis-reveals/.
Freedman, L. (2019) The Self Managed Learning College Study, Phase One Report. Brighton: Centre for Self Managed Learning.
Golding, W. (1954) *Lord of the Flies*. London: Faber and Faber.
HM Government, UK (2018) Integrated Communities Strategy Green Paper.

Holbrook, S. (2017) I can't answer these Texas standardized test questions about my own poems. *Huffington Post*, January 5. https://www.huffpost.com/entry/standardized-tests-are-so-bad-i-cant-answer-these_b_586d5517e4b0c3539e80c341?amp=1&guccounter=1.

Kahneman, D. (2011) *Thinking, Fast and Slow*. London: Penguin.

Kuhn, T. S. (1996) *The Structure of Scientific Revolutions*. 3rd edition. Chicago, IL: University of Chicago Press.

Marshall, B. J., Armstrong, J. A., McGechie, D. B. and Clancy, R. J. (1985) Attempt to fulfil Koch's postulates for pyloric Campylobacter. *Medical Journal of Australia*, 142(8), 436–439.

Mathews, C. (2016) An enquiry into how the role of self-motivation is sustained by previous students who attended a Self Managed Learning environment. Brighton: University of Brighton (also available from the Centre for Self Managed Learning).

Moss, S. (2017) Half of Britain's prisoners are functionally illiterate. Can fellow inmates change that? *The Guardian*, June 15. https://www.theguardian.com/inequality/2017/jun/15/reading-for-freedom-life-changing-scheme-dreamt-up-by-prison-pen-pals-shannon-trust-action-for-equity-award. Accessed 18/08/2019.

Powell, C. L. (1995) *A Soldier's Way*. London: Random House.

Robbins, D. (1988) *The Rise of Independent Study*. Milton Keynes: Open University Press.

Swann, J. (2012) *Learning, Teaching and Education Research*. London: Continuum.

Taleb, N. N. (2018) *Skin in the Game*. London: Allen Lane.

Ward, C. (1988) *The Child in the Country*. London: Bedford Square Press.

6

SOME EVIDENCE AND A RESPONSE TO THIS EVIDENCE – WITH A FOCUS ON SCHOOLING

Introduction

In this chapter I will follow up on the critique from the last chapter about the nature of research, especially the limitations of the kind of research being conducted on schooling, teaching, classrooms and curriculum. As much as possible, I will try to present evidence which is incontrovertible. In many cases there is what could be described as objective evidence, such as that on the implications of birthdates. In other areas, evidence may be of a different nature, but I would regard it as important. However, I'm not trying to be encyclopaedic. What I want mainly to do is to provide sufficient evidence to show that the work in developing a New Educational Paradigm is both desirable and highly justified. On the other hand, I want to show that the defence of the existing traditional schooling paradigm is not warranted.

The area that I want to cover in this chapter is that around the **social organisation of schooling**. I believe that there is sufficient evidence here for a New Educational Paradigm that moves away from the existing schooling model into other forms of learning. Clearly, some New Educational Paradigm providers continue to use the name 'school', but in many cases people are using other labels such as a 'learning centre' or 'home education'. My aim in this chapter is not to go into those particular structures, but rather to provide an evidence basis for later chapters and especially on the use of Self Managed Learning as one model of what can be achieved under this New Educational Paradigm.

The order of pieces in this chapter is largely a matter of convenience. Items could have been in a different order and certainly if the reader knows about some of these sections in this chapter, they may wish to move on to other sections.

In the next chapter I will focus on issues that affect learning and education, but that bring in research on wider issues than just the practice of schooling. To a large extent the two chapters need reading together to get a more complete picture of the many factors affecting education and learning.

Why the social organisation of schooling is failing

Summer born children

I am using the term children in this subsection (and others), because that's how it appears in the research but, as I have emphasised, I prefer to think of young people.

I initially became interested in the implications of the date of birth of boys aged 9–16 while working with the Football Association in England on the development of young players. We obtained important data from all the Premier League football clubs in England for 2005. At that time there were 2,025 boys in the academies of these professional clubs. Among the findings, when we looked at birthdates, were the following: 19% of players had a September birth while only 3% had an August birth. Aggregated by months, 58% of the boys were born in the four months from September to December, 28% were born in the next four months January to April and 14% in the four months of May to August. Please note that these 2,025 boys were the total of the 9–16-year-olds; it was not a sample. Every club has to send in the birthdate of the boys attached to their academies and we were in possession of that data. When we looked at other professional clubs, the figures were similar right down through the other leagues in England. This was caused by the fact that 1 September is the start of the academic year in England and that if you are selecting a boy at the age of eight, someone born on 1 September in that year group is almost a year older than someone born in August. Developmentally, this is a very large gap.

Incidentally, when we looked at amateur teams of young players, where they played in local recreation grounds, there was not this disparity. The difference came when there were selection decisions by scouts and managers from professional clubs.

Turning now to school specifically, the Department for Education's own research shows that at least 10,000 summer born (May to August) children gain worse results at GCSE than autumn born (September to December) children just because of their birthdate. Nothing else. The research shows that this gap appears as soon as children start at school and carries on right into higher education. It has been found that 18.8% of August born young people enter university at 18 compared with 21.3% for September born young people.[1]

The figures also show that summer born children are more likely to be labelled as special needs and more likely to have been identified as having a range of symptoms such as learning difficulties, and speech, language and communication needs. Indeed, by the age of 7 in primary school, August born children are nearly 90% more likely to be identified as SEN (Special Educational Needs) than September born children.

All this evidence points to the fact that current school arrangements and structures are inherently discriminatory. There is no way to make the classroom, the rigid subject-based curriculum and imposed timetables solve problems of inequality. The structures and processes of schooling are inherently faulty. They even encourage parents and teachers to make erroneous judgements. For instance, both parents and teachers of summer born children are more likely to underestimate the abilities of such children, according to the Government's research.

Response to this

In our College we encourage young people taking public exams to take them at the time that suits them. In school July and August born young people are taking the GCSE exams at aged 15 not 16 as is commonly claimed. In our College some students take these exams a year early if they want to, or a year later if that suits them. As we don't have classrooms there is no pressure to conform to the norm for what schools see as a year group.

School size

There has been a significant amount of research and exploration on the issue of the size of schools. Part of the problem with much of the research is what is defined as small or large. I am convinced by anthropological evidence and the work of people like Robin Dunbar (Dunbar, 2011) that 150 is the magic number. But it's a magic number for the size of a learning community that can operate in a humane way. Given that adults would be involved, it probably means that the maximum for learners is below 120. Much of the research clearly does not look at schools of that small size. For example, many studies regard 500–600 as a small size school. I do not.

The key issue here is more about having a school which I have heard described as one where: every adult knows every child; every child knows every adult and, most importantly, every child knows every other child. In such settings, it does seem from the research[2] that there are significant benefits which include learners feeling more engaged with the school; teachers and students being happier and feeling positive about the climate of the school; there is less violent behaviour and bullying; and in a properly designed setting costs can actually be lower, rather than the claimed economies of scale in large schools. Attendance also seems better in smaller settings and there is a potential better attainment and progression of learning, though we should not fall into the trap of just judging schools on exam passes.

The average secondary school in the UK is far larger than the 150 maximum. In such schools, which are typically more than 1000, the average teacher sees about 250 students each week (Wetz, 2009). It is not possible to know 250 people well. This is the conclusion of Dunbar's research and that of anthropologists studying hunter gatherer bands and similar small communities.

The other feature of the research is that we have to look at the issue of having small learning communities where, as Wetz points out, relationships are at the heart of the school. This means that small on its own is not something to be valued. Small schools can be created with a hierarchy and an authoritarian style of teaching. In such settings the advantages that have been identified for small schools do not seem to manifest themselves.

Response to this

Our College currently has 40 students and in the near future the maximum will be around 48. Even longer term, we would not think at all of getting to the size of 100 students. Rather, we are more interested in helping other people set up smaller settings so that we can maintain an even smaller size than a hundred students per organisation.

In our work in schools we insist on working with learning groups of six students as a maximum. Alongside this, we use specific processes and structures so that we quickly get to know the participants in the group. It is common for us to find out in a day things that the school has not discovered in four or more years. I remember being given a group of 13/14 year-olds in a local school. The year head selected them as poor performers. Regarding one girl, Marie, she said that they knew nothing about her. For instance, Marie never put her hand up in class and she seemed very closed and withdrawn. In the group she talked about being shy and introverted. Another girl in the group, Chevelle, said that Marie would know the answer to a question posed by the teacher, and she would whisper it to her. Chevelle was then able to put her hand up and answer the question. As is common, school works better for extraverts than introverts and no one had found out that Marie was actually quite knowledgeable.

As an aside, as explained in Chapter 4, at one stage we explored with our local authority the idea of setting up a free school under the Government's rules. We pointed out that it would be easy to use existing resources such as offices and shops to run small learning communities that would have the advantages that have been shown for small schools. The problem is that the current Government is in general fostering an environment where schools are getting larger every year on average and therefore making problems of bullying, violence, poor attendance, school refusers, etc much worse.

Coupled with this stance is a conservatism that ruled out our approach, so we did not pursue it. However, when people challenge me as to how one could meet the needs of many thousands of children via small settings my response is that it is simple and not as bad for the environment as building new schools, which are poor for our carbon footprint. As an example, locally there are retail premises and offices that are vacant that are fine for places like our College (we occupy an office building). In rural areas there have been examples of the use of converted barns, yurts and unused farm buildings.

If one has a large school building it can be divided up into smaller, self-governing units. This has happened in a number of countries including the USA. In the UK some schools have been designed to have small units as mini-schools and then resources such as playing fields are shared facilities. The problem with some of these is that the mini-schools have been larger than 150 and the advantages of small size are lost.

Violence

This heading is really a subset of the above because I hope to say something about the social organisation of schools and their size as part of my case here. Firstly, though, I can summarise some of the more psychological evidence that comes out of school shootings in the USA, though there been school shootings in other countries. Clearly the USA has had more problems with this partly because of the easy access to guns. However, school shooters there obviously had some of the following problems: fragile identities; a lack of social skills; depression; anxiety; loneliness or isolation; suicidal tendencies and a lack of empathy towards others. These factors have been identified in research by Langman (2009), Newman et al. (2004) and Cullen (2009). Note that not all school shooters had all of these characteristics.

There are interesting interpretations as to why these shootings occurred and the Alternative Education Research Organisation in its newsletter after one of the school shootings explained that the main factors seemed to be that it's shootings in schools. The newsletter said, 'We don't have teenagers doing mass library shootings, museum shootings or park shootings. What is the difference? Libraries, museums and parks are not compulsory or authoritarian, you go there when you want. You do what you want and leave when you want. They don't judge you, test you, grade you, suspend you or kick you out. Schools need to change. Democratic and learner centred schools don't have mass shootings. Statistics verify that'.[3]

Research by Langman (2009), Newman et al. (2004) and Cullen (2009) confirm the opinions expressed above. Newman et al. point out that the 'attacks have been on institutions' (p. 264). Langman is convinced that the 'murders they [the shooters] committed were not inevitable outcomes of their personalities, but actions they committed in a state of crisis. Had they been safely maintained through their crises, there is no reason to assume they would have become murderers later in life' (p. 154). He goes on to suggest that a strategy is that students who are struggling socially need to have connections to adults to help them through that. But he also points out that students need to feel safe in school and that while 'bullying itself does not cause student school shootings anything that contributes to students' misery, fear and rage can play a part in driving them to violence' (p. 193).

Newman et al. point out that the social structure of the schools leads to what they call 'information loss', and that there were warning signs such that tragedies could have been prevented if the information that was available had been shared. The problems that they identify are problems about the system itself and structural arrangements of secrecy, and that information that doesn't fit the operating paradigm is dismissed. As they point out 'problems can go unnoticed in school precisely because they do not disrupt its basic function. Individual student problems often do not interrupt daily routines and may therefore fester unnoticed until a major eruption, such as shooting, thrusts it into view' (p. 102).

Further 'that the culture and social structure of public schools leads to information loss, which in turn obscures the pain and anger inside some students – emotions that, in rare cases, boil over into rampage shootings. The question is not how individuals could have missed the warning signs, but rather how the organisation of public schools prevents them from recognising and processing the information correctly' (p. 79). This evidence 'of systemic distortion: information that does not relate to an organisation's ambitions or survival gets filtered out. Important information "disappears", not because of intentional decisions to ignore it, but because "people deliberately do not seek out unfavourable information"' (p. 88).

Response to this

What I have described above is, of course, on the dramatic end of the spectrum of school problems. However, this notion that students take out their anger on schools as an institution is relevant. In the UK we don't have easy access to guns, but there is easy access to incendiary devices such that we find that school students do attempt to burn down their school and, in some cases, succeed. For us as a small college we work hard at making certain that we do know what's going on amongst all our students, and this can sometimes mean being appraised of issues that might occur away from the College. But if one is taking a stance of working with the whole person, then these other outside influences, such as through social media, may need to be accommodated.

The only time that I faced anything approaching the issue which was of the magnitude described above occurred in the School for Independent Study, North East London Polytechnic. I had a student who joined the group that I was working with and he obviously had a lot of issues about his own life and how he saw himself. At one stage he asked me to meet him privately away from the group. I asked him if he was prepared to talk in the group with his peers and, in the end, he agreed. He explained that he had problems with writing and, basically, he was functionally illiterate. We were able to provide help with this. However, there was evidence of more unhealthy interests when he decided to make a study of warfare and weapons and where it appeared that he might be wanting to take an inappropriate view of the use of weaponry. He had a number of the characteristics that have been described above from the psychological evidence about school shooters in the USA. Therefore, it became very important to make certain that the peer group worked with him and helped to deal with his anxieties and what they saw as his hang-ups.

This was an example of what researchers have said is crucial with young people who have a range of psychological issues, and that is to provide a supportive safe place in which they can talk and where any concerns can be monitored, not through some bureaucratic process, but rather through direct human interaction.

The negative response of schools to difference

It is well known that certain groups do not do as well in school as they should do due to a school environment which has not accommodated their difference. Some of these examples are very well known so I will make small reference to them and refer the reader to notes and references. Other examples are perhaps less well known and may benefit from a little more explanation.

The groups that are well known to do less well in school in the UK and are less likely therefore to go into higher education include the following: children in care (looked after children, as they may be labelled); autistic children; those who are adopted; those on free school meals (which is evidence of poverty); young people with ADHD; working class children, especially from white and Afro-Caribbean backgrounds; and young people with a severe physical disability.[4]

The group that is often not recognised as having different issues in school includes those who are very introverted (see above my comments on Marie). Cain (2012) presents important research evidence about the discrimination against introverts, who she suggests make up more than one third of the population. As she argues, 'many schools are designed for extroverts' (p. 253). She suggests that 'we tend to forget that there's nothing sacrosanct about learning in large group classrooms, and that we organise students this way, not because it's the best way to learn, but because it's cost efficient and what else would we do with our children while the grown-ups are at work?' (p. 253). I would argue that the attempt is low-cost, but actually inefficient for learners grouped in large classrooms. She does point out that, too often, what children have to do is to be prepared to learn how to survive in a school day, just because they are more introverted. You could argue that that is similar to all the other negative differences, as perceived by the system, that I've indicated above.

Cain (2012) has a list of what she would regard as a desirable environment for introverted children. This list includes the following criteria for such a school:

- prizes independent interests and emphasizes autonomy
- conducts group activities in moderation and in small carefully managed groups
- values kindness, caring, empathy, good citizenship [...]
- strongly enforces an anti-bullying program
- emphasises a tolerant, down-to-earth culture (p. 257).

Response to this

In SML College we genuinely do support difference. The student who needs to work a lot on their own is valued as much as those who enjoy group activity. Everyone is allowed to learn in the ways that suit them and, as we have found at least 57 ways that young people can learn effectively, there is plenty of choice. However, it's important to point out that given the fact that students have this choice, the quieter, more introverted, students are often happy to join in on collective activity because they know that they are allowed to be quieter and more introspective.

There is no average learner – at all

It may be useful to focus on the fact that there is no average child. Therefore, by school classrooms working on the assumption that they can pitch teaching to the level of the average they are seriously at fault. The key author here is Rose (2015).

I need to start at the beginning of Rose's book. The opening piece of research he refers to is that conducted in the US Air Force. There were a lot of problems of pilot error in the 1950s. The cockpits were designed to suit what was seen as the average pilot. However, pilot errors and crashes were an issue. Research was conducted on 4,063 pilots. When they took 10 dimensions of pilots such as length of arm, length of leg, etc they found that there was no average pilot. No pilot came anywhere near the average of the 10 dimensions used to design cockpits. What they had to do was then to respond to the fact that individuals were different and that they could reduce pilot error by designing cockpits around the pilot, not around a mythical average. There is no average – it is a mythical invention.

The second piece of research that Rose refers to is that conducted by a US newspaper, *The Cleveland Plain Dealer*. They had worked with the local health museum, which had created a statue based on average data from 15,000 young adult women. The statue was to represent the truth about the average woman based on this research. The newspaper started a competition to see who might meet this average. They assumed that there would be quite a number of people and instead what they found amongst the 3,864 contestants was there was not one that even came close to all the dimensions of the average adult woman.

Rose then points out that too many organisations work on the basis of a myth of an average. His most important, evidenced statement is perhaps on page 8 when he says, 'any system designed around the average person is doomed to fail'.

He also emphasises that the fact that there is no average at all 'is a scientific fact' and that this does not apply just to body size, but there is 'no such thing as average talent, average intelligence, average character, nor are their average students or average employees or average brains for that matter' (p. 11). He turned his attention then to various sectors, including education. He shows that any educational model based on the assumption of an average child is in error. He comments that schools still follow the same rigid patterns as they did a century ago 'with fixed class durations, fixed school days and fixed semesters, proceeding through the same unyielding sequence of "core courses", all of which ensure that every (normal) student graduates from high school at the same age with, presumably the same knowledge' (p. 125). He conclusively demonstrates that this is a complete nonsense.

He goes on to develop his notion of 'pathways' and, as he comments, 'there is no single normal pathway for any type of human development – biological, mental, moral, or professional' (p. 129). He particularly points out that speed of learning varies enormously, but has no bearing on the ability of the individual learner. Due to the fact that speed and learning ability are not related, he states that 'we have created an educational system that is profoundly unfair, one that favours students who happen to be fast while penalising students who are just as smart yet learn at a slower pace' (p. 133). He goes on to show how this fast/slow dilemma is genuinely discriminatory in a very dangerous way. He points out, based on his pathway model, that there is 'no universally fixed set of sequences for human development – no set stages everyone must pass through to grow, learn and achieve goals (p. 135). Finally, on page 188 he states, 'We continue to enforce a curriculum that defines not only what students learn, but also how, when, at what pace and in what order they learn it. In other words, whatever else we may say, traditional public education systems violate the principles of individuality.'

Response to this

Rose's justification for the fact that everyone has their own individual pathway and that there is no average ideal pathway is an important support for the Self Managed Learning model. There is no justification, in fact, for continuing with an educational model that is in direct contradiction to scientific evidence. In our College each student can learn in any way they choose and they can learn at their own pace. The absence of classrooms and an imposed timetable is the only way to be fair to the differences in the ways young people learn best.

The positive value of difference

I want to make the case here that we need difference among people, that diversity in any society, community or working organisation is to be valued. The best text on this is Page, 2007, entitled *The Difference: How the Power of Diversity Creates Better Groups, Firms, Schools, and Societies*. He presents rigorous research evidence to support this proposal.

The implications for education, which are examined later, show that we need to not just respect difference amongst learners, but actually support that difference. We should value it and, if necessary, encourage it, rather than assume that we want a uniform output from a school.

Page's two most important findings are, firstly, that diversity trumps homogeneity – that is that people with different perspectives and experiences will outperform people who have more homogenous perspectives and experiences. Secondly, he shows that diversity trumps ability – that random collections of intelligent problem solvers can outperform collections of the best individual problem solvers.

His book reminded me of an old exercise that we used to use on courses with managers. It's called the NASA Space Shot Exercise and the process is to give individuals a sheet devised by NASA. On the sheets is a list of items that could possibly survive in a crash on the moon. Individuals are asked to rate these items in the order of importance and to try to get as close to NASA's own ranking of these items as possible. They are then put into teams of about six or seven and asked to work in these teams to come up with an agreed collective ranking. I have done the exercise dozens of times, as have many other people, and every time the group scores are better than the best individual score. By using the diversity of approaches and ideas of individuals the group is always a better performer than the best individual. This kind of result is confirmed in Mercier and Sperber (2011), who cite eight significant research studies that confirm this.

This is one demonstration of what Page shows in his book about problem solving and also about prediction. Further, he goes into more detailed research on specifics. Here is one quote:

> Careful empirical studies show this benefit to cognitive diversity: teams of people with diverse training and experience typically performed better than more homogenous teams. Studies that isolate diversity and skills, such as between the types of engineers, show evidence that diversity improves performance. Studies of creativity and innovation concluded that cognitive variation is a key explanatory variable. Studies also show that management teams with greater training and experiential diversity typically introduce more innovations. Based on this evidence organisational scholars generally agree that cognitive diversity improves rates of innovation (p. 323).

Response to this

The implications of this for the education of young people are that it is crucial to honour difference, to respect it and to encourage it. We actually need diversity in all sorts of areas in societies. Page and many others show that intelligence alone is not sufficient, or indeed often an important factor, in effective problem-solving, innovation and predictive capability.

Unfortunately, schools often put negative labels on people. For instance, we have students coming saying that they are no good at art. An art teacher has not liked their work and indicated that they were not going to do well at art. Our artist staff member often just put out materials so that passing students could inquire about them. She would then encourage them to play with materials, to mess about with clay or just daub paint on paper. Gradually they would get more into particular media and over time show real ability. Others didn't warm to materials but loved to take photographs. With encouragement they really developed their abilities such that one student won a photography competition against much older school students.

In our learning community the diversity that exists is of great value. For instance, a couple of our autistic girls have developed a very good PowerPoint presentation on autism, which they use occasionally in community meetings. This helps new students in particular understand issues of autism and how those students on the autistic spectrum can be helped within the community, whilst at the same time being valued as individuals who bring something to the community.

What is appalling is that the organisational world is starting to get interested in neurodiversity and to value employees who may be on the autistic spectrum or may have dyslexia or dyspraxia, whilst most schools clearly often take the opposite stance. Schools in England that are chasing exam results in academic subjects, as encouraged by the Government, end up valuing only those who can pass exams in academic subjects.

As Page says, 'People often speak of the importance of tolerating difference. We must move beyond tolerance and toward taking the world to a better place' (p. 375). He shows that by valuing diversity and welcoming it we can genuinely make the world a better place, but only if we move away from the educational model that says, at best, differences might be tolerated and at worst are suppressed.

Bullying

Bullying is a major problem especially in secondary schools, which of course are generally larger than primary schools. The exact figures for bullying vary greatly, but common percentages quoted are that 40 to 50% of young people post-age 11 have been bullied sometime in school.[5] Whilst there are all sorts of initiatives, such as anti-bullying weeks and bully buddies to support bullied children, the problem of bullying in schools has not been solved and the situation is not getting any better, if one looks at national figures. The big problem seems to be that because it's regarded as inevitable and endemic within secondary/high schools, it is usually not really taken seriously. I know that last comment will come as a surprise, because schools say they take it seriously, but they don't actually stop it. If it was really taken seriously, bullying would be a rare event.

One problem that I've seen locally is a growing trend to 'blame the victim'. At a meeting where an educational psychologist was talking about their role with bullied children, they seemed to feel that the main thing they should do was to develop resilience in bullied children. This does nothing to address the systemic issues within a school and can seem to those who are bullied that they are somehow lesser persons, because they need to have some training in resilience. As an aside, it seems to be also problematic that some psychologists have no interest in wider social problems and only wish to address the individual, as has been their training.

The second problem is that it's assumed that children will be bullied and it's just part of the growing up process and once they leave school it will all be okay. Nothing could be further from the truth. A number of really rigorous research studies have shown that effects of bullying last into adulthood.

Lewis et al., 2019, cite research funded by the Medical Research Council UK. It is estimated that nearly one hundred thousand children in the country are suffering from post-traumatic stress disorder because of severe bullying. The study also revealed that half of young people with post-traumatic stress disorder had self-harmed and one in five had attempted suicide since the age of 12. A quarter were not in education, employment or training (NEET) and half had experienced high levels of social isolation and loneliness.

Evans-Lacko et al., 2016, performed an analysis using the National Child Development Study and the 1958 British Birth Cohort study. They showed that people who were bullied were more likely to use mental health services in childhood and adolescence, and also in midlife. Wolke, 2019, explained, 'We want to eradicate the myth that bullying at a young age could be viewed as a harmless rite of passage that everyone goes through – it casts a long shadow over a person's life and can have serious consequences for mental health.' His study showed that bullies and their victims have an increased risk of developing psychotic experiences in adult life.

Campbell and Morrison, 2007, showed that bullying was significantly associated with a predisposition to psychotic experiences. Varese et al., 2012, showed that children exposed to bullying and related abuse were 2.72 times more likely to have psychosis in adult life than the rest of the population. Moore et al., 2017, showed that victims of bullying are associated with a wide range of mental health problems such as depression, anxiety, suicide attempts and illicit drug use. Copeland et al., 2014, found high levels of markers of inflammation in young adults who had been bullied and Takizawa et al., 2015, showed the same in midlife. (Inflammation markers are correlated with both mental and physical health problems.) Brugger, 2019, showed that exposure to bullying is associated with symptoms of mental illness and that this continued beyond childhood.

Lieberman, 2013, makes an impeccable case against the harm done by bullying, arguing that it is 'probably the most pervasive form of social rejection that we have' (p. 69). For instance, he cites a Finnish study of over 5000 eight-year-olds. Those bullied by that age were more than six times as likely to have taken their own lives by the age of twenty-five.

One saying I used to hear when I was young was, 'sticks and stones may break my bones, but names will never hurt me'. This was to say that the name-calling and verbal bullying was not as serious as physical bullying. We now know, from the neuroscientific research, that this saying is untrue – see Lieberman, 2013. Emotional pain and physical pain occur in the same part of the brain and it is clear that verbal bullying is extremely serious and does lead to mental health problems. In monitoring suicides by children who have been verbally bullied it appears that verbal bullying is more likely to produce a suicide or attempted suicide by the young person than physical bullying. So again, the lack of serious attention to this situation is appalling. It is clearly grossly unprofessional to allow this to happen in schools.

Further Lieberman, 2013, cites research that social pain – such as from verbal bullying – significantly reduces intellectual performance. As he comments, 'This must be a profound distraction and a major strain on classroom learning' (p. 279).

Response to this

The whole issue of bullying is significantly more serious than schools seem to treat it. I've deliberately quoted a number of research studies, all of which show that bullying for under 18s so often causes problems in later life and, in studies cited, to the age of 50. The law in England requires that parents make certain that their children have, as the law says, 'a suitable education in terms of their age, aptitude, ability, and any special needs'. It is clear that for quite a number of our College students their education in school was totally unsuitable. Parents were doing their duty by the law, and by the young person, to take them out of school, where they were not getting a suitable education.

A good example was a boy who was badly bullied and didn't attend school for a year, and the school did nothing about it. A diligent educational psychologist discovered this and knew about us and therefore forced the school to pay for the boy to come to us. In another case, a girl came to us having been seriously physically bullied in school by other girls. The problem was that her picture and her information was passed around to girls in other schools, such that she would get attacked in the street or on the bus. On more than one occasion the police had to intervene in the assaults on her to bring her in a police car to the College. The police asked the local authority to provide transport such as a taxi, which they would normally do where a child is in danger travelling into school. The local council refused because we are not an official school. Even though the council has a duty of care to children, they were not prepared to meet their obligations.

These are systemic problems in schools, and therefore this is not intended to blame any individual teacher; although we have had complaints of bullying by a minority of teachers, that is, verbal bullying. In the past, it used to be physical bullying since teachers in England were allowed to beat children. Mercifully, that at least has gone away, but the verbal bullying can remain. However, it is clear this is a minority of teachers and the issue is one about the nature of school organisation, not generally about any individual.

One of the factors is the size of schools and since schools are getting larger each year in England there is clearly not going to be a reduction in bullying, despite all the short-term fixes that schools attempt.

In our College we've had one or two examples where things got out of hand online. We have had to step in. I can never remember a case of ongoing physical bullying occurring, but we have to intervene if what one student might call banter, another student might feel is hurtful. However, such situations are rare and students themselves say that the College is generally a bully-free environment.

In summary, we can see that globally millions of young people have their lives blighted just because they attended school. We should not allow this to continue.

The subjective curriculum

I have deliberately labelled this subsection about the **subjective** curriculum because that is a particular emphasis I want to make here. Any choice of curriculum for young people is a subjective choice. There is no objectively right curriculum. One of the interesting aspects of Britain is that there is devolved government in Wales and Scotland. The curricula for schools in Wales, Scotland

and England are all different. Yet there is no evidence presented by Governments that there are significant differences amongst children in the different parts of Britain, such that these large differences in curricula are justified. There are Welsh and Scottish young people in England who do the curriculum as imposed from Government for England. There are English students in Wales and Scotland who do the curriculum for those countries. One example worth mentioning is that of the English baccalaureate (EBacc). This supposed qualification drives the curriculum in schools in England. The requirement to get an EBacc is that a young person must take GCSEs and pass them only in academic subjects. The particular subjects that have to be passed are English, maths, a science, a foreign language and history or geography. Any learning outside these five academic subjects does not count in terms of the judgement against a school for its performance in the EBacc.

The Government in England introduced measures in 2011 for this qualification. The National Foundation for Educational Research has plotted changes since that time (see Hepworth, 2019). They say that between 2009 and 2019 the number of GCSE entries increased by 1.9% overall. Entries for the Ebacc subjects have increased by 12.6% over the time period while entries into non-Ebacc subjects have fallen by nearly 30%. Another way of looking at the figures is that 81.4% of all GCSE entries in 2019 were the Ebacc subjects compared to 73.6% back in 2009. They comment that this is an enormous shift. They show the impact for technology subjects that have decreased greatly in the 10 years from 2009, as have music and drama entries. The choice of having this English baccalaureate is a subjective choice from a Government that imposes this on schools, but where the case for this choice is not adequately justified.

A good example would be the reduction in subjects in what the Government Department for Digital, Culture, Media and Sport called creative industries.[6] That Government department has shown with its figures for 2017 that the creative industries sector of the UK economy has increased by 53.1% since 2010 and its contribution to the UK economy is estimated at £101.5 billion per annum. If we make a comparison between the creative industries and the rest of the UK economy, then that 53.1% represents almost twice as much as the growth in the UK economy overall, which was 28.7% over that time. For the country, creative industries and their contribution to the economy and to jobs is crucial. Yet the Department for Education has been guilty of reducing the contribution in schools to creative activity. It's clear that the two Government departments, if they talk to each other at all, must be at loggerheads because I would have thought that the Department for Digital, Culture, Media and Sport would be wanting more young people to be taking creative subjects in school and yet the Department for Education is making certain that there is a drastic reduction in provision in schools.

This is where I'm making a case that the subjective choice driven by politicians is dangerous and is having a negative impact on both the lives of young people and the economic future of the country.

Response to this

In our College we don't have an imposed curriculum; we work with students on their interests. The fact they have a very diverse range of interests and of activities is much healthier for both the British economy and for their own future career prospects than the narrow provision in schools. When we had the inspection from Ofsted, the lead inspector admitted, after he had interviewed all our students, that we have a broader curriculum than any school because our students can study anything they want. Our students do engage greatly in the creative sector and this is going to be of value to them in their careers. Indeed, research by Freedman, 2019, has shown that a high proportion of ex-students have taken up, or are planning to take up, careers in the creative sector.

What is taught does not equal what is learned

This seems to me to be a fairly obvious statement. If everything taught in the classroom was perfectly learned then, of course, every student would pass every test they took. This doesn't happen because what we know is that much teaching does not lead to learning. In earlier chapters I have shown how from research there is very little that is taught in school that transfers into useful skills or knowledge for adults.

In our research we have found at least 57 ways that young people can learn and in the 19 years that we been running our College we have never been asked to create a classroom, even though that is one of the 57 options. Our students have total free choice about learning modes and the one mode that they know very well is the classroom; and it's the one mode they have no interest in using. The closest we get to anything organised for collective groups are workshops where students choose to work together on some issue that they're interested in and they may or may not be supported by an adult. (Workshops are often led by students, if there is a leader.)

We tend to suggest that we have a process curriculum. That means we have a particular process way of working, which is about supporting the student in developing their own curriculum and, in doing that, developing their own modes of learning that suit the learning goals that they themselves choose. We have a passion for learning. However, we have no interest in classroom teaching.

This is an example of using the power of the process curriculum – the actual way of learning – as opposed to the content curriculum of traditional education. In the traditional classroom it gave rise to the notion of the 'hidden curriculum'. Writers identified that the hidden curriculum either encourages dependency on the teacher or counter-dependent rebellion. The process of a teacher-controlled learning environment has these effects on many learners, and this undermines the ability of young people to grow up as fully autonomous human beings.

The notion of a hidden curriculum was originally articulated by Jackson (1968) and then explicitly developed by writers such as Snyder (1970) who saw the socialisation of the classroom as reducing autonomous action and having longer term negative effects. Vallance (1983) makes the case for considering the strong role of the hidden curriculum in her statement that it includes 'the inculcation of values, political socialization, training in obedience and docility, the perpetuation of traditional class structure-functions that may be characterized generally as social control' (p. 10).

Response to this

These writers, and many others, on the dangers of the hidden curriculum only saw the process of learning in educational institutions as a negative factor. However, I have suggested that we can take a positive position on how, for instance, adults work with learners and how the design of programmes can actually assist learner autonomy. If we want to develop autonomous learners, then the process needs to match the aim – means and ends need to be harmonised.

In the College the idea is to use the process curriculum to good effect. The process is made overt and does not therefore constitute a hidden curriculum. We are designing and implementing a process to liberate learners from the constraints of classroom learning. A guiding principle is the development of effective autonomy for students so that they can go out into the world and operate as autonomous human beings.

Studying English is not the same as developing literacy

The kind of curriculum that is common in England for learning English has a great emphasis on writing essays, analysing Shakespearian plays and learning grammatical rules. I have already commented on the foolishness of the curriculum for primary school children and the need to learn grammatical forms. After the age of 11 in secondary education it gets even worse in terms of its lack of relevance to literacy. Literacy is about being able to read and write, so that you can function effectively in society. The evidence from research in England shows a rather depressing situation for school children. One in five children leave primary school unable to read or write properly. Sherwood, 2019, quotes research that says,

> It is estimated that 9 million adults in the UK are functionally illiterate and one in four British five-year-olds struggles with basic vocabulary. Three quarters of white working-class boys failed to achieve the government's benchmark at age 16. Research also shows that functionally illiterate adults are more likely to be socially isolated and lack self-esteem.

In comparison to this evidence from schooling, the research evidence from home educated children is much more positive. The best research on this is Pattinson, 2016. She showed from her in depth research on home educating families that children are not taught literacy, but develop it through practices in the home and the opportunities they are given to manage their own learning. The children in her study might have learned at different ages, but they all became literate without the use of classrooms or formal teaching. In some cases, the parents themselves did not know how the child came to be able to read and write. Because the parents responded to the needs of children, then in the absence of a uniform approach children could learn in ways that suited their own predilections.

Response to this

In our College we have had students who have come unable to function in terms of their reading and writing. However, our approach is always based on each individual and starting where the individual is. It is important that we find out about them and their levels of literacy when they join us so that we know what we need to do to help them; then we can provide individual support as needed. It is a much more cost-effective approach and it works since the norm is that students leave us fully literate, although some will not get good grades in their English exams.

Where students need to pass an English exam because of future career choices, then of course we help them with it, even though we know that in later life they will never have to analyse a Shakespeare play or a poem or have to write a creative essay. We have to accept that they have to play the game in order to get the qualification that may be needed. Of course, those rare individuals who take up a career in writing will value the ability to write creatively. But we know that that is a small minority of the population.

Travel supports learning

In my earlier discussion of our research on adults I mentioned that travel tends to come out as a very positive experience from the point of view of learning. It may not be always positive from the point of view of enjoyment, because sometimes travelling goes wrong. People learn from these things. Also, earlier I supported Taleb's notion of having 'skin in the game'. There is nothing like going to another culture to understand more about that culture than you get from dry textbooks. The textbooks have their place but, for instance, on my first visit to India, I knew about the history and cultural differences and the religious differences, and so on in India. What I hadn't experienced before was the sheer scale of the country and the population and the impact of not just the sights, but the smells and the feel of the place. That can't be obtained from a textbook.

Travel is of enormous value even if it is in one's own country and visiting areas that one doesn't know about. All of this can provide tremendous learning, often unconsciously. Therefore, it is interesting that the Government in England is ferociously against parents taking their children out travelling during term time. A BBC report of March 21, 2019[7] commented that the number of fines issued to parents in England for taking children on term–time holidays almost doubled in the year. Penalty notices rose by 93% to almost 223,000 in 2017–18.

Government sources have tended to suggest that every day that the child misses school they are missing out on learning and that this is a terrible thing for parents to do to their children. What they do not comment on is that state schools have much longer term times than expensive independent schools. In our locality the terms for state schools are around 39 weeks per year and for some of the independent schools they are 34 weeks. In our College we chose 36 weeks so that we would be in between the two, given that we get most of our students from state schools, but some occasionally from independent schools. Now if parents are paying out a lot of money to send their child to an independent school and then not getting as much teaching as in a state school there can be a question as to why parents are doing this. The answer, of course, is that the amount of time spent in the school is not a measure of the quality or quantity of learning and that parents who take their children on holiday during term time are providing educational benefit.

Response to this

In our College we encourage parents to travel with students. The advantage we have is that we do not have an imposed schedule of teaching, so that when a student returns from holiday they just pick up from where they left off in any of their learning plans. In school, if someone is out for two weeks, then of course they do miss what has been going on in the classroom and that can be to their disadvantage. That is a comment on the error of the rigidity of the schooling model, rather than that parents and students should be punished for travelling.

The myth of neat linear progression

In our research on effective leaders we found that many had very erratic career paths. It is well known that many successful entrepreneurs left school with few or no qualifications. But even those who have climbed the corporate ladder may have started off erratically before developing their career successfully. My concern about schools is an expectation of neat linear progression. Performance is measured and tested regularly, and students are supposed to be on track for whatever predicted destination the school might come up with for that individual. The outcome seems to be unacceptably high levels of discrimination against individuals who are different, and who progress differently.

I will give just one example from many relating to our students. Coco (real name, as she has featured in our local newspaper) joined us from school when she was coming up to 13 years old. She got into trouble at school because they didn't like her doodling all the time and because she was diagnosed with ADHD and dyslexia. She wasn't particularly rated as a good student, to say the least. During her first year with us she mostly drew cartoons, sat on the sofa and chatted, and also made models of small creatures. There wasn't really any evidence of her doing anything else. Staff were a bit concerned about her progress and, as always, I urged patience – just 'trust the process' is one of my standard responses. By the age of 15 she had written a 250-page graphic novel; the publishers of the book said they were shocked at the talent of such a young person and the book rapidly sold out on Amazon.

Coco also took two GCSEs a year early, at age 15, and passed both of them. She commented that in order to pass her law exams she drew cartoons of barristers and solicitors, which helped her to understand their roles. As she put it, she just learns in a different kind of way and communicates in a different kind of way. She doesn't see it as a disadvantage.

What this simple example shows is that the notion of a linear progress in learning is a myth. That schools attempt to monitor progress as though it is something that will happen logically and incrementally is not borne out by the evidence. When we work in schools, we hear that people are seen to have not progressed as much as they were expected to and that this was somehow a problem – when it isn't necessarily.

Treadway, 2015, has done the serious slog of actually comparing real life situations within schools from extensive data. In the English system, there are a series of what are called Key Stages and the expectation is of a linear and predictable progress between each of the stages. These stages are Key Stage 1, which finishes at age 7, Key Stage 2 at age 11, Key Stage 3 at age 14 and Key Stage 4 at age 16. School pupils are judged for attainment at each of these stages, with the expectation that this will be a linear progression. Treadway has shown that this assumption is erroneous. As he puts it, children's learning is too idiosyncratic to be able to make these kinds of predictions. It also shows that children who have a low attainment at Key Stage 1 are particularly likely to show a development process which is so unpredictable that it's not worth attempting the task. The trouble is that this means that such young people are 'slow tracked' and discriminated against within the school system.

Learning is not a simple process of just adding new facts, knowledge and skills into someone and then measuring that accumulation. I've made the case that learning isn't all one thing and that it shouldn't be a surprise to us that development is an uneven process when someone is apparently not making progress. Indeed, I would like to get the word 'progress' removed completely from any kind of discussion about learning amongst young people.

Here are some examples of particular individuals that might help to flesh out the generalities of that research.

Nobel Laureate and President of the Royal Society Sir Venki Ramakrishnan was being interviewed on BBC Radio 4. Here is someone who is about as respectable as you can get. Yet when he was questioned about his education he was happy to say that he had been a poor attender at school and at university. One trick at university, he explained, was to sit in lectures by the window so that after the register had been called, and the lecturer had turned his back to write on the board, he could climb out of the window and go off for a coffee.

It reminded me of Bill Bryson's tales of school and that he was the worst attender in his high school. He was regularly hauled up for his poor attendance.

At one meeting with the careers counsellor she had trawled through career options, given his poor school records, and in the end said, 'It doesn't appear that you are qualified to do much of anything.' He replied, 'I guess I'll have to be a high school careers counsellor then!' For this response he was marched to the principal's office (and not for the first time). It's a shame that the school did not recognise his obvious comedic talents instead of punishing him.

He developed his writing talents by spending time on things that interested him and also learning a great deal from the world around him. He became an excellent self-managing learner.

Another example is of a boy in Bolton, Lancashire, with no apparent interest in his schoolwork. He tended to spend time with his mates or watched comedy VHS tapes that he had recorded. He gained one GCSE, then after school did a series of seemingly dead-end jobs, such as in the bingo hall and at the local cinema.

As he enjoyed cracking jokes and fooling around, he started to do some stand-up comedy gigs in local pubs. Eventually he developed a comedy stand-up act. He was officially entered in the *Guinness World Records* book for the planet's biggest-selling stand-up tour ever. His 'Tour That Doesn't Tour Tour … Now on Tour' show sold 1,140,798 tickets in 113 arena dates between February 2010 and November 2011, earning him a place in the 2013 edition of the book. His name is Peter Kay and he has also won awards for his comedy acting.

His time when he was seemingly loafing around and doing nothing was actually a crucial time of learning for him. He learned from watching comedians the art and craft of doing stand-up. He also used his time in the bingo hall and at the cinema to listen to people so that he could learn the potentially funny things that went on in daily life.

Looked at from a short-term point of view he was a complete failure. Taking a longer view it's the opposite. He was, and continues to be, a brilliant self-managing learner. This is also true of the scientist Sir Venki Ramakrishnan and the best-selling author Bill Bryson.

Response to this

In our College we do not have an expectation of neat linear progression. We often find that students coming out of school need time to de-school, and this may take a number of months. They can apparently be doing nothing but, in reality, what they are doing is getting their brain around the different way of working and starting to think about what they want to do with their lives. Giving space to do that is really important, because one of the big errors in school is for young people to be on a treadmill, where they are just churning along each year on an ever-narrowing path that they never really thought through. As it is meeting school requirements it feels like the right thing. I meet many graduates who realise that the track they got on was the wrong one and that has not helped them with their career. Others, of course, make rapid career shifts when they realise that their academic background has hindered their career development.

When we get new staff out of schools, it is often important to help them to be patient when it looks like a student is not delivering a lot of outcomes. But what we know is that it is important that learners have opportunities to daydream, to play around, to muck about – so that they can explore for themselves, without the pressure to perform against imposed standards. What we are doing is helping students to develop an internal locus of control when in school they have been expected to work with an external locus of control. The latter is where they have been through a school system that has told them what they should do and that their job is to go along with this. We know that, in terms of life satisfaction and developing an effective career, having an internal locus of control is crucial. This is where you realise that your life is in your hands and that you can take charge of your development in the ways that are important to you, so that you develop the life that you want to lead.

In SML College we've seen students who seem not to have settled and not to be doing much eventually get the idea and go on to successful careers. Patience is absolutely crucial in our work because structures and processes are not magic. Trying to force it is often unhelpful and it requires high levels of trust in young people from adults working with them to avoid inappropriate pressurising.

I have often described my own career model as more related to a four-crop rotation model. We know that in a typical English farm it might have four fields in a block, three of which would be growing different crops and the fourth would be left fallow. The notion of a fallow field was not to do with nothing useful happening. Fallow periods are really useful and indeed in crop rotation are essential. They, for instance, help with pest and weed prevention.

Certainly, I have found that it's useful to have a period of high energy and doing a lot of work which can be followed by fallow time where I can step back to do a bit of thinking and enjoy things I might have had to give up during a high pressured work pattern, and that these fallow periods are really crucial. It allows for a re-examination of what I have been doing, reflection on learning and preparation for the next phase in what I want to do.

We should encourage people to go at their own pace and not to expect linear progression. Our biggest problem can be with parents who find that sometimes difficult to grasp. Young people experience themselves going through these irregularities and once they can be reassured that that's okay, and that we don't have any expectations to the contrary, then they can be happier and more contented. Unless, of course, parents put pressure on, which can be detrimental.

Conclusion

In this chapter I have focused on aspects of the research and evidence about the impact of schooling. The next chapter will focus more on wider issues that also play a part in the education of young people. I have shown that factors such as when you were born, the size of the school you go to, the level of bullying, and the response to difference within the school will be important factors in whether the young person learns what they need to learn to be able to go on to lead a good life once they've left school.

I accept that there are some young people who enjoy school. With my son and daughter, I urged them to use the school rather than be used by it. I supported them in doing things that were in their interests, even if it was against what the school wanted. However, they both knew of the limitations of the schools they went to and were able to work through them with support of parents and others in the family and their friends.

I recognise that a child born in the first half of the academic year in a privileged family, whose extrovert confidence supports their presence in the school, may well feel more positive about their experience than a child born into poverty, taken into care, and diagnosed with autism, who is very unlikely to find school a positive experience. There is a crucial issue of social justice here that most societies seem prepared to sacrifice. It is also frightening that parents may do the same, especially if they feel that they must follow the crowd and do what everybody else is doing, even though their child is refusing to go to school and desperately unhappy. I know that many parents in England do not know the law and are not aware of their rights and that, along with the social pressure to do whatever everyone else is doing, can allow a young person to have a bad experience in the school system.

I hope that adding the material in this chapter to the next one will provide a convincing basis to then read the further information in the book about solutions to these problems. Even the confident, privileged extraverts who pass all their exams with flying colours can find that their lack of ability to manage their own learning can catch up with them. An example is in Oliver James (2007), who discusses research on female undergraduates in an Oxford college, one third of whom had had an eating disorder and 10% of whom had an eating disorder at the time of the research. Some of this evidence is discussed in the next chapter as we look at mental health issues that are neglected in the current schooling system.

Notes

1 The Department for Education evidence is in 'Month of Birth and Education', Research Report DFE-RR017 of 2010. However, this research has been replicated elsewhere and by independent academics. For example, in Bell and Daniels (2010). This paper shows that the effects are international. The issue is the start day of the academic year, which varies across countries.

   McDonald, 2018, shows that August born children were 30% more likely to be diagnosed with ADHD than older peers – from a study in the USA.

2 S. Grauer and C. Ryan (2016) 'Small schools: The myths and reality, and potential of small schools'. https://medium.com/communityworksjournal/small-schools-the-myths-reality-and-potential-of-small-schools-76a566c42f6e. Human Scale Education is a good UK site for information on small schools and their value: https://www.hse.org.uk

3 The Alternative Education Resource Organization produces an excellent newsletter on alternatives to school. The quote is from the edition of February 2018. The site is www.educationrevolution.org

4 Here is some evidence in relation to the problems that school creates for certain young people:

- Adoption UK, www.adoptionuk.org (accessed 01/07/2018), quotes their research entitled 'Bridging the Gap': 79% of adopted young people agreed with the statement 'I feel confused and worried at school'; two-thirds of secondary-aged adopted young people said they had been teased or bullied in school because they are adopted; 60% of adoptive parents do not feel that their child has an equal chance at school.
- *People Management* journal of May 2017, p. 48. Only 16% of autistic adults are in full-time employment – 'a figure that has remained static for the past eight years'.
- Royal Society for the Encouragement of Arts, Manufactures and Commerce (RSA), 'Pinball Kids: Working together to reduce school exclusions', www.thersa.org (accessed 02/05/18). The risk factors that predict the likelihood of exclusion are 2x as likely to be in care; 3x as likely to be 'children in need'; 4x as likely to have grown up in poverty; 7x as likely to have special educational needs and disabilities and 50% have a mental health problem. Four in five excluded children are likely to be Not in Education, Employment or Training (NEET).
- Wetz (2009, p. 106) quotes a study in one British city that 15% of young people aged 16–24 NEET (Not in Education, Employment or Training) died within 10 years due to risky behaviour.
- *RSA* journal (2018), Issue 3, p. 7: 'Only 6% of children in care went into higher education in 2016.'
- www.ambitiousaboutautism.org.uk/when-will-we-learn report 2018: 'As many as 26,000 autistic young people were unlawfully denied a full education last year'.
- R. Grant (2019): Research shows that grouping at any age is more to do with classroom management, and nothing to do with helping children learn.
- J. Astle (2019): 'Pupils who qualify for free school meals currently arrive at primary school an average of four months behind their peers and leave secondary school 18 months behind. Pupils with special educational needs and disabilities start 15 months behind and finish three years behind' (p. 41). Schools make the situation worse.
- F. Hainey (2019): Research study by Coventry University and the University of Roehampton cites the following, 'In 2017, more than 16,000 parents in the UK were prosecuted by the courts for their children being absent from school'; 'It is most commonly children with special educational needs who are regularly missing school and families feel these needs are not being met adequately in schools'; 'Of the parents prosecuted in 2017 71% were women and 10 parents (nine women) received custodial sentences.' (They went to prison.)
- L. Partridge (2019): 'Students eligible for free school meals, those with special educational needs and disabilities and those from certain ethnic groups are significantly more likely to be excluded than their peers.'
- Social class discrimination has been discussed in Chapter 4 but here is a more specific example: 'Panic! Social class, taste and inequalities in the creative industries', Edinburgh College of Art, the University of Sheffield and Create, April 2018. From a survey of 2,487 arts professionals the researchers found that people from working class backgrounds and Black, Asian and Minority Ethnic workers all confronted significant exclusion from the sector that is biased towards upper-middle class, white males.

5 Research by the anti-bullying charity Ditch the Label has the highest figure of 50% from its study of 8,850 people aged 12–20 (quoted in the *i* newspaper, April 19, 2016, p. 6). Brugger (2019) quotes a Department for Education figure of nearly 40% in a 12-month period, and 6% on a daily basis from Baker, et al. (2016).
6 This evidence is taken from the Department for Digital, Culture, Media and Sport Economic Estimates 2018 (the latest available figures were for 2017 at the time of producing the report).
7 https://www.bbc.co.uk/news/uk-england-47613726

References

Astle, J. (2019) Schools unleashed. *RSA Journal*, Issue 3, 38–41.

Baker, C., Dawson, D. and Thair, T. (2016) Longitudinal study of young people in England: Cohort 2, wave 2. London: Department for Education.

Bell, J. F. and Daniels, S. (2010) Are summer-born children disadvantaged? The birthrate effect. *Oxford Review of Education*, Vol. 16. Published online https://www.tandfonline.com/doi/abs/10.1080/0305498900160106.

Brugger, S. (2019) Bullying in childhood: cause or consequence of mental health problems. www.nationalelfservice.net. Accessed 04/03/2019.

Cain, S. (2012) *Quiet*. London: Penguin.

Campbell, M. L. C. and Morrison, A. P. (2007) The relationship between bullying, psychotic-like experiences and appraisals in 14–16-yer olds. *Behaviour Research and Therapy*, 45(7), 1579–1591.

Copeland, W. E., Wolke, D., Lereya, S.T. (2014) Childhood bullying involvement predicts low-grade systemic inflammation into adulthood. *Proceedings of the National Academy of Sciences of the United States of America*, 111(21), 7570–7575.

Cullen, D. (2009) *Columbine*. New York: Hachette.

Department for Digital, Culture, Media and Sport (2018) Economic Estimates.

Department for Education (2010) Month of Birth and Education, Research Report DFE-RR017.

Dunbar, R. (2011) *How Many Friends Does One Person Need?: Dunbar's Number and Other Evolutionary Quirks*. London: Faber and Faber.

Edinburgh College of Art, the University of Sheffield and Create (2018) Panic! Social class, taste and inequalities in the creative industries. April.

Evans-Lacko, S., Takizawa, R., Brimblecombe, N.et al. (2016) Childhood bullying victimization is associated with use of mental health services over five decades: A longitudinal nationally representative cohort study. Originally in *Psychological Medicine*, doi:10.1017/S0033291716001719. Reprinted in LSE Research Online, http://eprints.lse.ac.uk. Accessed 03/04/2019.

Freedman, L. (2019) The Self Managed Learning College Study, Phase One Report. Brighton: Centre for Self Managed Learning.

Grant, R. (2019) Grouping primary children by ability is indefensible. *Times Education Supplement*, January 30.

Grauer, S. and Ryan, C. (2016) Small schools: The myths and reality, and potential of small schools. https://medium.com/communityworksjournal/small-schools-the-myths-reality-and-potential-of-small-schools-76a566c42f6e.

Hainey, F. (2019) Parents threatened with jail for taking vulnerable kids out of school, according to study. *Coventry News*, March 24.

Hepworth, N. (2019) GCSE entries: How are non-Ebacc subjects faring since the introduction of Progress 8? NFER, August 22. www.nfer.ac.uk. Accessed 22/08/2019.

Jackson, P.W. (1968) *Life in Classrooms*. New York: Holt, Rinehart and Winston.

James, O. (2007) *Affluenza*. London: Vermilion.

Langman. P. (2009) *Why Kids Kill*. New York: St Martins Griffin.

Lewis, S. J., Arseneault, L., Caspi, A., Fisher, H. L.et al. (2019) The epidemiology of trauma and post-traumatic stress disorder in a representative cohort of young people in England and Wales. *The Lancet Journal of Psychiatry*, 16(3), 247–256.

Lieberman, M. D. (2013) *Social: Why Our Brains are Wired to Connect*. Oxford: University Press.

McDonald, K. (2018) Harvard study shows the danger of early school enrolment. https://fee.org/articles/harvard-study-shows-the-dangers-of-early-school-enrollment/ Accessed 05/09/2019.

Mercier, H. and Sperber, D. (2011) Why do humans reason? Arguments for argumentative theory. *Behavioural and Brain Sciences*, Cambridge University Press, 34(2), 57–74.

Moore, S. E., Norman, R. E. and Suetani, S.*et al.* (2017) Consequences of bullying victimization in childhood and adolescence: A systematic review and meta-analysis. *World Journal of Psychiatry*, 7(1), 60.

Newman, K. S., Fox, C., Harding, D. J., Mehta, J. and Roth, W. (2004) *Rampage. The Social Roots of School Shootings*. New York: Basic Books.

Page, S. E. (2007) *The Difference: How the Power of Diversity Creates Better Groups, Firms, Schools, and Societies*. Princeton: University Press.

Partridge, L. (2019) Is pressure to achieve exam results contributing to school exclusions? Yes, new RSA data indicates. www.thersa.org, blog, March 11.

Pattinson, H. (2016) *Rethinking Learning to Read*. Shrewsbury, UK: Education Heretics Press.

Rose, T. (2015) *The End of Average*. London: Penguin.

Royal Society for the Encouragement of Arts, Manufactures and Commerce (RSA) (2020) Pinball Kids: Working together to reduce school exclusions. www.thersa.org. Accessed 02/05/2018.

Sherwood, H. (2019) Britain's battle to get to grips with literacy is laid bare in H for Harry. March 3. https://www.theguardian.com/education/2019/mar/03/literacy-white-working-class-boys-h-is-for-harry.

Snyder, B.R. (1970) *The Hidden Curriculum*. New York: Alfred A. Knopf.

Takizawa, R., Danese, A., Maughan, B. and Arsenault, L. (2015) Bullying victimization in childhood predicts inflammation and obesity in mid-life: A five-decade birth cohort study. *Psychological Medicine*, 45(13), 2705–2715.

Treadway, M. (2015) Why measuring pupil progress involves more than taking a straight line. https://ffteducationdatalab.org.uk/2015/03/why-measuring-pupil-progress-involves-more-than-taking-a-straight-line.

Vallance, E. (1983) Hiding the hidden curriculum: An interpretation of the language of justification in nineteenth-century educational reform, in Giroux, H. and Purpel, D., eds., *The Hidden Curriculum and Moral Education*, Berkeley, California: McCutcheon.

Varese, F., Smeets, F., Drukker, M., Lieverse, R., *et al.* (2012) Childhood adversities increase the risk of psychosis. *Schizophrenia Bulletin*, 38(4), 661–671.

Wetz, J. (2009) *Urban Village Schools*. London: Calouste Gulbenkian Foundation.

Wolke, D. (2019) Childhood bullying shown to increase likelihood of psychotic experiences in later life. https://warwick.ac.uk. Accessed 03/13/2019.

7

THE WIDER EVIDENCE ABOUT LEARNING AND EDUCATION – AND ITS IMPLICATIONS

Introduction

In this chapter I want to explore some of the wider issues that affect education and learning, though they are not specific to particular school structures. The first item, for instance, is around the impact of private tutoring on student learning. This is clearly a process that interacts with what schools do,but occurs outside the school. Other sections in this chapter refer to what people do after school and what that might mean for schools. I am also interested in exploring, for example, mental health issues that clearly belong in a wider context. Schools impact on the mental health of students, but there are many other factors that affect young people.

Whilst I am saying these are factors that are outside school structures, I believe that they are important issues for schools to address. For instance, if schools claim they are preparing young people for life in the society in which they dwell, then educational activity must go beyond the learning of knowledge and skills. This cuts against the commentators on schools who merely focus on what goes on in schools and a supposed need to improve teaching in the classroom. I am making the case for any organisation that is involved in supporting the learning of young people to take a much wider interest than just school academic performance, as judged by exam results.

Tutoring

As with other sections in the book I will comment on particular evidence in relation to England, but it is well known that the role of private tutors is a global one. Markovits, 2019, cites evidence that the global market in private tutoring is approaching $100 billion. For instance, Asian countries are well known for out-of-school tutoring to support the education of young people. Markovits, 2019, mentions a study that shows that in South Korea private tutoring accounts for 12% of total family expenditure.

Weale, 2018, provides some pertinent evidence from the British context. She cites the estimate of the worth of the tutoring industry in Britain is £2 billion per annum. Evidently, parents are prepared to pay a great deal of money for this support. She cites the evidence of the Sutton Trust, which is a charity that wants to improve social mobility through education. Their annual survey of secondary students in England and Wales showed that 27% have had home or private tuition, a figure that rises to 41% in London.

Given that England also has selective grammar schools for the post-11 age group, there is a particular industry supporting exam passing. The Sutton Trust show that fewer than 10% of children from families with the lower incomes receive any tutoring, compared with 37% from households in the top quarter of income. About 70% of those who received tutoring gained a place in a grammar school or other selective school, compared with 14% of those in the same area who did not. Clearly, for many parents this is money well spent, if they are interested in selective education.

Other information suggests that this shadow tutoring workforce actually props up some schools, whether private or state, that have an outstanding rating from their inspections. When I resided in North London the local secondary school had an excellent record of passes at GCSE. The local tutoring agency said that more than 50% of the students who went to that school used their agency, and that therefore they were more responsible for the outstanding rating than the school.

Response to this

Parents who make a choice to use private tutoring are recognising that the classroom is not a good environment for their child to learn. One-to-one support for young people is superior to the average classroom. Otherwise, parents would not be paying out large sums of money – in some cases thousands of pounds – to support the tutoring of their children.

In our College one-to-one support is a norm. By getting rid of classrooms and other school structures it allows us to work in a more cost-effective way. The cost of students attending our College is less than the cost of running a local secondary school; the average in England is that local authorities get from the Government just over £6000 per annum per pupil for secondary education. Our cost of running is under £4000 per annum per student, though we have some parents who pay nothing because we support them, and other parents who are prepared to give a little bit more to support the poorer parents.

What we can show is that we can run a cost-effective operation that responds directly to student needs. Some parents might utilise extra tutoring for students, especially near to exam time. As long as we know what they are doing, so that we can fit in with them, that can work fine. However, we are very keen that parents who cannot afford this are not disadvantaged and that we help students to use a wide range of learning activities outside the College. This is where we refer to our research showing that 57 (at least) varieties of learning modes are available to young people under the age of 18 and tutoring is only one of these.

Not in Education, Employment or Training (NEET)

In Britain there have been a number of studies of young people 'Not in Education, Employment or Training' (NEET), after the age of 16. Although technically the leaving age from education was raised to 18, in reality many young people after the age of 16 are not in education, employment or training (NEET).

I will just quote one study here, but this evidence is confirmed by all the other studies that I have seen. For a change I will cite evidence from Scotland; it was published in 2015 by the Scottish Government as a result of some rigorous research.[1] The following are some of the findings from their research, and they make unpleasant reading:

- Young people, who were NEET, remained disadvantaged in their level of educational attainment 10 and 20 years later. More than one in five of NEET young people in 2001 had no qualifications in 2011, compared with only one in twenty five of non-NEETS.
- There is a 'scarring effect' on economic activity. In comparison with their non-NEET peers, NEET young people in 2001 were 2.8 times as likely to be unemployed or economically inactive 10 years later. [...]
- NEET experiences are associated with a higher risk of poor physical health after 10 and 20 years. The risk for the NEET group was 1.6–2.5 times that for the non-NEET group, varying with different health outcomes.
- NEET experiences are associated with a higher risk of poor mental health after 10 and 20 years. The risk of depression and anxiety prescription for the NEET group is over 50% higher than that for the non-NEET group.
- Young people who were NEET in 1991 and remained economically inactive in 2001 consistently demonstrated significantly poorer outcomes in 2011 than those who were non-NEET in 1991 and economically active in 2001 and those who were engaged in employment or education in either 1991 or 2001. This suggests that there is a cumulative effect of being out of employment or education on later life chances and this group is the most disadvantaged.

Response to this

In our College we see that one of our priorities is that individuals leaving at 16 – or earlier or later – are in a constructive place in terms of future learning or work. I deliberately say 'learning or work' because there have been a number of students who have left to be self-employed and, therefore, they are not in employment in the strictest sense of the word. We know that certainly in the UK there has been the growth of self-employment and it is not surprising that our students are part of that picture. Similarly, students might not sign up for a formal education course after the age of 16, but the evidence is that they continue to learn in other ways and that they are not showing the symptoms that have been identified for those NEET.

The biggest issue is where young people leave school at 16 and engage in unproductive activities such as merely sitting at home and watching YouTube or they take-up drug dealing or other criminal activity. My view is that any educational institution – school, university or college – should be judged and evaluated as to how well they equip the person to go on to a fulfilling, meaningful and productive life after they leave. They should not be evaluated on the basis of exam passes, as these do not necessarily equip the person to have a fulfilling, meaningful and productive life.

I will comment later in this chapter on the changing nature of the world of work, which impacts on all young people.

Metacognition

This analysis of metacognition might have belonged in the previous chapter, but I would argue that schools do a poor job in encouraging metacognition. At its simplest we are talking about thinking about the way you think, knowing what you know (and what to do with it), being aware of your own awareness and consciousness, and so on. It's often labelled as higher-order thinking skills and the word meta means 'beyond' or 'on top of' as its root, so this is going beyond just thinking.

What I want to do is to separate this notion from self-regulation. The latter idea has become perhaps more popular in school. It is sometimes linked to the idea of metacognition. However, in metacognition the core is that individuals set goals for themselves, and then monitor and evaluate how they achieve those goals and develop an ability to reflect on their action in order to make changes in what they do.

Self-regulation has to some extent become the means of conforming to the school requirements better. At its worst it is a notion of beating yourself up to do what the school wants. On Wikipedia the section on 'Self-Regulated Learning' talks about being able to concentrate on school subjects, finishing homework assignments by deadlines, planning schoolwork and motivating oneself to do schoolwork.[2] It is a reason why I'm not including this notion in metacognition. I am not interested in how young people can be made to conform better to what schools impose. Effective metacognition involves planning action based on your own goals, then monitoring that, being aware of how that works out and then evaluating how well any tasks are performed so that strategies might be re-evaluated. Students can then plan to do things differently based on any reflection about how their learning has worked out. It crucially involves active control over the process by the learner. This includes why an individual would be undertaking this learning in the first place.

Some theorists in the field argue for the value of social metacognition. This would be where you are not only aware of your own awareness but aware of other people's. It involves engagement with other humans in working towards goals that may be collective, for instance. Social metacognition seems a valuable process in areas such as team working. To be able to think about the way a team is thinking, and to be aware of what the team is aware of, must be of value.

Response to this

A metacognitive stance is important in Self Managed Learning. In the first week that students are with us we ask them to reflect on their life experiences and how they see themselves now. We then ask them to consider what kind of goals they might want for the future, in terms of both the life they want to lead, and a career that might be part of that. This leads to them coming up with immediate goals that can feed into their longer-term plans. They then work on these shorter-term goals and report back to their learning group on how actions they took worked out or not. This review process is crucial for individuals to continue to monitor and evaluate their learning.

We regard this as central to any notion of learning how to learn. Learning how to learn is not about just having some mechanistic study skills or tricks on how to remember things. It is much more a metacognitive activity. Students, by understanding that they can set goals (and that they can work on their own goals and can evaluate their own learning), are more able to pursue their learning after they have left us, and in all sorts of environments.

Students who have left us comment in evaluations on how they are better able to plan and organise themselves compared with their peers, for instance, in a university environment. Often students when they are with us are not conscious of the importance of these changes as they see it as part of the way of doing things. It is sometimes only when they leave that they realise that they have developed a way to learn how to learn in a much more sophisticated mode than if they had continued in school.

At the end of their first week with us they answer those five questions that I indicated earlier (see Chapter 2). They then share these in their learning group, where they also become aware of other people's awareness. Hence the dimension of social metacognition is really important. At the end of the first week they plan activities for their next week and then at the next meeting of the learning group a week later they can review how things have gone – what worked and what did not, and what they have learned about learning from what they undertook.

The world of work

There is a great deal that I could discuss about the world of work. The failure of schools to address the needs of pupils to work after they finish with their full-time education is a scandal. Having productive work in life is essential for our well-being – witness the poor mental health of the unemployed. However, work may not be paid or may not include employment. I am using the term in its widest sense as in the quote (erroneously attributed to Freud) that 'love and work are the cornerstones of our humanness'. And just to add to my criticisms of school, they do not do a great job on love either (meaning all forms of love and relationships).

I have split this section in two and start with issues of independence and interdependence.

Independence and interdependence

I have a slide that I use for presentations which has a few controversial words on it that I enjoy explaining. Two of the words indicate the value of 'cheating' and of 'stealing'. What I mean by 'cheating', is the notion that it is useful to help each other and work together. If in an exam people help each other, it is called cheating and they get punished for it. In work and in other things in life, helping each other is crucial to our humanity. This is important; it is a vital capability to learn along with a mindset that is oriented to an interdependent mode of being. At its simplest we become a fully-functioning 'self' through our interactions and relationships with others. Without these we cannot be who we want to be.

It has been fascinating working in the organisational world for most of my career. Some people have a misguided view of how to work in an organisation. There are concerns from employers that people coming out of the educational system are poor at team working. Note that I am talking about **team working** here. I do not mean **team building**, because it is not about building a team and people staying within one team. It is more that through work, life and communities we work with different people, and we need to develop the capability to work with different people. But it is not just a capability; it is about a mindset that says learning is not just something for the individual to keep to themselves or to use competitively. Rather, organisations and communities do not work unless people share and help each other. So in this subsection I want to talk about the notion of **interdependence** alongside **independence** and explain more about that as we go along.

The notion of 'stealing' is the idea that you take ideas from other people. The joke is that in the academic world if you take ideas from one person, it is called plagiarising and you get punished for it. If you take ideas from lots of people, it is called research and you get rewarded for it.

With organisational clients I get involved with issues of innovation. Clearly, people collaborating helps organisations to be innovative and hence the 'cheating' piece is so important. However, 'stealing', namely taking ideas from other people, is often the essence of innovation. Creativity, that is coming up with new ideas, is helpful but it is not innovation. The latter is rather about taking ideas that may be already thought through and utilising them in different ways. Ultimately for companies it is about taking products or services to market. Organisations that just promote individual creativity are not necessarily successful. What they find they need is to be able to take creative ideas and make them work in practice. That is innovation and it requires both capabilities and mindsets, namely the idea of taking from others and the idea of utilising ideas from others effectively.

In our College we encourage greatly the 'cheating' and 'stealing' mindsets. We want our students to work with others, to get used to the idea of collaborating and for them to also know how to take ideas and utilise them for their own purposes. Here is a rather simple example. At the end of each term we do some fun things.

I added in one time a sheet of examples from the UK citizenship test. People applying to be a citizen have to take a test, and the Government produces examples of the kind of questions that would be in such a test. I took the 17 hardest-looking questions, and ones that, in many cases, did not seem to be very relevant to whether someone should be a UK citizen. For instance, one of the questions was, 'Is the Isle of Man a Crown dependency?' So, these are tricky questions. I gave this out to students and said that those who would like to have a go at it might be interested in getting their scores on the test and seeing if they could get 100% right. I indicated that there would be prizes but they would be prizes for the whole community. No individual gets a prize separately from anybody else. Students formed small teams of usually around three or four and busily consulted Google and other sources quite quickly. The small groups came up with 100% correct answers. It was relatively quick, because our students are used to the notion that they work together and help each other.

An example from higher education was when I did an MA part-time whilst working in a learning and development role in local government. All of us on the course were people working in the field and therefore came with experience. We had some concern about the way in which we were being taught, and so we carried out a number of things. One was that we organised our own weekend residential and invited a select number of the lecturers to call in so that we could talk with them in a different environment. We also decided that for some of the lecturers we wanted to engage in dialogue and therefore, well before the person arrived for their lecture, we decided to move all the chairs into a circle so that when the lecturer came in we said, 'Would you like to join us in the circle and talk with us?' Obviously this was challenging to some lecturers. However, we found that they got used to the idea that there would be more of a dialogic mode of working. These kinds of changes meant that we, as a group, worked together really well. We supported each other in our learning and often met away from the university to collaborate on course topics. We also found that we were able to apply much more back into our own organisations than we might have done if we had carried on working in the traditional manner.

Whilst this was seen by the faculty as the best group they had had on the programme, it had within it a crucial weakness. The end result of the MA was that those who passed then got divided into those who got a pass, and those (approximately 20%) who got a distinction. As the academics pointed out, it is probable that in another year most of us would have got distinctions but, as the university had a rule about how many distinctions were allowed, we would in that sense be penalised. We had worked together well, such that we had learned an enormous amount and did well in both our research projects and our exams. However, only 20% of the candidates could get distinctions.

This example shows how what goes on in the educational world does not help what is required in the world of work. Interdependence is crucial. Another example would be Britain's health service. The title of a *British Medical Journal* article (Mayor, 2002) was 'Poor team work is killing patients'. Since that time there have been other research studies which indicate the same problem – there is a relationship between team working in hospitals and patient mortality (see also Epstein, 2014, for a US study).

An excellent report on the National Health Service (NHS) entitled 'An organisation with a memory' (2000) was produced by the Chief Medical Officer for the Department of Health. The report was clear that the NHS is not an effective learning organisation and that it is poor at collective learning.

The NHS, we should remember, is one of the world's largest organisations and it employs a largely highly educated workforce, which has usually undergone extensive training. What we are dealing with here are inadequacies of their approach to work-based, interdependent learning. The report says, 'the failure to learn reliably from adverse events – is illustrated by seven simple facts.' (Note that when the report refers to an 'adverse event' this is a polite way of saying that there was a major, sometimes life-threatening, error or mishap. Often people died who should not have.) Four of the 'facts' are as follows:

- Research suggests that an estimated 850,000 [...] adverse events might occur each year in the NHS hospital sector, resulting in a £2 billion direct cost in additional hospital days alone; some adverse events will be inevitable complications of treatment but around half might be avoidable.
- The NHS paid out around £400 million in clinical litigation settlements in the financial year 1998/9 and has a potential liability of around £2.4 billion from existing and expected claims; when analysed many cases of litigation show potentially avoidable causes. [...]
- At least 13 patients have died or been paralysed since 1985 because a drug has been wrongly administered by spinal injection.
- Over 6,600 adverse incidents involving medical devices were reported [...] in 1999, including 87 deaths and 345 serious injuries (p. 5).

The report goes on to chronicle the human misery caused by failures to learn collectively, as well as the billions of pounds it costs the NHS. If I take the last of the examples mentioned above, the report points out that the circumstances of the errors were similar and that there is a clear failure to learn from experience. I should reiterate that we are talking about highly trained people making these mistakes. The Chief Medical Officer was emphasising that without improved interdependent learning, such mistakes would continue.

The report does, however, show how such learning problems need to be addressed systemically. It suggests that the NHS has a blame culture which does not help learning. It comments, 'When an adverse event occurs, the important issue is not who made the error but how and why did the defences fail and what factors helped to create the conditions in which errors occurred' (p. 21).

Later in this report is the following damning indictment of the current education system as well as aspects of the work context:

> There is little culture of individual self-appraisal. The education of NHS professionals depends to a variable, but generally significant, extent on clinical apprenticeship – that is, on learning by example. This process rarely counteracts a burden of public expectation of infallibility, and may often reinforce it. Yet for the NHS to learn effectively from experience, these individuals must be able to admit that perfection is not always attained: firstly to themselves, and then to their fellows. Where the ability to self-appraise openly and frankly is absent, the negative effects of the 'blame culture' will be reinforced (p. 77).

Also, what the NHS report shows is that the educational system acts as a disincentive to 'self- appraisal'. As the report shows it needs a culture where there is collective interdependent learning. But the education system does the opposite by focusing on the individual only.

An interesting dimension to this problem is cited by Dolan, 2019. He shows that working–class values are more group based and less individualistic, interdependence is more valued and that middle–class values are more about the individual. He cites research where evidence was that in education, working–class students are more likely to be motivated by interdependent goals than middle–class students – and the problem is that such interdependent motives predict lower levels of academic attainment. This is confirmed by research I have already cited.

Dolan argues that there is a strong case that working–class students would gain if universities, in particular, placed more emphasis on interdependence and collaboration. Unfortunately, he doesn't go on to show that there would be enormous social benefits if the education system supported a more working–class orientation to a more interdependent and group-based approach.

Response to this

Please note that in the above, I'm not rejecting the notion of independent learning. Clearly, we do learn a great deal on our own, for example, reading a book, watching a film or talking with a tutor. The issue is the balance between the individual and the collective. In Self Managed Learning we naturally focus a great deal on the individual through our recognition of the fact that every person is different and therefore we need to respond to those differences. However, the importance of both the learning group and learning community is that we balance these. Somehow schooling, especially based on the classroom, neither focuses on the individual nor the collective. As one former teacher described it in a meeting – education is not about teaching individuals, but teaching a class. It's a batch processing model from manufacturing. The batch of say 30 children move from one subject to another subject, just as you would have batches of widgets moving along through a production line. The problem is that widgets are all the same and children are not.

Specific qualities needed in work

The CEO of a major company and I were discussing what the educational world needs to provide for his leading-edge business. After the discussion, he emailed me the following list:

> Building the right mindsets, critical reasoning, understanding of biases, creative thinking and problem solving, fluid and flexible thinking, love of learning, design thinking, communication and influence, impact and changing the world around us, community, interpersonal dynamics and relationships, well-ness and mental health; spiritual path; self-esteem, resilience, grittiness etc. Meta cognition. Ethics, personal accountability and integrity. Teamwork. Emotional intelligence. Pattern matching and recognition. Self-knowledge and understanding of own patterns. Curiosity, cultural awareness.

In a way there is nothing remarkable about the list, in that every survey of major employers in the last 30 years has come up with demands for better teamwork, better creativity, more self managing capability, and so on.[3] Also, our research (along with that of all academics who have also made studies of leaders) shows that, for effective senior leaders, school, college, university and training courses contribute at most 10 to 20% of what makes the person effective. In other words, the billions of pounds and dollars that are spent every year globally on education are largely wasted.

Response to this

If we are going to respond to the CEO's list of requirements, then we have to have a **process** that encourages those qualities. It is not about exhorting young people to behave better, it has to be about creating a context for working in this way.

I replied to the CEO's email as follows:

> I have taken your original list and just started to show how our process curriculum meets what you suggest e.g. in terms of our students:

- They learn to be creative and to solve problems by doing it. For example, they have to plan their own personalised curriculum – that is real creativity and problem solving. It also requires the development of self-knowledge.
- They have to learn to get on with others as they are all part of a self managing community that comes up with its own rules and assists its members not just to develop independence but also inter-dependence. They collaborate and support each other's learning.
- They develop a love of learning by being given the chance to learn anything that they like and in any way that works for them.
- They directly address issues of wellness and mental health by focusing on each other's needs and by being hugely tolerant of differences.

- The development of metacognition is intrinsic to our process and students are challenged to think about the way that they think in their first week with us – and through interactions with others throughout their time with us.
- Ethical issues are to the forefront of many of the informal conversations in the College. Also more formal debates are initiated by students – the latest one was on whether it is ever OK to steal.

It would have been possible to go on to pick up every word in his email but hopefully the idea of how we work is reasonably clear.

Artificial Intelligence (AI)

We know that AI can deal rapidly and effectively with the content side of running a business, and in other parts of our lives. What AI cannot do – and will not be able to do – is to deal with, for instance, those qualities that organisations need and what my colleague Rose Luckin (2018) has identified as including a social intelligence: the ability to engage with others and to think creatively.[4]

In her book, she is especially careful to locate AI in its full educational and social context. For instance, she emphasises how as humans what we offer is an ability to work together and to bring a social intelligence to decisions about the application of AI (something AI alone cannot do). She shows how the limited view of learning that has dominated education is unhelpful. If education is just about drilling students in facts and data, then the role of the teacher can be replaced by AI. However, for proper human learning the collaboration of learners is central and it is where AI cannot contribute.

She takes a broader view of intelligence than the stance of IQ-driven educators. Social intelligence is central to human development and how we can best utilise AI in the future. The title of her book, *Machine Learning and Human Intelligence: The Future of Education for the 21st Century*, is apt because a great deal of it is actually discussing the way we think about intelligence and the importance of, for instance, metacognition. We can develop our knowledge and skills in a broader context. One of the many areas that she points out is the notion of achieving mastery in a subject. It requires us to develop a way of thinking about what mastery means and to pursue that to the full, not through competing with others, but from having a real sense of what we mean by the learning we want to undertake. This includes the ability to self-assess – again a process mostly omitted in formal education, but which is an important part of Self Managed Learning.

This capability is part of what is technically labelled as self-efficacy. To quote from the book:

> An accurate perceived self-efficacy, based on accurate judgements about what we know, is a key ability for learning and will be so to an increased extent. It

will be *the* most important ability for our future lifelong learning. It is also something that is unavailable to AI (p. 131).

Response to this

I have to own to a bias in the above as Professor Luckin is the Honorary President of our College. However, the reason for her being appointed to that post is because of the kind of work that she has been doing and, more explicitly, its link to much-needed changes in education. She is pioneering approaches which show the radical impact of AI in schools and the way that it can replace a great deal of the traditional classroom teaching. However, it cannot replace the social interactions necessary for learning and the other features of learning mentioned above – such as the development of metacognition. It is important to note that what we mean by Self Managed Learning is not selfish individualistic activity. The notion of self managing is about students both working together and working on their own.

Careers and jobs

It is clear that AI will impact hugely on jobs that will be available to young people. In discussing 'What's wrong with education' Simms, 2019, cites the report from the World Economic Forum in 2016, which states that the most in demand occupations and specialities did not exist even five years earlier. And it estimates that 65% of children entering primary school in that year would end up working in roles that similarly did not yet exist. The exact impact of the changing nature of work is not easy to predict as Taylor and Wallace-Stephens, 2019, accept. They quote predictions from several universities and think tanks about the number of jobs at risk of automation. Their range is 35% (University of Oxford) to just under 5% (McKinsey Global Institute).

Whatever the future holds, some of it is already present as automation is already eliminating jobs, especially many of the middle-range jobs. Paradoxically, given governmental support for STEM subjects (Science, Technology, Engineering, Maths), it is clear that many of the jobs in that area can be mechanised out with artificial intelligence.

All commentators suggest that the most important issue for young people is learning how to learn and to be able to make sensible choices about careers. It's about being well prepared for any eventuality rather than the idea that you can predict the future. We cannot predict even a few years into the future. Therefore, a knowledge-fixated education system is, as Simms, 2019, shows, quite wrongheaded.

A major problem is that schools are generally ill-equipped to help pupils think through career issues. Without a good knowledge of the individual and how they think it is tricky to engage with each pupil about choices. Rubin, 2019, cites some important research. For example, many children start to rule out career choices as early as seven. Also, evidence from the charity Education and Employers, shows that career interests are often based on gender stereotypes, socio-economic backgrounds and social media. Their figures show 36% of young people based their career aspirations on someone they knew and 45% because of TV, film or radio.

The need to assist young people with exploring more widely is crucial as poor career choices lead to much frustration and unhappiness. Willmott (2016) cites research on dissatisfaction with career amongst adult employees. The research found that over a quarter (26%) of those whose career has failed to live up to their expectations identified poor-quality career advice and guidance at school as a key factor to blame.

An interesting piece of evidence cited by Simms is that it is not always easy to be clear what impact the experience of young people will have on future employability. She cites Roger Kneebone, Professor of Surgical Education at Imperial College in London, as saying that medical students have spent so much time in front of their screens, and so little time using their hands, that they have lost the dexterity required to cut and stitch up patients. He argues that surgeons need craftsmanship as well as academic knowledge. Skills that might once have been gained at school and home, such as cutting textiles, measuring ingredients, holding instruments and doing woodwork, have been neglected. Kneebone explains that he has actually resorted to using lace-makers and expert chefs to help build these fine motor skills in students.

This is an example of the difficulty in spotting that this might happen. As Kneebone has indicated, you have to then respond to a situation where young people may not have learned what is required. This is back to the requirement for an openness in being prepared to learn as you go along and not assume that school and university have fully equipped you for the world of work.

In my own working career, especially as a chief executive, I have had to select many staff. At its simplest I have said that the people I am looking for have to be good learners and prepared to learn anything, literally anything, and be trustworthy with a strong moral and ethical stance. Basic knowledge and skills can be gained along the way. In many roles the kind of qualities that I indicated above are the most important and, of course, it is a bonus if people are very knowledgeable and skilled in the areas that are needed. But, given the pace of change, unless somebody is a good learner they can be a liability.

Response to this

I suppose I do not really need to reiterate that what we are doing in the College is attempting to prepare people for whatever eventualities come their way. Certainly, we do not wish to encourage students to think that there are easy decisions to be made about career choices. One of the things that we pay particular importance to is helping students to understand, in depth, more about the kind of work that is available, and what it means in terms of the qualities needed to do it.

An example would be the role of focused work experience. By 'focused' I mean work experience that is an area of interest to the student. More generalised work experience, such as just sending students out to experience any setting that employers can provide, is less useful. It is not completely useless, but the motivation to learn from work experience is greater where students have thought about options, and have already done some exploration about them. The following is just one example of what I mean.

On a couple of occasions, we have had students who thought that being a vet would be a good career as they liked animals. A local vet explained that often young people, especially girls, think that it would be nice to work with cuddly animals. But what they do not realise is that the job is smelly and dirty, with much blood, urine and faeces. The animals are generally easy to deal with (as they are usually anaesthetised) and it is more of a problem to deal with the pet owners, who are stressed and anxious, and therefore need careful handling. If a vet is running a small animal practice it is essentially a business, and if you do not satisfy the pet owners, you go out of business.

The vet explained to me that in five years' training to be a vet at university never once was there a session around dealing with humans. Yet he argued that unless you are good at dealing with humans, you will not make a career as a vet. So, we arrange for the students to be able to spend a week working in the vet's practice and sitting in on operations, cleaning up and sweeping the floor. Obviously, they also get the chance to talk to the staff who work there. If after that work experience, they still figure on being a vet, then they have to know that they must get very high grades in their exams in science subjects for them to have any chance of such a career. We have to help them to put all the elements of the picture together. It is about having the academic learning. But, unless a person has the other dimensions and qualities to be able to handle the kind of work involved, then the academic learning, on its own, will not be sufficient.

Mental health and related issues

The issue of mental health problems for young people gets much publicity and, in a sense, the issues are so well known that people almost switch off because there is so much concern. Too many of the suggestions are related to dealing with the symptoms rather than preventive measures. For instance, in England there is great pressure for more people to be employed in children and adolescent mental health facilities. There is also a tendency to make easy prognostications related to, for instance, the growth of social media and the time that young people spend in front of a screen. There is a tendency for schools to blame mental health and suicidal issues to factors outside their control. The normal culprits that schools blame include the media, parents, the medical profession, lack of counsellors and therapists, lack of money, and, most perniciously, the young people themselves.

I mentioned earlier (see Chapter 6) in relation to bullying that educational psychologists were pushing resilience training as a way of blaming the victim, who they claim should be more resilient. Wright, 2018, makes an excellent case against those who want to blame the individual and the tendency to say 'that whatever is going wrong in society, personal life and work is as a result of your own moral, biological, psychological or spiritual weaknesses that, with a bit of mindfulness work, you can put right' (p. 22). And if you cannot, it is your fault. His more generalised comments about society can be applied even more devastatingly in the school context, with the growth of mindfulness programmes and other self-help tools that ignore the responsibilities of adults towards young people. I should say that, in its proper place, mindfulness can be helpful for individuals, as can other self-help methods. The issue is of schools ignoring their responsibilities to young people by dumping the problem on the individual. This adds up to a notion that school itself has little or no impact on mental health and related problems.

In relation to the latter, we now have a wealth of evidence from the USA that is undoubtedly relevant to other rich countries, like Britain. This shows that there is a direct link from the mental health and suicide issues of young people to their school. Gray, 2018, has an excellent summary of rigorous research studies. As he points out he had, four years earlier, provided evidence from a mental health facility in Connecticut. This data revealed that the average monthly number of emergency mental health intakes for school-age children declined from 185 in May (the last full month of school) to 102 in June (the month in which school is finishing), and then down to 74 and 66 respectively in July and August (the two full months of freedom from school). In September, the rate starts to climb up again. This is very clear evidence that when young people are out of school, they are less likely to have emergency mental health requirements, and that school quite clearly has a negative impact on the mental health of many young people.

Since Gray's earlier evidence he cites other studies now that support what he found. Lueck et al., 2015, studied the rate of psychiatric visits to a large paediatric emergency mental health department in Los Angeles. They found that the rate of such visits in weeks when school was in session was 118% greater than in weeks when school was not in session. In other words, the rate of emergency psychiatric visits was more than twice as high during school weeks as it was during non-school weeks. Plemmons et al., 2018, found the rate of hospitalisation of school-age children for suicidal ideation and attempts increased dramatically by nearly 300% over the seven years of this study from 2008 to 2015 and each year the rate of such hospitalisations was significantly higher in school months than in the summer. Gray summarises these research studies by saying 'increase in suicidal ideation and attempts over time is the result of the increased stress from this of school over this time period, and not attributable to some factors independent of schooling' (p. 2).

Anecdotal evidence from the UK supports this more thorough research from the USA. Our own experience is that some students come with a range of mental health problems and that these reduce over time while they are with us. This has come from parents who have been asked about the impact of the College.

Response to this

When we look at the evidence of growing mental health problems amongst young people, this is a global phenomenon where there is intensive schooling, as in the UK. We are, then, into the territory of what is the role of a school in relation to the young people who attend. Clearly, for many it is a notion of teaching facts so that individuals can leave and perhaps go on to further education beyond school. Even less extreme advocates of a teaching approach in schools tend to take the view that problems of young people belong with a psychiatrist or psychotherapist or counsellor. Many schools, of course, employ counsellors for this very reason that it is not regarded as something that teachers should get involved in.

When we were working in one school where we had introduced a Self Managed Learning programme, the Deputy Special Needs Coordinator worked alongside our team to learn the approach. She then started to run a very effective programme with children who had problems, as defined by the school. On one occasion she had unearthed some significant family issues, which raised child protection matters. I had to go to the school to defend her against criticism from the senior leadership of the school that she should not have been unearthing these problems. She was criticised because this was seen as a matter for professionals, such as the mental health experts. Note that she had made such a referral once she knew the problem, but the issue was that she should not have identified the problem in the first place. I was staggered that the individual was virtually being disciplined for doing what seemed the most moral thing to do, which was to highlight that there was a problem and that a girl in the school was potentially in a harmful situation. The notion that, by discovering it, the individual was thought to be in the wrong struck me as extraordinary.

In our College we want to know about the whole life situation of students and we do know that the majority of students with us have a number of issues to deal with, the most common being anxiety and depression. Often we have to address those issues before the individual is in a space where they can actually pursue any academic learning. Not having a classroom structure and having high levels of support means we don't get trapped into a notion that we should get on with teaching, irrespective of the emotional state of the individual.

International comparisons of mental health

The standard test for international comparisons is that run by the Organisation for Economic Co-operation and Development (OECD) and is called the Programme for International Student Assessment, commonly abbreviated as PISA. These tests are used to compare performance across different countries. This has influenced choices in some countries as to how to educate young people. In England there has been the importation of maths teachers from Shanghai, because of Shanghai's performance on the PISA tests, especially in maths.

I have been working with a colleague, Ann Qiu, in Shanghai to help her develop an alternative school, because of the horrors of the Chinese education system. As she puts it, if China is doing so well why is it that the wealthy Chinese parents spend a lot of money sending their children to the USA or England for their education. In the view of Ann Qiu, who is an experienced educator, the huge pressure put on school students to perform in written exams starts early with extended out-of-school academic learning imposed on them. The implications of this are that they do well on the PISA tests. However, this is a direct quote from a paper that she wrote about the situation:

> The suicide rate among young students in China is the highest in the world and is continuously rising. In Shanghai 23.39% of students in primary and secondary schools admit that they have had an intention to suicide, 15.23% considered the suicide methods and 5.85% seriously planned suicide, 1.71% experienced an actual suicide attempt.
>
> *(Qiu, 2013)*

She points out that this has been reported by the 39 Network, one of the biggest health networks in China.

She also cites the physical health problems of children and teenagers, which have been getting worse. The rates of near-sighted students in China are also the highest in the world and a deputy chief inspector at the Ministry of Education admitted the anxious pursuit of performance and lack of physical exercise are the major contributors to this.

Before we entered into a partnership with colleagues in Shanghai we had a visit from a group of alternative practitioners from South Korea. At that time they claimed the highest suicide rate in the world and they were also one of the most highly rated countries in the PISA tests. As they put it to me, 'Our students study like crazy, have no free time, end up with excellent academic results – and then a lot of them kill themselves. Is this the way to have a sensible education system?' These Koreans were people running alternative education ventures of which there are now well over a hundred in South Korea, because of the horrors of their education system.

Response to this

As a college we have no interest in exerting the kind of pressure that has been put on some students in other countries. Pressure for academic results has been growing in England and is not helping the growing suicide rate amongst young people in the UK.

The paradox of the Chinese situation is that I had a colleague who was asked to work in Beijing University because the Education Ministry there was concerned about improving the creativity and innovation in students. Chinese companies are worried that their education system, with its heavy emphasis on rote learning and high pressure, may not be fit for purpose in the future.

We are committed to our more holistic approach and I have given information about this already. However, this does not mean an either/or choice: help young people with emotional well-being or push for academic results. It is a both/and situation: our students improve their emotional well-being so that their academic learning can be more productive.

Life satisfaction and emotional well-being

In this section I will draw on what I perceive as the best two heavily researched pieces of work on life satisfaction and emotional well-being. Clark et al., 2018, bring together a wealth of evidence focused on the work of the Well-being Programme at the London School of Economics' Centre for Economic Performance. The other document drawn on here is Goodman et al, 2015, in their bringing together of the most impressive research on social and emotional skills, and effects on adult life. Both studies are based on huge amounts of direct research and also bring together research material from a range of sources and, in the case of the Clark study, much international evidence as well.

Clark et al. introduce the notion of happiness over the life course as based on aspects of what should be attended to in childhood. They say there are broadly three main aspects of child development: intellectual or cognitive, behavioural and emotional. The intellectual development is about knowledge and task-oriented skills, whereas behavioural development is primarily about behaviour to others. Lastly, emotional development is about how the child feels. Their interest is in which are the most important of these as predictors of subsequent life satisfaction. They summarise research by saying that the strongest childhood predictor of a satisfying adult life is emotional health in childhood. The intellectual and the behavioural developments are less important, though not irrelevant.

They show that, as we know, there is large influence from parents, but they also say that schools are key. They comment that so many people only think about schools affecting academic performance and maybe behaviour, but that the emotional health of the child may be left to the family. They are very clear that this is a totally wrong view. The effect of schools is huge. Even if you hold constant the child's family background, the primary school still has an enduring influence, and for behaviour and emotional health, it has as great an influence as the secondary school. In their overview of life satisfaction, they summarise that income has only a small part to play. Human relationships are much more important and mental health is the most important single factor in explaining the variation in happiness in the population.

In digging into the issue a number of the headline features include the fact that emotional health in childhood reduces adult illness, physical as well as mental, and that intellectual performance has no effect on the number of physical health problems someone experiences. They show that there is a two-way interaction between happiness and health and that healthy people are happier and happy people live longer. They actually prove that helping pupils' well-being does not detract from, but rather adds to, their academic performance.

I can only recommend to readers if you have a choice of any books around happiness, to pick this one, because the thoroughness of their research beats other texts that I have come across.

Now I would like to turn to the Goodman et al., 2015, report made for the Early Intervention Foundation and funded by the UK Government. Their focus is on social and emotional skills in childhood and its effects on adult life. They pick what they call five broad groupings of social and emotional skills affecting children and adult outcomes. This is their list, in their words:

1   **Self-perceptions and self-awareness.** These relate to a child's knowledge and perception of themselves and their value, their confidence in their current abilities and a belief in their efficacy in future tasks.

2   **Motivation.** This can be characterised as the reasons for which individuals strive towards goals. It includes the belief that effort leads to achievement, distinguishes whether goals are set by other people or by oneself, and the value that is attached to the goal in question, aspiration and ambition.

3   **Self-control and self-regulation.** These refer to how children manage and express emotions, and the extent to which they overcome short-term impulsivity in order to prioritise higher pursuits.

4   **Social skills.** These describe a child's ability and tendency to interact with others, forge and maintain relationships and avoid socially unacceptable responses. They cover communication, empathy, kindness, sharing and cooperativeness. They are absent when a child is solitary, shy or withdrawn.

5   **Resilience and coping.** These are demonstrated when an individual is able to adapt positively and purposefully in the face of stress and otherwise difficult circumstances. Resilience is not so much an aspect of character as a developmental process – the ability to summon strength when needed and 'beat the odds' of adversity (p. 7).

I have a few quibbles with some of these definitions, which I will return to, but, by and large, it is, I would guess, quite recognisable to people that these five factors can be important for young people in growing up. One additional point they make in relation to these is to add in to self-perceptions and self-awareness notions of 'locus of control' and 'self efficacy'. It would not be a surprise to know that I would link these to ideas of self managing. The notion is that you can take control of your own life, within reason, and that this is a valuable focus taking one into adulthood.

Taking each of their five areas in turn they have identified potential positive and negative factors that may come out of childhood development. They do discuss the fact that some may have a stronger relationship than others and I can only refer readers to the actual report if you wish to go into more depth about which factors have a stronger predictive value. Given that proviso, it is the worth looking at what they see as coming out of each of the developmental areas.

Self-perceptions and self-awareness. Here they see mental health, well-being and life satisfaction being related to these factors along with some of the other adult outcomes, such as potentially having a higher income and being less likely to be unemployed or to be in social housing. From the point of view of physical and mental health, good self-perception and self-awareness seem to be positively related to self-rated health. Also with this factor there is less likelihood of obesity, clinical problems, smoking and drinking problems. They comment on the possibilities of implications for other areas of adult life and that such self-perceptions and self-awareness may reduce propensity to crime and increase positive outcomes in partnerships (meaning relationships).

The motivational area. They see this as having less clear outcomes, although they consider that it may affect positively on education and reduce the likelihood of smoking, but otherwise they don't find much in this area. I wonder if this is because their definition includes goals set by others, i.e. where there is extrinsic motivation. This might be a reason why the implications of this factor are not present.

Self–control and self–regulation. Here again, I have some issues about their category and I mentioned earlier about different ways that the idea of self-regulation can be interpreted. If it means taking charge of your own life, it is a positive thing. If it means being better at doing what other people tell you – self-regulating to achieve other people's goals – then it does not seem to me quite so useful. However, given that, it seems likely that an appropriate kind of self-control and self-regulation does link to life satisfaction, mental health and well-being in adulthood and that again this is likely to produce better outcomes in terms of jobs and income. It also seems possible that self-rated health may be more positive and that clinical problems, obesity and drinking problems may be reduced. This also links to a lower propensity to crime and more positive partnerships.

Social skills is another problematic area in that being solitary or shy might be where Cain's, 2012, study would have been helpful in showing that more introverted modes do not have to be negative, and that it may well be that the problem with both the world of work and of education is that extroversion is more valued. However, given that proviso, life satisfaction and well-being are clearly helped in this area along with income and job satisfaction. And again, self-rated health and likelihood to create positive partnerships are relevant factors in adult life.

Resilience and Coping is another area in which both concepts can be misinterpreted in terms of expectations as to how an individual copes with a world around them that is intrinsically unfair. However, given that, there is a positive relationship in their research with life satisfaction and a good occupation in adulthood. Emotional health is a clear winner in terms of a usually positive value for mental health and well-being and also partnerships.

One of the factors they suggest in terms of life satisfaction is that higher self-esteem at age 10 is positively associated with more life satisfaction at age 42. However, higher cognitive ability at age 10 is not significantly associated with life satisfaction at age 42. To sum this up they suggest that the effects of self-esteem, conscientiousness and sociability on life satisfaction are not gained through the pathway of formal qualification attainment.

When they look at poor health, their evidence shows that it is strongly predicted by almost all social and emotional skills. However, these results are unaffected by the inclusion of formal education attainment as a control, suggesting that these associations were independent of education.

They conclude their findings with the following statement:

> our work supports the view that developing a balance of skills in childhood, both cognitive and social and emotional, is important for success in adult life. With this in mind, well-evidenced interventions that support parents, schools and communities to develop children's emotional well-being, self-regulation and young people's sense of their own efficacy in the world alongside their cognitive development, are likely to be very beneficial in the long term (p. 75).

Response to this

By now it will come as no surprise that I see the importance of the evidence presented in areas such as well-being. It is interesting that the authors of the report above want well-evidenced interventions directed to parents, schools and communities. They are unlikely to get this, because they do not put forward what that would mean in practical reality, and schools see well-being as an add-on to academic performance. Until that focus is changed, nothing will change in the state system. The unbalanced exam-happy, performance-oriented model of schooling that is present in most countries is not fit for purpose.

In our College, we look at the whole person to help the individual to develop in all the areas relevant to them in having a good life after they move on from us. It is why I am suggesting the need for a New Educational Paradigm. It requires a different mindset and a different way of thinking to start to take seriously the notion that childhood should be a good preparation for adult life, and that currently for many young people it is not.

Conclusion

In this chapter I have raised a number of wider issues that impact on young people and that ought to be taken seriously. I have cited much evidence in favour of this. My frustration is that if people do actually read any of these texts, they clearly do not take them seriously, except those of us who are working to develop a New Educational Paradigm.

In this book I am suggesting that Self Managed Learning is part of an emerging New Educational Paradigm, and that we will have a lot of struggles to create a new way of thinking. The advantage in science is that eventually the evidence wins out: in the area of education that has not been happening. I am not confident it will happen in the near future. However, if we are serious about paying attention to the life of our young people, then we adults have to at least have a go. 'Skin in the game' is needed if we are to take a genuinely moral stance as adults.

Notes

1 Scottish Government (2015) 'Consequences, risk factors, and geography of young people not in education, employment or training (NEET)'.

Other reports, e.g. by the Audit Commission in England in 2010, confirm the findings in the Scottish study. While there are claims by the Government that the NEET problem has lessened in terms of numbers of NEETs there is still a clear indication of the disadvantage caused by the lack of gainful activity of such young people.

2   The sections on Wikipedia on both Metacognition and Self-Regulated Learning are well worth consulting for those who want to know more about the background to these notions. However, as I have said, the self-regulated learning section does not address serious issues about who controls the learning.

Material on metacognition can be accessed also at the Education Endowment Foundation. It has some interesting material in it based on experiences in the UK and has useful references. https://educationendowmentfoundation.org.uk/tools/guidance-rep orts/metacognition-and-self-regulated-learning/

3   Here is a sample of evidence and views on the needs of the world of work:

'Speaking on a panel at the inaugural CIPD Festival of Work, Matthew Taylor – whose review formed the basis of the (UK) government's recent overhaul of workers' rights – said "We talk about coding – we won't need coding in 20 years but we are going to need empathy, we're going to need teamwork, we're going to need resilience," he said.' https://www.peoplemanagement.co.uk/news/articles/skills-of-the-future-are-empa thy-teamwork-resilience-matthew-taylor

'International research by LinkedIn picks up messages from earlier bulletins, with 92% of employers saying that so-called "soft skills" are equally or more important than hard skills.' https://www.edge.co.uk/sites/default/files/documents/skills_shortage_bulletin_5_ final_-_web.pdf

'The most important human traits in 2062 will be our social and emotional intelligence, as well as our artistic and artisan skills. The irony is that our technological future will not be about technology, but about our humanity. And the jobs of the future are the most human ones.' T. Walsh (2018).

The notion that the business world is best captured with the term VUCA has caught the attention of many. The initials stand for Volatility, Uncertainty, Complexity and Ambiguity. See Bennett and Lemoine (2014) for an explanation of the importance of this approach.

4   See also A. Beard (2018), who comments as a robotics expert that he had found that for a robot the acquisition of language was abstract and formulaic whereas for humans it is embodied, emotive and subjective. The future of intelligence would not be found in machines but in the development of our own minds.

References

Beard, A. (2018) *Natural Born Learners*. London: Weidenfeld and Nicolson.

Bennett, N. and Lemoine, G. J. (2014) What VUKA really means for you. *Harvard Business Review*. https://hbr.org/2014/01/what-vuca-really-means-for-you.

Cain, S. (2012) *Quiet*. London: Penguin.

Chief Medical Officers, NHS (2000) An organisation with a memory. London: Department of Health.

Clark, A. E., Flèche, S., Layard, R., Powdthavee, N. and Ward, G. (2018) *The Origins of Happiness*. Princeton: University Press.

Dolan, P. (2019) *Happy Ever After*. London: Allen Lane.

Epstein, N. (2014) Multidisciplinary in-hospital teams improve patient outcomes: A review. *Surgical Neurology International*, 5 (Suppl 7) S295-S303. Published online, doi:10.103/ 2152-7806.139612.

Goodman, A., Joshi, H., Nasim, B. and Tyler, C. (2015) Social and emotional skills in childhood and their long-term effects on adult life. London: UCL Institute of Education. Report to the Early Intervention Foundation, March 11.

Gray, P. (2018) Children's and teens' suicides related to the school calendar. May 31. https://www.psychologytoday.com/gb/blog/freedom-learn/201805/children-s-teens-suicides-related-the-school-calendar.

Luckin, R. (2018) *Machine Learning and Human Intelligence: The Future of Education for the 21st century*. London: UCL Institute of Education Press.

Lueck, C., *et al.* (2015) Do emergency paediatric psychiatric visits for danger to self or others correspond to times of school attendance? *American Journal of Emergency Medicine*, 33, 682–684.

Markovits, D. (2019) *The Meritocracy Trap*. London: Allen Lane.

Mayor, S. (2002) Poor team work is killing patients. *BMJ*, 16, 325(7373):1129.

Plemmons, G., *et al.* (2018) Hospitalization for suicide ideation or attempt: 2008–2015. *Paediatrics*, 141(6).

Qiu, A. (2013) The Real Shanghai Secret. (Unpublished paper, available from Centre for Self Managed Learning).

Rubin, C. M. (2019) The global search for education: How employers help children design their futures. www.cmrubinworld.com/how-employers-help-children-design-their-futures/. Accessed 15/09/2019.

Scottish Government (2015) Consequences, risk factors, and geography of young people not in education, employment or training (NEET). https://www.gov.scot/publications/consequences-risk-factors-geography-young-people-education-employment-training-neet-research-findings/pages/1/.

Simms, J. (2019) What's wrong with education? Work. *CIPD Journal*, April, 26–31.

Taylor, M. and Wallace-Stephens, F. (2019) Work in progress. *RSA Journal*, Issue 1, 10–15.

Taylor, M. Address to CIPD Festival of Work. https://www.peoplemanagement.co.uk/news/articles/skills-of-the-future-are-empathy-teamwork-resilience-matthew-taylor. Accessed 09/09/2019.

Walsh, T. (2018) *2062: The World that AI Made*. La Trobe, Australia: University Press.

Weale, S. (2018) An education arms race: Inside the ultra-competitive world of private tutoring. *The Guardian*, December 5.

Willmott, B. (2016) Third of UK employees disappointed with their career progression. https://www.cipd.co.uk/about/media/press/150316-eo-skills-careers. Accessed 15/09/2019.

Wright, S. (2018) Making (sacred) space for staff renewal and transformation. *Paradigm Explorer*, 1, 21–24.

8

THE EXPERIENCE OF SELF MANAGED LEARNING

Introduction

I want to start this chapter with the voices of young people. What follows are reflections on the experience of young people attending SML College. In order to ensure anonymity, the names are fictitious, and I have amalgamated aspects of different students' stories, so that any individual in real life is not identified. However, the two stories are very representative of student perspectives.

After these stories, I will summarise some of the research evidence on students' views of Self Managed Learning on programmes not in the College but mainly from a variety of schools. Finally, there is an extract from research on parents and carers and their views of the College as well as material from a follow-up study of past students.

Dean's story (aged 13)

When I came to do a trial week, I found it quite a surprise that a place like this existed. It seemed quite strange, as there were no classrooms and I didn't have to put my hand up to leave a room but could wander where I liked. Students here seemed to be doing all sorts of different things in different places and initially it was a bit confusing. However, I quite liked the fact that it was a calm space that I seemed to be welcomed into.

I was pleased to get a chance to do the trial week because I had not been enjoying school. I quite like to work on things on my own and to follow my own interests, and school didn't seem to want to let me to do that. I got really interested, for instance, in film and wanted to make films, but it wasn't possible in school. I wasn't really interested in the sports that the school was interested in and in fact enjoyed playing roller hockey outside school. I guess I quite like to do things a bit differently from others. Often it wasn't welcomed in school.

I also didn't like the bullying that went on. Although I wasn't personally bullied, it didn't make it a nice place to be. On the trial week it just seemed quite different. A world where there wasn't any bullying – people just got on with things.

When I arrived for the first day of the start of the new year, we spent the first day working out things like rules for the place, which again was a bit of a surprise for me. Mostly it seemed people were quite happy with the rules they'd already agreed, so I went along with that. Then we were put into learning groups and I had a meeting with five other students, of the same age as me, and a learning group adviser. We had to answer these five questions in the first week. It was interesting answering the first question about past experience because I hadn't really thought about it at all. So, when I was asked about how I saw myself now, I guess I was like others in the group in more emphasising negative things. I said I like writing, but the school didn't like what I wrote. I also said something I think about not being too confident in class, even though I think I did pretty well in most subjects. In fact, apart from English, I seem to get reasonably good marks in tests.

Being asked about what I want to do in the future was initially quite difficult. I could think of the kind of life I might like to lead, like being happy and having enough money, but I hadn't really thought of any kind of career, apart from in film. However, in talking with others, I could see that there are other kinds of media like TV and journalism that might also be interesting.

I didn't really think too much about how I could learn things at that time, and I struggled a bit with this. However, the group and the learning group adviser were helpful in saying things like, well, we could go on visits or invite people in to talk about things.

I seem to remember we went out on a trip to the lifeboat station in the first week as well and it was nice that it was optional. I went and I found it quite interesting to find out about what the people did there.

At the end of the first week we had a learning group meeting to talk about what we should each do in the next week. And I seem to remember I talked about wanting to try and find ways of learning the things I want to learn and maybe look at other opportunities. I said that although I was really interested in making films, I didn't really know about it and the learning group adviser said he could find a filmmaker who might come in so that we could talk to him. I thought that was a great idea and in fact is something that we did some weeks later. What was useful with that was the learning group adviser invited in the filmmaker and he came to our group and one or two others joined us. We asked him lots of questions about how he came to make films and also what was involved. In the end, he said I could come and watch them when they were doing a film for an organisation. And that was great when it happened, because I could see that it was a lot more complicated than I had thought, and especially with things like lighting and sound and just how you storyboard it and all those things.

I've also found it useful to join in with other people on things. I'm a bit quiet at times, but it's pretty easy to go to a workshop where people are doing something. For instance, in science they were doing dissections. Although I wasn't too sure to start with, I found it quite interesting to understand more about biology.

What I like is also that I got the afternoons and evenings and weekends to myself as we don't have homework. Well, we have work we can do at home, but it isn't like school homework. I can spend time with the roller hockey team, and I can watch movies, but now with the view to try and find out more about how they work. I also enjoyed reading a lot in the past but with all the homework we had in school I didn't read as many novels as I used to, and so it's good to get time to read.

Where I'm at now is that I still think films might be really interesting to get into, but I'm keeping my options open and making certain to learn other things. I figure if I want to go to college, then I will want to do GCSEs and get good marks. I'm not totally committed to college at the moment as I might find an apprenticeship is more interesting. I'm quite a practical person so that might be a good thing to do.

The idea of doing something in the media like journalism, like writing for different kinds of magazines, could be a thing to do. I've enjoyed some of the debates we've had in College and I think I have become more confident to speak out on my own opinions.

Sarah's story (aged 11)

I came to SML college earlier this year. I was very unhappy in school and was getting into a lot of trouble. I like to argue, especially with the teachers. I didn't like all the tests that we did. I was okay in English, but I just can't do maths and have been told I am dyscalculic, which means I can't do maths.

When I came to the trial week, I was a bit surprised that I wasn't being pushed to do things like maths when I really can't cope with it. I liked the fact that it seemed like people are quite free and do what they wanted, so I was really glad when mum agreed that I could come here as a student. In trying to work out what I wanted to do, it was quite difficult to think about things I liked, and I'm still not sure about a career. I know that I want to be happy in the future. And also, probably will want to have a nice house to live in and have a bit of money, because we don't have much money as mum is on her own with me and we find it a bit hard at times.

I have quite a few things I'm interested in. I join in with the other girls in our group in doing projects together. I've always loved listening to music and now I can start to learn an instrument. Our music learning adviser is helping me to learn some chords on guitar and we are trying to get a group going. Since the group is short of a bass player, I think I will concentrate on learning bass guitar. It's great that there are instruments here as we can't afford one at home. Because we have an afternoon music and art club, I can carry on with my guitar playing in the afternoon as well.

The other subjects, apart from maths, I think are going okay. I was pleased that the maths learning adviser wasn't going to push me into doing things I don't want to do, though he said he'd try and help me as best he can with my dyscalculia. I started to enjoy writing now and I didn't enjoy school having to learn all the grammar and stuff, but now I can just write poems and do creative writing, which I enjoy. And I'm starting to do some drawing about the things that I am writing about.

I quite enjoy that we can go out and use the playing field opposite – whenever we get one of the adults to take us – which most days is OK. One thing that I didn't expect to get interested in is languages. I have never been abroad, but I'd really like to. With adults here who can teach German I'm starting to learn how to speak German. I also like using Duolingo for learning German and a group of us have been playing around with learning other languages. For instance, last week we had a go at some Dutch.

I see the older students thinking about getting organised to take GCSEs. Someday I might have to think about that, but not now. I think that next year I would like to do the Bronze Arts Award as I'm told it's like a lower level GCSE and I could do it with music, if I get good enough. I have already been thinking about what I would need to do. I might record myself playing guitar, and I would have to teach someone else how to play guitar. I'd have to write about someone I admire and there are lots of guitar players that I love.

I want to stay here for the rest of my education and there is talk of being able to go beyond 16 now, which would suit me. As mum has got funding for me from a trust that supports the College, we should be OK about that.

A summary of aspects of research on student perspectives

Of the research studies carried out from the University of Brighton, the following eight are particularly informative in this context: Capps, 2014; Dufflen, 2010; Edmonds, 2015; Mayes, 2008; Mathews, 2016; Mehtola, 2013; Sankey, 2008 and Worley, 2015. There are also evaluation studies of programmes at Neale-Wade Community College, Cambridgeshire; South Harringay Junior School, London; St Luke's School, Portsmouth; Tetherdown Primary School, London and Uckfield Community Technology College, East Sussex on the Centre for Self Manage Learning website.[1]

Some of the issues identified by students in five schools that experienced SML[2]

Students found the chance to talk to each other, and to be listened to, was a real feature, as was the fact that they had time to step back and think, as opposed to the normal rushed school day. They appreciated the value of sharing ideas and contacts amongst each other so that, as a peer group, they were able to support each other. They also commented that the peer group provided a good influence as regards behaviour in the school. The idea that they could help each other is important as they mostly commented that in class they didn't get that opportunity.

The fact that the process was enjoyable was something that they saw as a nice relief from the pressures of school life. The fact that it wasn't lessons and it was something else was very much appreciated. Incidentally, I have found that in the College students get used to a way of working. Some are more likely to grumble about anything that goes awry. However, in school, the contrast between their normal studies and being in a learning group, where they helped each other, was such a large contrast that their level of appreciation was higher.

They liked being able to talk with adults as equals and we kept up our model of being on first name terms with students we worked with, even though this was not the norm in the school. They appreciated not being shouted at, but rather having an opportunity to talk on an equal basis with the learning group adviser.

Whilst they appreciated the support that they gave each other, they also realised that challenges within the group were of value. One student had been particularly critical of teachers and their peers in the group challenged them about their own behaviour, suggesting that that may have brought on the problems they had with teachers.

They talked a lot about having personal control and being able to think for themselves. This fits with the locus of control idea, namely that at a meta-level we were encouraging the notion that they could take control of their own lives, even if they felt there were limitations within the school.

They liked the opportunity to be creative and develop real ideas and put them into practice. Some commented about moving beyond just dreaming about something to actually making it happen, and the challenge that they had to do that. Within that, developing their priorities was seen as an important feature, as many were used to the school laying down priorities and the fact that they were challenged to think through what was important and what wasn't so important was new and useful.

The idea of looking to the future and thinking about their lives and careers was valuable to most students, as was the fact that there were no limits being put on what they could think about. This opportunity to have thinking time, they felt, made a real difference.

They liked the fact that it was confidential, that we as learning group advisers would not share anything outside the group without permission. The only time we might want to take something out was if there was a real child protection issue, though that never occurred in any of the in-school programmes that we were involved in. They believed that this confidentiality rule allowed for more personal connection and that just being with others where they would not be being judged or laughed at was really important.

Some recognised that their own confidence levels had increased by being on the programme and that they felt more secure in trying out new things. This was also linked to the fact that they felt they had got a wider view of learning; they started to realise that learning was something that went beyond what was in the classroom. The opportunity to learn from each other and from going on trips or from bringing in visitors allowed them to see that there were many ways in which they could learn things that would be of value to them.

Parents'/carers' views of SML College

The following is an extract from Mayes, 2008, which is in her words (except for the fact that at that time we were the South Downs Learning Centre, so I have changed 'Centre' to 'College' to bring it up to date).

> How the students had changed collectively fits into three key themes: a boost in confidence, motivation and aspirations, and to the majority of parents were what they considered unexpected outcomes.

> > *'He's much calmer, he's much happier, he's much more confident, his self-esteem has been enormously boosted and he has got a forum for his voice – he's found a voice for himself that people will listen to.'*

> Several lessons have been seen to have been learned:

> > *'[Child's name] has finally realized that he has got to be responsible for himself and if he doesn't start identifying what it is he wants to achieve in his life, and how he is going to achieve it, then it is not going to get done and he will have no-one to blame apart from himself.'*

> This acknowledgment may seem harsh for a young teenager but is indeed a necessary outcome for a self managed mindset and he has thus embraced responsibility in order to reach his goals, or at least knows he has to, to do it.

> What I found to be the most rewarding remark was the fact that every parent interviewed exclaimed their delight in the fact that their child hasn't wanted to miss a day since they started at the College and all morning fights or absence excuses were a thing of the past.

> The parents' perceived ability for their child to use SML and how it reflected in other areas of the student's life was encouraging. If they hadn't seen a definitive improvement already, the parents at least recognised potential or saw parts of it in how their children approached their work.

> > *'I think that as she has only got a couple of years left before she applies to college, she sees that that is kind of imminent and she sees that two years is really not a lot of time, so she is now getting herself together.'*

> The experience so far in terms of the College's influence on her child's growth has left one mother oozing confidence.

> > *'There are 14-year olds here and obviously they are looking at GCSEs and things like that. My son is not at that stage yet, but I think the longer he is here, the*

more he will be focusing on his future and what he wants to do – finding out what GCSEs he wants to take if he does!'

The determination not to impose expectations or superfluous anxieties is prominent here and typical of the parents' position on education at SMLC. The fact that the students were trying all sorts of different things, and were obviously relaying that prospect to their parents, satisfied those I interviewed greatly.

When asked if there was anything they would like to see their child additionally doing or pursuing, all parents were adamant that their child would make their right choices or were actively already doing so.

'Obviously I want [him] to fulfil his potential, but that is much further down my agenda now, on my list of priorities, because I think that [he is] so much more confident.'

For one parent, although happy and convinced the College suited her child exceptionally well, admitted she was finding it difficult not knowing what could lie in store for her daughter, saying: *'I think like every mum, it is just wanting that crystal ball thing – I would just like to know what she is going to do when she leaves here.'* She then added that as long as her daughter was progressing, that would be enough to assure her.

Outside of the College, and in other areas of their lives, the students were seen to self-manage their own social lives and financial situations. Confidence, again, was a major factor and it was maintained that the College's influence contributed to their new-found self assurance.

Being asked to elaborate on this, one parent deliberated:

'I suppose from [the students'] point of view, it is a sort of inspiration because whatever they want to do, a way is found for them. So, they start thinking that most things are actually possible. Whereas the other way is that nothing is possible, and everything is too hard … and then you just get "I can't do this, I can't do that."'

Follow-up study of former students of SML College

This section contains extracts from an independent research study by Freedman, 2019. The study is still continuing at the time of writing, but the researcher believes that the evidence collected so far is quite conclusive in the areas that are covered in this report (Freedman, 2019). Part 1 of Freedman's research was based on a questionnaire-based study. In his Part 2 (discussed here) he has been conducting interviews with past students, generally those who have left some years ago.

The main reason for the research has been to test our assertions that the experience of Self Managed Learning has positive effects after the individuals have left the College. Like other research cited it has been important to have the study carried out by someone independent of the College.

In summary, the evidence is hugely positive. In the small number of examples where ex-students were less positive there were no negative effects of attending the College. All this compares with research on school leavers, many of whom report significant long-term damage from attending school (see, for example, the evidence already cited on the damaging effects of bullying and of the negative impact on individuals' careers through schooling). The opening lines of the report are as follows:

> SML College is an environment for learning which operates almost entirely counter to the prevailing logic of the educational mainstream. Its stated aim is simple: 'Preparing young people for the test of life not a life of tests.' This study seeks to provide an answer to the question: Has Self Managed Learning College been successful in its aim?
>
> The simple answer is yes. Evidence from survey responses and in-depth follow up interviews demonstrates an overwhelming majority of successes defined by any measure. This is despite a student intake which contained a disproportionately high number of additional support needs, some of whom had been written off by mainstream education.
>
> While it is impossible to know how students would have fared had they not attended the college, their responses demonstrate that in their view SML College almost always had a positive, and in some cases transformative, effect on their lives. This effect was most pronounced in students who arrived with profound psychological needs, but was present across the sample. What is it about SML College that made this possible?

Freedman later comments:

> The hypothesis that it was often the negative experience of school that caused issues, rather than the other way around, is supported by interview data; of the students interviewed who suffered from depression and/or anxiety, all of them attributed the development of their mental health issues to their experiences in school. One explained, '… it was all of it from going to the school. Bullying was the biggest part. I was fine and happy at home.'
>
> Further support for the idea that the experience of school was a significant cause of these issues is provided by the simple fact that young people and their families expected, or at the very least hoped, that leaving school and joining the SML College would help to address them. In many cases this expectation was proved correct.

The core of Freedman's report is around what he labelled, 'Life After SML College'. Here are extracts from that section of his report:

> Evidence suggests that for a significant number of students it was attendance at SML College which enabled them to get to a point where they were able to attend further education or sixth form college. In some cases this meant facilitating

the development of the emotional and psychological wellbeing needed for further education; in others this meant support in achieving the necessary qualifications, in others it meant support preparing applications, for some it was a combination of such factors, and for a few it meant facilitating the identification of new interests which motivated young people to continue studying.

Interestingly, of the five students who had not continued to pursue further education, four are currently engaged in work they love, and two are operating at a level which far surpasses the norm for young people of their ages. One (aged 18) is head of tech for a research and development company, one (aged 19) is the production manager for an events management company which organises major UK festivals, one (aged 26) is playing in bands, running events and teaching music, and one (aged 22) is a pub supervisor, a job she does because it is fun. With the right attitude and support, further education is not necessary for an excellent work life. The remaining twelve in-work ex-students are in a diverse range of occupations; two carers, two designers, two shop assistants, a psychiatric nurse, a plumber, a chef, an SEO specialist, a sound engineer, and a PR specialist for a charity. Are there any identifiable patterns in the work choices of ex-students? It does seem that there is a tendency towards creative (5/16 or 3.125/10 compared to approx. 1/10 UK jobs) and helping professions (3/16).

In a later part of this section of the report Freedman considered issue of well-being. As I indicated in Chapters 6 and 7 on research, well-being at a young age is the most important factor in later life satisfaction so his evidence on this is important. Here are extracts from that section of the report:

Psychological Wellbeing

As detailed in Interim Report 1, the survey included a measure of psychological wellbeing taken as a combination of scores in six distinct domains; autonomy, personal growth, purpose in life, positive relations with others, environmental mastery, and self-acceptance. The intention of including this measure was not to produce data which would enable the assessment of the impact of SML College, or comparison to other groups (impossible without valid control or comparison groups beyond the scope of this study) but to identify potential trends worth exploring further in the interview phase. The two most pronounced trends warranting further exploration which emerged are discussed here. Other more subtle trends are addressed in the subsequent section.

1) In general, students appeared to have relatively high levels of psychological well-being. This is notable given the number of ex-students who had at some point been identified as having being pathologically psychologically unwell.

It is abundantly clear from both the survey and interview data that in the opinions of ex-students, attending SML College very often had a positive impact on mental health and psychological well-being, both considered globally and in terms of the sub-domains described above. In some cases, as the students themselves see it, attending meant the difference between the relatively stable and happy life they enjoy now, and the misery and mental ill-health they imagine had they not attended. Further, the positive impact on wellbeing was not limited to students who arrived with an identified affective disorder and was also described (especially in terms of impact on subdomains such as self-acceptance and purpose in life) by students with no additional support needs.

2) Students scored extremely highly in the measure of personal growth. Does this relate to the experience of the college's learning groups which emphasises detailed consideration of future aspirations and the route to achieving them?

The scores of ex-students on the personal growth domain were so phenomenally high that it was necessary to consider the possibility that this was a relic of the measurement tool rather than a reflection of the characteristics of ex-students. While the metric has been validity tested for use with younger populations, it seems fair to suggest that the items used to measure attitudes to personal growth – for example 'For me life has been a continuous process of learning changing and growth' – could cause a skew towards high scores in young populations such as this one. Though it is thus possible that part of the cause of high scores in attitudes to personal growth may be the way this domain was measured, data from the survey and interviews does indicate a very positive attitude to personal growth, both in ex-students who were highly satisfied with their lives at this time, and in those who were less so. Several explicitly connected this attitude to their time at SML College.

Freedman's next section looked at the positive influence and benefits of attending SML College. As he explained in this extract:

The forms this positive influence took can be divided into two broad domains; cognitive benefits (e.g., development of a particular skill), and non-cognitive benefits (e.g., developing confidence). Of these, non-cognitive benefits were the far more frequently mentioned category. This may be because improvements in non-cognitive domains were more common. It is also possible that this type of influence was more likely to be mentioned retrospectively because it has had a more significant influence on students' lives.

In the text below, benefits have been divided into categories. Where relevant, subgroups within each category are mentioned and a brief explanation of how the college facilitated the benefit is provided. For each category, two direct quotes from ex-students are provided to enable insight into the way students understood the positive influence of the college as well as the sources this analysis was drawn from.

Cognitive Benefits
Specific Skills / Qualification: For many students, the development of particular skills and the achievement of qualifications was an important benefit of attendance at the College. In some cases, the achievements of skills and qualifications represented huge improvements on personal and external expectations.

'It helped massively with my confidence and English and maths skills.'

'The heartfelt kind and understanding teachers helped me get my horrendous basic academic skills (English and math) up to the best level I believe was possible in the amount of time I was there.'

Attitude to learning: Frequently mentioned in parallel to specific skills were improvements in attitudes towards learning and the development of a specific passion or a general passion for learning and education. Attitudinal changes were facilitated by the lack of compulsion and freedom to choose.

'SMLC taught me to be creative by giving me the option to learn about music from really lovely people which in turn made me decide I wanted to do something in the music industry which led me to what I do now for a living, a job I absolutely love.'

'I know, appreciate and respect the value of education because it has not been forced upon me in a careless and rigid way.'

Non-Cognitive Benefits

Autonomy: Many students described benefits which coalesce around the term autonomy; the capacity to self manage, independence, responsibility and self-motivation. These developments were enabled by the self-managing process and the combination of freedom and real responsibility students are required to take for themselves and the College.

'I can say that everything I've done has been my own choice. And knowing that I have this freedom continues to inform my decisions and thus makes me very happy. I can't blame anyone else for these choices and I can't be "sour" because things haven't worked out for me.'

'I think it was really important for me to be in charge of my learning. I need flexibility a lot of the time and that wasn't at all possible in mainstream school. I'm a lot more confident in myself to be independent now.'

Sense of Self / Mental Health: SML College supported students to be and become themselves, accept themselves for who they were, and improve and maintain mental health. These processes were described as being enabled by the non-judgemental accepting atmosphere in which students felt valued, safe and secure.

'It made me feel like an actual individual rather than just another name on a sheet, I have so many good memories from SMLC.'

'I find myself to be much more emotionally mature than my peers. I know myself – who I am, what I need, what I want – much better than anyone else I know.'

Life Direction / Sense of Purpose: For several students, SML College supported the development of a clear sense of direction and purpose in life, either in terms of a short or long term strategy or in terms of a specific passion to pursue. In both cases, it was the combination of freedom and support which facilitated this benefit.

> 'It allowed me to focus on what I wanted to do with my life and provided support for that.'

> 'Helped me to make a strategy for my future.'

Social Skills: The most frequently mentioned benefit was the opportunity to make friends and develop social skills. For many individuals, this was absolutely the most important thing they needed at that point in their lives. The atmosphere of the College combined with the freedom of choice and movement facilitated the development social skills and making friends.

> 'SMLC provided a safe environment in which I could learn and enjoy social interactions.'

> 'I think socialising was the biggest and most positive thing I got out of my experience.'

Self Efficacy: One of the most commonly mentioned benefits was improvements in confidence and self-efficacy. It seems likely that this improvement was mediated by some combination of all the factors mentioned above, with the relative contribution of each depending on the individual.

> 'It helped me to be confident in being myself and knowing that I was free to be interested in and love whatever I want.'

> 'Although I don't think I got a lot out of SMLC academically, I think it really helped me to increase my confidence and connect back into society after having been very isolated.'

Freedman identified a small minority for whom the College did not work out. This example from an interview is indicative:

INTERVIEWER: How did you relate then to the idea of managing your own learning?
EX STUDENT: Oh I can't.
INTERVIEWER: It seems like you were still expecting the learning advisors to manage your learning for you.
EX STUDENT: Yeah.

In an earlier discussion of internal versus external locus of control it could be interpreted that this student had an external locus of control. They expected others to make things happen and the notion of freedom was unwelcome.

Freedman commented:

> Students may have moved out of the physical space of mainstream education, but their mentality towards learning, education, and adults involved in these

processes did not always immediately change. For some students, this meant a process of transition or de-schooling, characterised by initial struggles with freedom, which ultimately resulted in positive and often transformative experiences of self managed learning. However, for a minority it seems that maintaining a 'schooled' mindset in an environment whose principles and practise did not match this mindset was problematic.

Locus of control issues

Our experience has been that there have been, over the years, a small minority of students who were under the significant influence of their schooling, their parents, their peer group outside the College and the media – all of which have promoted an external locus of control. They still focus on someone doing things for them and especially wanting adults to tell them what to learn and how to lead their lives. If learning does not happen 'properly', then someone else is always to blame.

Locus of control seems to be a pertinent theoretical framework to explain some issues that we face. Clearly, we are explicitly promoting the value of an internal locus of control. The idea of self managing is about the person taking charge of their own life and not expecting others to make decisions for them.

One interesting example of this influence is that of a student who came in one day saying that she felt stressed. This girl was taking six subjects at GCSE and was progressing on track as far as the relevant learning advisers were concerned. She had left school at the start of year 10 (the year before she would take her GCSEs) and the comments she made were at the end of year 10 when her friends in school had been taking mock exams. They were all stressed out with the pressure and had made this plain in meeting with her. She then started to feel that she must be behind in her learning as she had not been feeling pressurised and stressed. This prompted her to feel anxious about how she was doing. The learning advisers commented that it took quite a bit of explaining to her that she was doing fine and that there was no need to get stressed. In the end she took and passed all her exams with very good grades – generally better than her peer group from school. This kind of result is supported by the research of Whyte (1978) that students with a more internal locus of control perform better in higher education in terms of academic results.

I have to acknowledge that our students live in a world which says that what we are doing does not make sense. The messages to young people can be about having an external locus of control and we can't have our heads in the sand and ignore this influence. It does make me feel bad that sometimes we haven't managed to help a few students to make the breakthrough. One factor, though, is that we have no evidence of doing harm to any of this minority. In that sense we meet a kind of Hippocratic measure – 'first do no harm' – and that this is better than the influences of school on many young people. We also have evidence from parents who have made their student leave and go to school. They have said that the young person has shown more personal commitment to their own goals in school and their personal motivation to learn has improved.

Here is an email sent in January 2020 by a parent who was not keen on the SML approach but reluctantly sent her son to us following problems in school. She returned him to another school as she was concerned that he was not progressing rapidly enough with us.

> I just wanted to write a letter of appreciation to you all and generally for the existence of SML College. Fin gained something priceless from his time there that has made his transition back to mainstream school easy. He returned with a confidence that I couldn't imagine him having before his year and a half at SML College. And despite some quite hefty knocks in the beginning he has maintained a sense of self-assurance that I attribute completely to the time he had there and the space he had to find himself and his way of learning. He approaches learning differently and with a sense that it is achievable – not a panicked sense of being overwhelmed and bored simultaneously! He is flourishing in English and, much to my astonishment, maths. Having missed a year in mainstream I expected him to be behind – but, and this is what strikes me the most, he doesn't seem to be 'behind' in any of the subjects, even ones he didn't give a second of thought or attention to for his entire time away. It's true that he isn't achieving his 'expected target' but he is engaging and learning and this is a big big change from the situation when he left school in year 7, and much more valuable.
>
> I thought it might be useful for other parents who may be worried that their children aren't doing enough with their time at SML College … it appears that when he did apply himself, it went in. And that is gold.

This is an example where the student did move from an external to an internal locus of control but we have to admit that there have been a few, as cited by Freedman, who didn't stick it for long enough to make the switch and for whom all the external influences were too much for us to deal with.

Be that as it may, the fact that most students who arrive with an external locus of control do change to a more internal mode is really encouraging. We should note though that, as Rotter (1975) – the inventor of the model – indicates, this is more of a spectrum than a sharp distinction between two modes.

Wallston and Wallston (1978) show significant benefits for more internally focused individuals and therefore suggest 'training' to help people to change. I would obviously say that it's learning that is the issue and instructional modes have not been shown to be successful. If we are then to encourage a more internal locus of control it's worth summarising the research evidence on the impact of locus of control.

Wallston and Wallston (1978) have indicated particular potential health benefits of a more internal locus of control. Research evidence has included:

- smoking cessation (internals are less likely to smoke and those that have been smokers were more likely to respond to evidence to give up)
- birth control – internal single females were more likely to use contraceptives
- seat belt use

- dental care
- weight loss.

The Wikipedia entry on Locus of Control[3] covers later research, with an excellent summary of other benefits from an internal locus of control. These include (for internals):

- less likely to suffer from stress
- less likely to be depressed
- more likely to take positive action to change an unsatisfactory job
- higher self esteem.

For us one relevant piece of British research found that an internal locus of control at age 10 predicted that the person would be less likely to be over-weight at age 30. Given the negative health implications of obesity, this is really important.

The evidence, then, points to the value of an internal locus of control – especially alongside related qualities such as higher self efficacy. It confirms our view that we should encourage a self managing attitude to life. It also explains where young people with an external locus of control may prefer school-like instruction – and why there may be some who just don't get it during their brief time with us. My worry is that the research evidence suggests that maintaining an external locus of control (as schools tend to promote) can have a negative effect on the person's life. Another reason for a New Educational Paradigm.

Conclusion

The research now available on Self Managed Learning as used for young people is quite extensive and, I believe, conclusive. The process works in the way that we predicted it would. When I say that it is as predicted, I recognise that proponents of the existing schooling paradigm would presumably make different predictions as to the outcomes of what they do. The fact that schooling is not working for large numbers of young people seems to be accepted as collateral damage in a system designed for sifting out the supposedly less able from the more able via a punitive testing regime. For those with no real interest in social justice, the existing paradigm is presumably judged to be perfectly fine, and I acknowledge that it is not easy to change people's minds on this. However, for those who proclaim a desire for social justice for young people, I would hope that they might start to pay attention to the evidence and consider the need for a New Educational Paradigm.

Notes

1 For the school cases, see selfmanagedlearnng.org/for-young-people/ (accessed 03/10/19).
2 These are taken from the independent research studies.
3 https://en.wikipedia.org/wiki/Locus_of_control (accessed 04/01/2020).

References

Capps, J. (2014) An enquiry into learning groups within a Self Managed Learning environment and how past students perceive this approach to have developed their ability to self manage within the context of their current vocation. Brighton: University of Brighton.

Dufflen, T. (2010) How does the physical environment of a Self Managed Learning centre enhance the learning experience of students who have previously struggled in mainstream schooling. Brighton: University of Brighton.

Edmonds, N. (2015) An enquiry from the trial week which supports and promotes plans/strategies to allow students aged 9 to 16 deal with transitions from mainstream school to an Open Learning College. Brighton: University of Brighton.

Freedman, L. (2019) The Self Managed Learning College Study, Interim Report 2. Sussex: Self Managed Learning College.

Mathews, C. (2016) An enquiry into how the role of self-motivation in sustained by previous students who attended a Self Managed Learning environment. Brighton: University of Brighton.

Mayes, S. (2008) Parents' views of South Downs Learning Centre [now SML College]. Brighton: University of Brighton.

Mehtola, J. (2013) An enquiry into students' perceptions of learning within a Self Managed Learning environment. Brighton: University of Brighton.

Rotter, J. B. (1975) Some problems and misconceptions related to the construct of internal versus external control of reinforcements. *Journal of Consulting and Clinical Psychology*, 43 (4), 489–493.

Sankey, N. (2008) Student experiences of Self Managed Learning. Brighton: University of Brighton.

Wallston, B. S. and Wallston, K. A. (1978) Locus of control and health: A review of the literature. *Health Education Monographs*, Spring 6(2), 107–117.

Whyte, C. B. (1978) Effective counselling methods for high-risk college freshmen. *Measurement and Evaluation in Guidance*, 6(4), 198–200.

Worley, L. (2015) An enquiry into the students' perceived outcomes of the process of restorative justice that resides in an alternative education provider. Brighton: University of Brighton.

9

THE ROLES OF ADULTS

Introduction

As I have shown in earlier chapters, there are many influences on young learners. Research evidence proves that generally the peer group is the most influential, especially for teenagers, but that does not mean that adults have no role (Blakemore, 2018). It is apparent that some critics of approaches such as ours would tend to assume that young people are left to their own devices without any support, just because we don't use classrooms, fixed lessons and imposed timetables. However, nothing could be further from the truth. It is especially important that adults create the structures and processes which can provide an anchor for learning.

Given that the peer group is so important, it is crucial to create an environment where the peer group operates in a positive and fulfilling way rather than in a negative way, for instance, like violent gangs and where risky behaviour can be encouraged through group pressure (for example, drugs) to the detriment of individuals. Paradoxically, in schools which have very controlling structures, they often know little about what is going on amongst young people, as we have found from working in schools. We are often given young people to work with because those in authority are confused about their behaviour and have a sense that the person is not learning anything. We usually discover, through the process of learning groups and the structure of using the learning agreement, a great deal more about an individual than the school has discovered in three or four years.

My case, then, is that adults have to play an important role, but the question is what kind of role and how we can best help in the personal development of the individual. There is a major influence of adults outside our College – not just parents but other family members, people in the local communities and other adults young people meet through social activities such as playing sports. We know that all of these can have an influence on the growing young person. We, therefore, have to locate our role within that context; we cannot ignore, for instance, the role of parents.

Hence, we have one structure where we have a meeting with parents, one of the staff and the student every term so that there can be a discussion about the overall development for the young person. We also have termly parent meetings at which we can talk about what we are doing, so that parents can be better informed. In addition to this, parents can be in touch at any time with staff, especially the learning group adviser for their student, as well as the Coordinator within the college.

Staff roles

The first part of this chapter is about what could be called staff roles. I use the term 'roles' (plural) here because it is not just one role. In a school it is much easier to identify a subject teacher as having a particular role to teach their subject to a class of students. And within that there may be subsidiary roles that they take on within the school. Our situation is obviously considerably different given that we don't have class teaching.

The notion of 'staff' is common in schools and I have used this term in the heading. In reality, we don't have staff in the way that schools see the role. Hence, I will need to explain in this chapter what our arrangements are for adults to support the learning of young people.

My own doctoral research[1] was a great deal on roles that are played by those who are assisting learners to learn. I developed a five-factor model, which is shown here.

The four outer circle roles (see Figure 9.1) are discussed below. The centre circle represents the integrative dimension. This latter is about ensuring coherence between the four roles. It is essential that the values and beliefs underpinning all activities are in sync. Argyris (1990) is very good at showing that often in organisations there is a mismatch between 'espoused theory' and 'theory in use'. For instance, if our theoretical base is in a caring, learner-centred mode, but then staff bully students, there is a clear mismatch. If the model could be represented in 3D then the integrative dimension would sit over the top of the other four.

Organisationally, it is my role, alongside that of the Trustees, to act as guardians of the fundamental values and beliefs about Self Managed Learning. It is apparent that many alternative schools have failed by not sticking to their fundamental values and beliefs. One area has been when parents do not buy into these values and beliefs. For instance, at least one school I know of failed because it tried to be all things to all parents. Over time they became less learner-centred and more like traditional schools. This meant that it no longer provided for the needs of many students, and parents who wanted a more learner-centred approach pulled out. The school fell between a radical alternative and a place that was closer to a standard school. In the end it did not have enough students to continue and so it closed. It is crucial to stick with basic values and beliefs about the nature of learning and of appropriate social arrangements to meet the needs of young people.

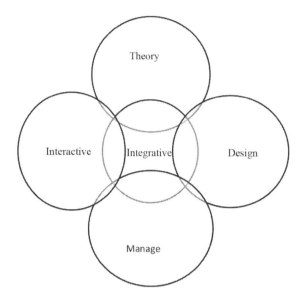

FIGURE 9.1 Model of roles

I get criticised every so often for being too rigid and uncompromising. Parents sometimes say, 'English and maths are crucial so we would like that, at least in these subjects, students are taught them and made to learn them.' My response of, 'As you know, this is Self Managed Learning so we will never impose any teaching on young people,' does not go down well with those parents, and I am accused of uncaring rigidity and a lack of response to parental needs. I see it as my role not to respond to the wishes of parents who do not understand what we are doing. I am always clear that if their views are in favour of enforced teaching, traditional schools are available to them. The problem is that often such parents have tried traditional schools and they have failed them and their offspring. They seem to want something that is a bit nicer than school, but based on the same principles of enforced teaching. Unfortunately, the influence of Government, local authorities, schools and the media all point to an enforcement model, so it is not surprising that parents struggle with the misinformation that they are provided by supposed experts.

Four basic roles

I want to make the case here that there are four basic roles needed to make a learning programme work effectively. These roles are linked to particular processes that are essential. These processes are described as follows. Firstly, action is based on appropriate theory. I'm using the notion of theory in quite a broad sense, but every learning programme is based on a theory of some sort. In school this is largely based on a theory of teaching and also, as part of that, there are theoretical assumptions about having a curriculum. Also, the idea of testing and assessment is

all part of a theory about how to make children learn through a compulsory educational programme. Self Managed Learning is based on a different kind of theory.

The second process is designing programmes and activities. School is designed
on the basis of classrooms and the associated idea of a class of pupils. Part of the
design is a hierarchy, with generally a principal or head at the top and various other
people undertaking activity within the school. Self Managed Learning is based on a
different kind of design.

The third process is how to manage all this. In school the traditional model is for
a principal or head to be a leader but that administrative duties may be carried out
by other people, such as a secretary or a finance officer.

The fourth and last role is that of interacting with learners. This is assumed to be
largely a teaching mode in traditional school, although there are other roles such as
teaching assistants in English schools and often there are counsellors, mentors and
others who interact with the pupils. Self Managed Learning has a different model.

I will now need to take each of these in turn to say little bit more about what is
required in each of these roles. I'm suggesting that it is both necessary and sufficient
to have these four roles carried out, so long as they are also integrated. If you miss
one, the process may not work very well. Some more idealistic alternative education programmes have, for instance, assumed that you can get away without
managerial roles and that somehow things will happen, even though money has to
come in, resources have to be bought, and so on. It is quite clear that that sort of
utopian notion – that you don't need a management, administration and leadership
function – is a delusion and many of the 1960s and 1970s alternatives failed because
of this. Summerhill School has survived for so long because A. S. Neil, and then
his wife, and after that his daughter have been strong, influential leaders.

Theory

Effective practitioners are able to articulate the theory that is the basis of their
professional activities. In the context of the College we are clear about specific
learning theories that underpin what we set out to do. Some have been indicated
in earlier chapters, such as the role of a process curriculum. Our theory about the
future nature of work has an impact, as does our theory of first and second order
learning. We work from the theory of Self Managed Learning and why that should
be the basis of the College.

We attempt as much as possible to make our theoretical basis as transparent and
clear as possible. This is not necessarily true in traditional schools, where there is a
kind of implicit theory, but much of it is not made explicit. Nor is there a link
between the theoretical assumptions and evidence. Hence the unscientific nature of
the theoretical assumptions that underpin traditional schooling.

I have been clear that the theoretical basis of Self Managed Learning has come
from bringing together a range of positions on learning. In thinking about a New
Educational Paradigm, I suggest that there are some common features of projects
and programmes that currently exist. One of the important dimensions is, for

instance, the recognition of particular concepts such as autonomy and freedom for students: that is to say, who has the power to make what decisions and what rights should young people have.

There are some important threads connecting schools and other organisations around the world. The International Democratic Education Conference (IDEC) is one such connecting process. In Britain, the Freedom to Learn network and the Centre for Personalised Education are examples of organisations where people come together under a common desire to promote a model of learning that challenges authoritarian schooling. What is common to these organisations are particular values and beliefs that underpin the learning process. What is different is in relation to the design of such programmes. For instance, schools like Summerhill School in England have a curriculum but the students are not made to attend classes; they have complete freedom as to what and how they learn. Also, Summerhill is unusual in being a boarding school. This automatically leads to a different design of the learning process.

Design

I take design to be the process whereby the theory is fleshed out in order to provide a basis for action. It is used in a metaphorical sense, since one does not literally design a product. Programmes and processes are not, in that sense, things that are designed; however, it is a term that is commonly used, and it does make sense to think about it as design.

There are two parts to designing:

Macro designing is about having the strategic capability to design total processes. The requirements here are to think strategically and to implement theory in practical ways. In the College there was a clear basis to the macro design from day one. We set out to create learning groups with learning agreements for all students within a supportive community. Our design has been deliberately different from that of schools by not having classrooms, imposed lessons and imposed timetables. We had to consider the whole programme and the interplay of the various factors in the design.

Micro designing is about creating specific processes. For instance, the learning agreement is part of the macro design and then the actual structure of it, including the Five Questions, is part of the micro design. Learning groups have a structure such as the agreement by the group about its own rules. Also, the notion of each person having their own time to talk about any needs they have is a micro design decision.

Constraints in this area included resourcing factors: annual budgets have to be met and we have had to work around constraints of the building.

It could be argued that these first two roles are, or could be, largely paper exercises or brain exercises. By that I mean that when we were starting the College, there were no students or other adults involved. I worked on the theory and design aspects, which we then talked about with parents and others, and eventually created the

College based on the theory and design aspects discussed in this book. The theory has not changed over time, but there have been some design modifications, especially in the micro design. For instance, when we started, we just gave students space to learn in any way they wanted, and we had no particular structure to the week, apart from a daily community meeting and a learning group meeting each week.

As we progressed, it became evident, through discussion with students, that we might fruitfully do some redesign. We experimented with students being supported in writing a kind of timetable for each morning of the week. It was almost as a replacement for a school timetable, but one that they wrote with our help, and it was looser. That seemed a bit rigid, so we have dispensed with that (unless students want to do it, which is rare) but rather try to think in terms of activities of learning that the person wants to undertake in the week so that each week individuals make some plans and then the learning group meeting, a week later, reviews those.

This approach to designing structuring is based on a particular way of thinking that I have found useful.

In Figure 9.2 I have represented two approaches to designing. First we can consider the first drawing with curved lines. After the Second World War the UK Government created New Towns. These were artificially created in selected locations in order to meet the needs for new housing. The designers of these New Towns often arranged for what they saw as a nice planned area in the town centre with carefully pre-designed walkways.

The first diagram in Figure 9.2 represents the kind of layout that was created. The problem is that people generally prefer to walk in straight lines to minimise the time to get from one place to another. So, they did this and did not stick to the designated paths. The management then started to put in fences to try to keep people to the paths.

The second diagram shows how paths were created in another New Town. The managers of the New Town grassed over an area in the middle of the town and left it grassy. People walked on it and in their own ways. Gradually, the grass became worn and, in the winter, slightly muddy in places where it was well used. It was then that the paths were put in on the areas where the grass had been worn and made muddy. So, these paved paths, as indicated in the diagram, were in response to how real people in the real situation actually moved across the space.

This is my analogy about how to create organisational structures. It could be argued that this is more democratic, if one wants to use that term, or more anarchic in the sense that initially no one was in charge of creating the paths. It was left entirely to individuals to walk where they wished across the grassed area, and then the role of management was to respond to what people were doing by putting in paving where it was needed.

An example of this in the case of the College was when we moved from renting premises in a Youth Centre to our own premises. I arranged for all the resources, materials, desks, chairs, and so on to be put into the largest room and left there. On the first day of the new term, we then held a discussion in the room. The 'we' is the adults and the young people. We discussed where we should put the different

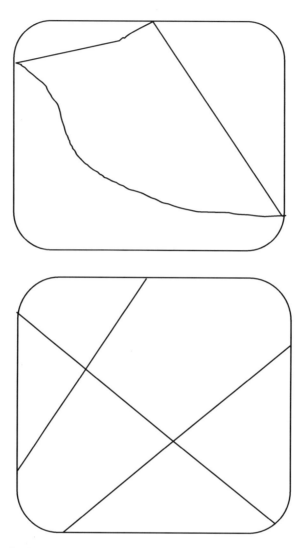

FIGURE 9.2 Designing a space

resources and what each room might be used for. I had some general ideas like having one end of the building as a quieter area and the other end as a less quiet area where, for instance, the music room would go.

A plan was generally agreed, and we set to work – all of us – in moving things to where it made sense for students and for adults. We also had to name the rooms in relation to what was going on in the room and it seemed to me, and was agreed by everybody, that the youngest group would take on that task and design labels to go on each of the rooms. They came up with some interesting ideas. The only banal one was to label the office, the office. Otherwise one quiet room was named after a TV character, another room, which is a small room where students can chill out, was called Bob. I have no idea why it was called Bob, but that is what it is now called.

This approach is based on the same model as the kind of non-design of a series of paths across a grassy area. Too often, adults feel that they need to decide on arrangements of this nature and young people have to fit in. I've seen some appalling new schools where clearly the architect has been going for a prize-winning design, but which was not at all popular with the pupils in the new school.

Another example of more open micro design is the notion that students can talk about anything in their learning group and they can put anything in their learning agreement, so long as they answer those five questions that we put to them. We do not need to control the process and indeed it would hinder any student's learning if we interfered inappropriately.

Manage

Here again the role can be divided into two:

Leading the programme has been important and different people have provided this leadership function. I set up the College, but others worked on specifics. Aspects such as selling, marketing and recruitment have been increasingly shared. At the start I fulfilled the marketing and recruitment role whereas now we have a marketing consultant assisting us with this work.

The charity has trustees, who are technically also directors of the company (we are a company limited by guarantee – a very English structure that limits trustees' financial liability, while providing a legally compliant structure). Trustees are responsible for the overall operations of the charity. I used to chair the trustees, but when we created the College, I stepped down to chair the governing body of the College (the latter is only one aspect of the work of the charity – the Centre for Self Managed Learning).

Incidentally, the creation of the governing body is another example of an evolving design. Initially, we had a management committee for the College consisting of all adults who worked in the College along with a couple of outsiders. As we progressed, and had more interaction with the educational establishment and with schools, it seemed apposite to create a body that could face-off to school governing bodies so that we could look structurally like a school but within our operations could be different. So, we created a governing body with a representative from each constituency that we recognise, namely students, staff and parents. In addition, we have representation from the local community, the business world, a parent of a former student, and those with expertise in learning. The major difference from schools is that the student representative has the same speaking and voting rights as everyone else.

Administering a programme is also crucial. Budgets have to be managed, systems created and managed, emails answered, files kept, and so on. Just because we don't follow the processes of schools, and other institutions, does not mean that we can ignore practical administrative activity. Initially, I did all this work, but now we have a finance officer working part-time for us and also a co-ordinator, who is our only full-time employee, and who manages the College on a day-to-day basis.

The efficient management of current projects is absolutely vital, as are the other three roles. However, it is one that can sometimes be neglected as a bureaucratic chore, even though it is crucial that budgeting is done effectively.

However, effective budgeting does not necessarily mean control by adults. We have a Joint Resources Committee as a new element in the design, which has been added as we developed, and where it's been important to start involving others more widely in the administration of budgets. Each learning group sends a representative to this committee, which is chaired by the co-ordinator, and another staff member is also on the committee. This committee has power to handle budget decisions such as for learning resources, cleaning and maintenance, trips, and food and drink.

At an early meeting of the committee, everyone could see that we had had to budget for quite a large amount of cleaning and maintenance. It was agreed that day-to-day cleaning would be carried out by students. Therefore, we only need to pay for professional cleaning every half term. The money saved was then allocated to the food and drinks budget, so that everything in the kitchen could be freely available to students at no cost. This includes tea, coffee, hot chocolate and bread-and-butter, and so on, so that all students can at least get basic food and drink throughout the morning. This is especially important for students who fail to get a proper breakfast before they come to the College.

This is another example of a changed design element. By having this new committee instead of the governors dealing with these budgets, it ensures fair and open decisions on relevant aspects of our finances.

Interact

Interacting with learners is often the most visible part of developmental activity. I will comment more on this below as this dimension raises some specific issues for educational professionals.

Note that the four circles or segments interact and overlap. Also, they need to be brought together in a harmonious whole. It's no use getting three out of the four right – all four have to work together. All are necessary and sufficient to make a programme work. I have tested this over the last 30 or so years and the model stands up. Note that it is a general model that is applicable to any organised activity of this nature and not just our College.

The interactive roles in learning

Ideally, learning needs to start with what I have called the 'P MODE'.
    P stands for:

- PERSONS – we need to understand the person if we are to assist their learning. Each person is different, and they have different needs.
- PATTERNS – each person will have patterns of behaviour and of thinking.
- PROCESSES – each person has their own processes of working and living.

- PROBLEMS – one way of thinking of learning is as a solution to a problem. For example, if you can't speak French and you need to, then you have a problem and the solution is to learn French. Or if you need to write well to progress in life and work then the solution is to learn to write well. And so on.

Note that in the latter examples, problems come before solutions. The process of writing a learning agreement could be seen as 'problem creating'. By this I mean that the person identifies what they can do now – for instance, basic arithmetic – and then may choose to aim for learning maths in order to pass the GCSE in the subject. Hence, they have created a problem for themselves. They could decide that they are happy just being able to do arithmetic, and that they do not want to get a GCSE in maths. Then they do not have a problem, unless at some stage they want to do a degree, which requires maths at GCSE level. They could decide not to go to university (so there isn't a problem) or they may then decide to create a problem for themselves by learning maths to GCSE level.

In our approach, the P MODE comes before the S MODE.

The S MODE stands for:

- SOLUTIONS – to respond to the person and their problems, there may be a need to look for solutions
- SUBJECTS – subject knowledge may help to meet the 'P' needs
- SKILLS – may be needed to progress
- SPECIALISATIONS – may contribute

as may

- SYSTEMS – such as IT systems.

Institutional education too often starts with 'S' – people have imposed on them Subject knowledge and Solutions to Problems that they have not yet formulated. Or the Solution distorts the way the Problem is tackled. By learning being seen as about Subjects it distorts how people are encouraged to view the world. Ecological thinking requires thinking about connections. Our environmental problems are created by silo thinking that creates the idea that you can change one aspect of our environment and not consider the other effects. For instance, the use of cars for the school run has increased over time.[2] In looking at the analysis by the Government in the UK one aspect is missing, namely that schools have been increasing in size and small rural schools have been closing, so parents have to resort to the car to get their offspring to school. This kind of silo thinking, whereby the increase in school size is not factored into policy decisions, is disastrous.

In the College we spend much of the first week finding out about each new student. The first of the Five Questions tells us ('us', note, includes others in the community – staff and students) about the person's past experiences and how they have shaped the person now. The second question tells us how the person sees themself now and the third question indicates the directions possible for their future. The fourth question proposes the way to bridge the gap from where the person is now to where they want to be – and this indicates modes of learning that are appropriate. The last question indicates how the student would know that they have achieved what they wanted. All of this tells us not just about the person's knowledge, skills and capabilities but also about their values (what they care about) and their beliefs (what they hold to be true).

So, in thinking of the role of staff, we start in the 'P' Mode. Once learners are clearer about what they want to learn, and how they want to learn it, they are likely to need to draw on expertise in the 'S' mode. In the past teachers might have been seen as the main source of 'S' learning. Now we have the vast array of material on the internet and the use of teachers changes. Our 57 varieties of learning come to the fore in addressing the fourth question about how to learn.

All of the adults I have called staff. We prefer to call them 'learning advisers'. Actually, I prefer the term 'learning assistants', because that's what we are here to do – to assist learners to learn. However, other adults get concerned that the term 'learning assistant' is low in status and could be mistaken for teaching assistants in school. Teaching assistants are often perceived to be subservient to the proper professionals and therefore not seen as having a status role. (In reality, we have found a lot of teaching assistants in schools are wonderful in understanding students better than the teachers and are great to work with.)

We have, then, one learning adviser attached to support each learning group. We call that role the learning group adviser. The learning group adviser is the key person to work with a group of six students on understanding the Person from that P mode position. It is the role of the learning group adviser to really know all six students in the group. The focus is on a holistic understanding of the young Person – the kind of Patterns of behaviour they have and the Processes by which they think. Learning group advisers need to help them to create good Problems through the process of answering the Five Questions. It is the learning group adviser who would typically meet with parents at the end of each term, along with the student, to discuss general learning issues relevant to that individual.

The learning group adviser does not need any particular subject expertise or skills to offer to the students. As an example, when I work in organisations with senior leaders, I'm often not at all au fait with the particular work that the individuals in the group do. For instance, in a recent programme to develop senior leaders in a university I had professors in the group heading up research teams doing high-level, complex work that I could not understand at all. That was not an issue. My role was to assist the people in the group to learn whatever they needed. It did not need me to deliver anything to them; for instance, when they all said they wanted to know more about the finances of the university, we invited to the group the finance director so that he could answer their questions. My role was to help them to clarify what they needed to learn; that's one of the most important things that I do.

It's important that the learning group adviser has a sense of the totality of what each individual student is working on. If the student then needs to learn, say a Skill, the learning group adviser can point them in the appropriate direction. Classically where individuals, for instance, want to learn particular Subjects, then we have subject specialists in the team. If I'm working with a student and they want to learn music, I can talk to our music learning adviser about meeting with the student to go into that or if they want to study Shakespeare, I can pass them on to our Shakespeare expert.

In recruiting learning advisers, we are keen that they can offer a number of things to individual students. Indeed, we post up information about each of us adults who work in the college, as well as introducing ourselves in the community meetings, so that students can take their own initiatives in approaching adults. However, sometimes students need help from the learning group. So, the learning group adviser has to know all the people on the team so that they know who they can go to if needed.

When I am providing my services as a learning adviser, it might well be helping a student with some writing or I might help them with science, since I have a science background and a chemistry degree. I might teach students Tai Ji, since that is something that might interest a group.

Offerings in the S mode could be from adults who are not part of the learning community. One girl in the group that I was working with wanted to be an actor. I discussed with her in the group about if she had a plan B. She said that she didn't, that she wanted to act and nothing else. So I found the figures from Equity, the actors' union, that showed that at any one time, the vast majority of its members were not actually acting but were waiting on tables or sitting at home waiting for the phone call. In the end she came to the conclusion that she might like to develop a skill as a backup and she thought maybe decorating cakes for birthdays, weddings and such like could be possible. I knew of a local person called Veronica, who was brilliant at providing birthday cakes for my daughter. I therefore contacted Veronica and asked if she would be prepared to come in and show the girl something about cake decorating. She agreed to that and brought in her equipment, including a recipe and ingredients to make gluten-free brownies, as she indicated that gluten-free food was a growing need.

She came in and did not just work with our acting girl, but also with other students who took an interest in it. They took over the kitchen and she showed them how to make particular decorations, such as flowers, out of icing. Veronica came in in the S mode: she was providing a particular Skill and a Specialism that she could offer. We draw on lots of people in our local area to offer such S mode support. Sometimes this means that the person comes to visit us, but it also might mean that we go out on a visit to see what other people are doing.

For instance, a recent example was a couple of students who were interested in architecture. A group went to an architect's office and had a whole morning session with an experienced architect. Again, the architect was offering their Subject knowledge and their Specialisation to help students to think about what would be useful. Therefore, it does not require us to have meetings on site.

When we started the College with 12 students in my house, there was just me and two learning group advisers, who also had to carry out the S role alongside the P role. It worked pretty well, though we did draw on resources from the local community to help us and students used a variety of resources beyond working with another adult. One example of that is of students working together engaging in mutual learning. Sometimes a student who is knowledgeable in some area might run a workshop for other students to learn more about that. Of course there are also students who just want to use other resources such as books and the internet to learn a subject and they, therefore, may rarely feel the need to call on staff, other than the learning group adviser.

Conclusion

In this chapter I have introduced the idea of different roles for adults in working with young people. I've restricted most of my comments to people working within the remit of SML College. I have not talked specifically about the role of parents and other adults who individuals will work with. However, I recognise that these other adults will also influence students' learning along with other influences from the media, and so on. However, I've pointed out that we make certain that we meet each term with the relevant parent or carer and the individual student in order to talk through issues about the role of the parent/carer. Since parents vary widely in terms of the interest that they take in their students, we have to respond to those differences.

In identifying particular roles that are important in supporting the learning of young people, I wanted to consider the way we think about it and also to indicate that although there are separate roles, they need integrating in a coherent way to make a learning programme work. In this sense what I've covered here is relevant to any programme that is located in what I'm calling the New Educational Paradigm. I have given one example, of Summerhill School, where the fundamental philosophy of freedom of the individual is common between our College and that school, but where they use a different design for the way they run that boarding school.

While the emphasis in this chapter has been on the role of adults, I would not want it to be seen as suggesting that the adults have the premier position in influencing the learning of young people. I mentioned in earlier chapters the role of the peer group as being absolutely crucial and therefore creating a community in which students feel able to support each other's learning is central to the way we think about our College.

I've also tried to show that, whilst we might be quite rigid in our theoretical base and not open to change, we have evolved the design in the light of experience and obviously the way we manage the College has also changed over time. However, in terms of our interaction with learners that does tend to be an area where we do not compromise.

There is much that could say about developing people to undertake these roles and that discussion belongs elsewhere as it would need to go into a lot of detail. There is some reference to this in a previous text, Cunningham, 1999.

Notes

1 See I. Cunningham (1984). In the research I studied practically what I was doing working in groups on programmes without a defined curriculum. I studied others who were working on similar programmes such as action learning and synthesised the evidence alongside the known theories of learning.
2 There is plenty of evidence on car journeys for the school run. For example, from the Public Health Agency, 2017. As long ago as 2006, Moreton gave the following information for the UK: 1 billion school trips are made annually by car; 500 million litres of fuel are consumed by cars doing this; 2.1 million tons of CO_2 are emitted and 570 million hours are spent in cars on the school run.

References

Argyris, C. (1990) *Overcoming Organisational Defences: Facilitating Organisational Learning*. Boston: Allyn & Bacon.

Blakemore, S. (2018) *Inventing Ourselves: The Secret Life of the Teenage Brain*. London: Doubleday.

Cunningham, I. (1984) Teaching styles in learner centred management development. PhD thesis, University of Lancaster.

Cunningham, I. (1999) *The Wisdom of Strategic Learning*, 2nd edition. Aldershot, Hants.: Gower.

Moreton, C (2006) The school run. *The Independent*, April 30. https://www.independent.co.uk/news/uk/home-news/the-school-run-476231.html. Accessed 27/09/2019.

Public Health Agency (2017) Leave the car at home for the school run. https://www.publichealthagency.hscni.net/news/leave-car-home-school-run. Accessed 27/09/2019.

10

SOME CONCLUSIONS AND SOME DIRECTIONS

Filmore (2018) starts his piece about taking action with the following quote from John A. Shedd, 'A ship in harbour is safe, but that is not what ships are built for.' This ties in with my earlier comments about the need for 'skin in the game'. In arguing for a New Educational Paradigm I'm also arguing for the need for those of us who want to see changes in schooling to take action. There is another old saying that it is better to light one candle than just curse the darkness. The hope is that we can see a significant change in the world, though I am sure I won't live to see it personally. As late as the 19th century there was a global acceptance amongst the ruling and middle classes of slavery. Slavery was also an important part of the successes of both the Greek and Roman empires. And we still seem to look up to them, even though slavery was an accepted part of the so-called democracy in Athens. So, change can occur, and iniquitous practices can be made illegal. The treatment of young people who are called 'children', and treated as less than persons, has been improving and maybe the school system will be the next for radical change.

Meighan (2005) wrote one of his many brilliant books about 'learning systems'. To some extent I'm using the word 'paradigm' to postulate a different take on what he was getting at. However, his book is still an excellent piece. In supporting the possibility of change he cites Gerald Haigh, a former headteacher, about an optimistic possibility of a world without schools. Haigh commented:

> Fanciful nonsense? Don't be so sure. My grandparents knew about work-houses. An accepted part of the social landscape for centuries, they now seem impossibly inhumane and counterproductive. One day, school will be seen like that – a transient phenomenon destined to fade gracefully away as the forces that created them gradually lose their impetus (p. 111).

Paradoxically, there are glimmers of some recognition about the issues in the formal system. An interesting example is in the Department for Education's guidance of April 2018 about home education, in which there are some quite liberal ideas, for example:

> Children learn in different ways and at different times and speeds. It should be appreciated that parents and their children may require a period of adjustment before finding their preferred mode of learning and that families may change their approach over time. Parents are not required to have any qualifications or training to provide their children with a suitable education. It should be noted that parents from all educational, social, religious and ethnic backgrounds successfully educate children outside the school setting, and these factors should not in themselves raise a concern about the suitability of the education being provided (p. 30).

If the current Department for Education were to implement these ideas, it would be a revolution in education. It clearly states that all adults are in a position to help to educate young people and that no teacher training is required. Indeed, my argument is teacher training does great harm to many humanistic young adults who enter the teaching profession. If children do learn in different ways and at different times and speeds (which they do), then there is no justification for the existing structures in schools.

I appreciate that there is a counter argument to this level of optimism. It could be argued that we have had false dawns before and an assumption that radical change is possible. This was certainly true from about the mid-1960s to the mid-1970s. When we established the School for Independent Study in 1973 in North East London Polytechnic, certain elements in the team saw what we were doing as an opportunity to revolutionise higher education by proving that anyone could come into university, or an equivalent institution, and be helped to learn. That optimism was killed off as the Polytechnic became a university and went down the usual traditional route.

But what is interesting from what might be seen as false dawns is that those ideas have lasted. Summerhill School in England is still based on the ideas of A. S. Neill, who started his first radical free school in 1921. Those ideas have lasted; indeed we can go back much further, to our hunter gatherer ancestors who very clearly never had schools and where young people learned to be able to live effectively in the environment in which they were growing up. Schools have been a recent invention in human history. For at least 95% of the time of Homo sapiens on the planet there have been no schools. It is therefore quite conceivable to consider the world without the existing schooling system.

Of course, what many argue is that our world is not like that of the hunter gatherers. It is much more complicated. And that is true. However, we have the same genetic make-up as we had at that time. We are brilliant learning animals, and we do that without schools, colleges and universities. The connected world, at one level, offers an opportunity for people to work together globally and ignore national boundaries in promoting new ways of thinking. This is definitely what is achieved through the International Democratic Education Conference. It's a brilliant event bringing people from all over the world together every year so that we can actually understand what is going on each culture and we can help and support each other.

Apart from the Roman Catholic Church, I can't think of an institution that has lasted a long time. Certainly, companies that I've worked with have often disappeared within 10 years; they have either gone bankrupt or been taken over. However, ideas last. This is why writing books, putting up material on the internet, talking at conferences, and so on, is so crucial, because not only can we provide support for each other, but we can ensure that these ideas continue, irrespective of what official systems of government want to stop.

Plenty of writers have discussed how strange it is that some countries that say they value democracy clearly do not have a notion of a democratic approach to education, where those involved in education should have rights about their own freedom to learn in ways that are important to them, and about the things that are important to them. So democratic education is one banner that we can march behind. However, others prefer other terms and, in the UK, we have recently had the formation of a Freedom to Learn Network, where concepts of freedom have been promoted as a rallying point. I'm suggesting that a New Educational Paradigm can encompass these and other labels and badges. We need to work together to be able to keep the ideas live, even if in many countries, especially the UK, there is considerable effort to suppress any practical implementation of these ideas.

It's back to the idea of 'skin in the game' and, in a sense, the ship out on the sea taking the risks. I talked to a principal of a school in Asia that was operating illegally, and the principal was clear that he was prepared to go to prison if there was any attempt to close it. He had carefully worked with politicians and people in power, such that the school continues, but it does need some savvy to be able to deal with authorities that are committed to controlling individuals.

Having in the past had to work with politicians, I often say to people that they need to be aware that politicians are not like normal people. I know that this is a bit of an exaggeration but for me it's a useful starting hypothesis when dealing with politicians. In the UK Parliament I have certainly met so-called backbench Members of Parliament who, of course, have little power because they have to follow party rules but who have been quite enlightened. Be that as it may, people in power that I've had to have discussions with, such as politicians in the Cabinet, tend to demonstrate that the one thing that matters above all else is power. The objective always is to gain power or stay in power. They may have other things that are important to them, but ultimately being in power trumps any other values that they may have. It's something that I think is difficult for people to grasp and therefore individuals can be naive in dealing with these power systems.

Unfortunately, as well as the powerful politicians such as the Secretary of State for Education who tried to close Summerhill School, there are those lower in the hierarchy who also stand in the way of change. Most teachers find it difficult to think of any other way of working than running school in the current mode, even though we have proved to sceptical teachers in schools where we've run programmes that there is no reason why any of the pupils in the school cannot benefit from a Self Managed Learning programme or something like it. We knew that we were taking risks when we went into schools, because we might be asked to compromise on our principles. But where you have schools that either are desperate, or are keen to see something different, it is feasible to say that we will run programmes where the participants will decide for themselves about the rules of the group and the things that they want to learn. And that there will be no limits, apart from what is in the school rules, which we have to accept. However, there are ways around that, as one small example in Uckfield Community Technology College may help to show.

This was when I was working with a group of year 8 boys (namely, aged 12 and 13) who were in and out of exclusion and who were judged by the school likely to be permanently excluded by the end of the year if they carried on in their current mode. One of the things that I realised was that when they came in to school in the morning, they had either had something sugary for breakfast or had been drinking caffeine-saturated carbonated drinks, and so were generally somewhat hyper. We discussed how to deal with this, and the students suggested that they'd like to play football at the start of the day. They thought maybe an hour and I suggested 10 minutes – and we negotiated 20 minutes playing indoor football in the school gym. These were students who were at the time not in class because of their behaviour, so as we went to the gym one of the teachers challenged them as to what they were doing, also because some of them were not actually supposed to be in school due to their exclusion. The students indicated they would be going to play football. They had hurried down the corridor so I was a little behind when I overheard them replying, 'Well Professor Cunningham said it was okay.' Hence it was.

At the time I found it useful sometimes to use that title – one that I was entitled to use. Of course, professor trumps teacher regarding status, so they were able to have their football session in the gym. And they organised themselves really well into two teams of three; they also played some silly games and all I had to do was stand and watch and then call time at the agreed time. They were quite happy to agree to that and return to our meeting room, where we could then get on with other work.

I appreciate that not everyone can utilise the title of 'professor' or something similar, but what I want to argue is that we have to be creative in the way that we deal with schools, and that we need to find ways especially to help those teachers who realise the horrors of what's going on and want to change things.

Other barriers to change

In a meeting about alternatives in education an educational administrator raised the issue of the application of alternative education initiatives to the larger population.

After all, although I have shown that there are very many hundreds of what are called alternative schools or democratic schools around the world, they are clearly in a minority compared with the many thousands of traditional schools. It's one of the difficulties of establishing a new paradigm in an area where it is not subject to research evidence. It's where the analogy with science does fall down, I'm afraid, because eventually in scientific evidence people have to respond to the best available research studies. And science is, of course, not democratic. As one colleague put it, when thinking about the change of view of the atom, nobody complained that Rutherford just split one atom. Once the atom had been split, we had to accept that atoms were not the basic units of matter. It only needed one example. In social areas such as education, clearly this doesn't work.

As part of the educational administrator's critique of so-called alternatives, he alleged that these were merely 'boutique operations'. Now, many people prefer shopping in boutiques rather than online or through large stores. So, at one level, it's not an apt criticism. However, he clearly meant it as a criticism, and to say that there wasn't anything relevant in small organisations like ours for the larger educational population. I have wanted to emphasise in this book quite a bit of the evidence from schools, alongside evidence from the College, to show that it is perfectly feasible to consider a radical change in education, if research evidence is acknowledged.

I am aware that acknowledging this evidence is trickier when people have an emotional attachment to current practice. After all, teachers have been taught to teach. And they wish to teach in a classroom to a class of young people on the basis of what they have planned to offer the young people. This is what their training has trained them for.

Teachers develop an identity as a teacher through their training, including interactions with existing teachers. Part of this identity is to do with the tools that teachers use in their daily work in schools. Examples of these would be planning a lesson, keeping order in a classroom, covering the syllabus through instruction and imposing tests on pupils. These tools are part of an identity as a proactive teacher. By proactive I mean that the teacher comes up with what is to be learned, using tools such as writing, speaking in a classroom and marking work.

I want to turn to work by Weick to show how much of a problem this is. Weick (1998), and in subsequent material (Weick, 2001 and Weick, 2007), looked at situations where firefighters had lost their lives. What he found was that in a particular disaster of a major fire the firefighters had had to run for their lives to escape the spread of the fire. They were instructed to drop their tools and equipment. Those who did, survived because they were able to run faster and escape the fire. However, many did not. In the 1949 Mann Gulch disaster 13 firefighters died and they had all kept their tools. This was repeated in 1994 in Colorado, where 14 died still with their tools and in four other separate fires 23 firefighters refused orders to drop their tools and died. Note that those who obeyed the order, and dropped tools and ran, survived. The interesting thing is that it was known that firefighters need to drop the tools to survive in these situations.

Weick points out that similar phenomena occur in other areas, such as a problem at sea, where Navy seamen ignored all the orders to remove their steel toecap shoes when they abandoned ship and, therefore, they drowned or punched holes in the life rafts, causing others to drown. Weick argues that tools define the social group. It's indicative of their identity such that to ditch these, even in an emergency, is to cease to be who you are. It appears that kind of over-learned behaviour becomes very ingrained in an individual, such that they don't feel able to separate themselves from the tools that represent their trade or profession. As he points out in Weick, 2007, 'dealing with the complexities of a highly interconnected and fast-moving world requires a new set of approaches to complement, if not entirely replace, traditional tools' (p. 5). He addressed these remarks to management educators, but clearly any teacher needs to consider the implications of his evidence.

I would argue that it is quite difficult for teachers to deal with the notion that they are no longer required to teach a classroom, and that most of the skills they've learned are undesirable in the kind of complexity that Weick refers to. In our College, and in similar programmes, our role is a more reactive one than the proactive one that teachers are trained to do. For instance, as a learning group adviser I ask questions because I don't know the answers. Teachers tend to ask questions because they do know the answers and they are testing the students. When I say I don't know the answers to questions, it's because I'm asking questions like: What's important to you? What do you want to learn? How do you plan to learn it? How are you getting on? What help do you need? What's stopping you doing what you need to do? What if you tried something different? and so on. My job, then, is to react to the answers I get, and probably then ask more questions. Once I have good information from the learner, I can then link to others who may be able to help the person. But it might not be another person, given our 57 different varieties of learning that are available. And even if it is a person it is a reactive role – a reaction to the needs of the student.

Here I am commenting on the P role as defined in Chapter 9. I showed that this work must pre-date any offer of helping the student to learn specific subjects or skills. However, there is a place for the S role once the young person has clarified and agreed what and how they want to learn something. Learning advisers who are helping students to learn specifics will then be responding to the identified needs of the student. And some of those conversations might have similarities, on the surface, to some teacher-to-pupil conversations in schools. The problem in school is that such teacher–pupil conversations are in a context of the drivers for teachers to control classrooms, to teach the fixed curriculum and to get students to pass tests.

Directions

The penultimate point that I want to make is about directions. I'm not going to try to be encyclopaedic here about all the possibilities for the future, but one that comes to mind is particularly pertinent at the time of writing this. It is March 29, 2020 and we are in the early stages in England of the coronavirus or Covid-19 crisis.

Schools have been closed and many problems are occurring from this. One example is around the well-being of children. Walker, 2020, comments that even at this early stage of the crisis, the National Society for the Prevention of Cruelty to Children (NSPCC) and its phone service, Childline, have been inundated with calls from worried children. For instance, she reported that 'last week, Childline delivered over 50 counselling sessions with children who are having suicidal thoughts, exacerbated by coronavirus as they felt trapped and isolated.'

Many children said that they felt increasingly lonely and vulnerable and mental health issues were being exacerbated by the crisis. However, even amongst the majority that have not previously had mental health problems, it's clear that these problems are growing because of the concerns about isolation and the worries about their future.

A number of commentators have indicated the error of schools in attempting to replicate the normal schooling model in the home. Merrow, 2020, comments 'a lot of school systems seem to be reflexively behaving as if they could simply transplant school's routines to the home.' In reading advice given by, and for, schools about dealing with the fact that children are not in school it is all oriented to continuing to utilise the schooling model, but in a new environment. It is clearly in most cases failing. Woolcock, 2020, cites a mother of three saying, 'We've been sent a timetable that details each activity and even the amount of minutes it should take. I feel stressed, just looking at how much should be crammed into the day' (p. 9).

Merrow is particularly good at critiquing the notion that the current crisis demands home-schooling. He cogently points out that it is an opportunity for home learning, which is an opinion that I would obviously support. The attempt merely to translate school systems into a home environment is clearly not working and the problems will undoubtedly get worse.

When the crisis occurred, we closed our building, but our stance with parents and students is that the building is shut, but the college is open. We immediately created a new online environment with three Zoom (video-conferencing) channels that allowed a great deal of interaction between learning advisers and the 38 students on roll. The use of platforms such as Discord has allowed for a lot of chat and interaction between the students away from the video-conferencing environment. Good old-fashioned phones and emails have also played a part.

The important feature of this is that students have been able to continue the learning community in this new environment. The feedback from students has been mainly positive. After the morning Zoom sessions there's a lunchtime open meeting where anyone can enter a designated Zoom channel and raise anything they want. Students are often just wanting to connect with others and continue the relationships that they had developed when the building was open. Most feel that it works really well and indeed one of our autistic students actually feels it's better in some respects since she is someone who finds noise and the closeness of others a problem.

Parents have started to adjust to this new world and the following is a comment at the end of our first week of working:

> Just have to say how amazing it is – despite tech hitches and Discord/booking in confusion – that the SML College team have turned EVERYTHING around so quickly to create a really broad and accessible online system.
>
> First full week for J [son] done and I just wanted to feed back to you that he is in a really good place. And a big part of this has been the opportunity for consistent face to face contact with college advisors and students. Of course, some teething issues around self managing at home and getting information about session timings etc but considering how huge the task at hand was to provide everyone access to an online alternative I think what you have achieved is really remarkable. Congratulations.
>
> The week has also been a time to suss out what I need to do in order to support J accessing the college's offer – so I also really appreciate all the communication with staff around how the new system works.
>
> I'll continue to feed back to staff of course as things crop up but just wanted to say a big direct thank you to everybody for their dedication and adaptability!

At one level, we are just replicating the Self Managed Learning mode in a new environment where we can't all be physically together. I would reiterate that it only works because we have a learning community where people know each other and are trusting and open and prepared to work together. Clearly, for some students the transition is proving a bit more difficult than others. But one of the points that we want to make is that in the world that we are operating in we do need to be able to connect with people without direct physical contact. Videoconferencing has been around for some time and it's clear that it will become more important, given the impact on the climate of human travel. In addition, improvements in air quality have already been identified as travel has been reduced. Whatever the future holds after this crisis, it is evident that the trend that was already there for increased homeworking by adults is going to continue. And indeed, it is desperately needed.

However, it only works if there is already that sense of trust and comradeship and connection that is the key part of a community way of working. It seems valuable that students who are not finding it easy do learn to deal with this environment, because it is going to be part of the future for them. And we are back to the problem that, even if schools used some of this technology, because they are generally not caring communities that empower students there will still be increased mental health problems for their students.

Another development from the closing of schools for the majority of children has been the large growth in parents booking one-to-one tuition via online arrangements. Clearly, if this is done well it can respond to individual needs; however, evidence suggests that a lot of it is around preparing young people for exams and therefore sticking to existing curricula. The other problem with this mode is that, of course, it misses the community dimension. As I pointed out earlier in this book, it's crucial for young people in this age group to relate to their peers and the notion that parents can fully provide for their offspring by one-to-one tuition is not likely to be realised.

This new environment is challenging teachers to be open to it to rethink their role. An article in *The Guardian* newspaper's Teacher Network from March 29, 2020 quoted a headteacher who was looking after a small number of key worker children who were allowed into the school. Currently, schools are expected to stay open just for the small number of children whose parents are seen as key workers, such as those working in the health service. This head-teacher commented, 'It just seems very calm and lovely — a bit of an oasis.

TABLE 10.1 Traditional schooling paradigm versus New Educational Paradigm — a reprise

Traditional Schooling Paradigm	New Educational Paradigm
Learning is organised by institutions such as schools and colleges. This is the only proper learning.	Learning anywhere — and not necessarily in an organised setting.
Young people have to be controlled otherwise they won't learn — extrinsic motivation is required.	Young people naturally want to learn given the right support. Intrinsic motivation works.
Imposed content curriculum.	Free — no imposition.
Teacher in charge.	Learner in charge — works with adults as needed.
Imposed timetable — pupils must follow.	No imposed timetable — students learn as and when they choose.
Decisions made hierarchically.	Joint decision-making between adults and young people.
Teachers impose tests.	Students choose if they want to take tests.
Formal relationships between teachers and pupils.	Informal relationships — all on first name terms.
Steady progression of learning expected.	Learning goes at a pace that suits the learner.
Taking public exams expected.	Taking public exams if the student chooses.
Dress code or uniforms.	No dress code or uniforms.
Students required to be in fixed rooms. No access to toilets or refreshments without permission from staff.	Students free to access rooms, e.g. toilets, as needed. No permission needed.
Learning is preparation for life, so it stops at some point and people start living.	Learning occurs from birth to death — it never ceases while you are alive.
People who can memorise a lot of facts are better people than those who can't.	Everyone is important and can contribute in different ways to communities and organisations.
Homework is required.	Learning can occur anywhere and there is no compulsory homework.

Children have never had this experience before, where they get to just play in their primary school. It's going to be strange. I'm no longer a headteacher, I'm a leader of a playscheme.'[1]

Perhaps headteachers might contemplate what the possibilities are when the schools reopen. Somehow, I think quite a lot will just revert to what they were doing before, and may even use the fact that many children have struggled while out of school to justify the notion of recreating school as it was before. It would be a great shame as there is an opportunity here for people to rethink. Only time will tell if that happens.

A New Educational Paradigm

I am repeating here the table comparing traditional schooling with a New Educational Paradigm (see Chapter 1). For now, I have said my piece and hope for more people to acknowledge the new world that we need to create.

Note

1 *The Guardian* Teachers Network, March 29, 2020. https://www.theguardian.com/world/2020/mar/23/parents-heeding-calls-to-keep-children-home-from-school-say-heads?utm_term=RWRpdG9yaWFsX1RlYWNoZXJOZXR3b3JrLTIwMDMyOQ%3D%3D&utm_source=esp&utm_medium=Email&utm_campaign=TeacherNetwork&CMP=teacher_email

References

Department for Education (2018) Elective home education. Guidance for local authorities – for consultation.

Filmore, P. (2018) A ship in harbour. *Paradigm Explorer*, Issue 2, 2.

Meighan, R. (2005) *Comparing Learning Systems*. Nottingham: Educational Heretics Press.

Merrow, J. (2020) Please don't call it Homeschooling. March 26. https://themerrowreport.com/2020/03/26/please-dont-call-it-homeschooling/

Walker, A. (2020) There have been more than 900 calls to Childline from children over coronavirus worries since schools closed. March 27. www.msn.com/en-gb/health/lifestylefamily/there-has-been-more-than-900-calls-to-childline-from-children-over-coronavirus-worries-since-schools-closed/ar-BB11N3CN?MSCC=1585317192&ocid=spartandhp

Weick, K. E. (1998) The collapse of sensemaking in organizations: The Mann Gulch Disaster. *Administrative Science Quarterly*, 38(4), 628–652.

Weick, K. E. (2001) Tool retention and fatalities in wildland fire settings, in Sala, E. and Klein, G. A., eds., *Linking Expertise and Naturalistic Decision Making*. New York: Psychology Press.

Weick, K. E. (2007) Drop your tools: on re-configuring management education. *Journal of Management Education*, 31(1), 5–16.

Woolcock, N. (2020) Assemblies online, mentors and hymns as teachers get learning. *The Times*, March 28, 8–9.

INDEX

weight loss 142
well-being: emotional 122–125;
  psychological 136–137; and work 109
work: changes 26; future needs 126n3; and
  learning 30–31, 34–38, 43; qualities
  required at 114–115; and well-being 109;
  see also work experience
work experience 117
working-class children 65n3, 86
working-class students 113
working-class values 113
workshops 94

World Economic Forum 2016 116
writers 35
writing 31–32

young people: developing identity 38; and
  locus of control 39, 100, 140–142;
  mental health 32, 118–121; and
  motivation to learn 38; suicide among 32,
  47n2, 90, 118, 119, 121

Zen and the Art of Motorcycle Maintenance 54
Zoom 164

Printed in Great Britain
by Amazon